For My Fri... ...ear
Love,

Alice's

BRADY BUNCH

Cookbook

Ann B. Davis

Ron Newcomer and Diane Smolen

June 2011

Rutledge Hill Press

Nashville, Tennessee

Published in Nashville, Tennessee, by Rutledge Hill Press, Inc., 211 Seventh Avenue North, Nashville, Tennessee 37219. Distributed in Canada by H.B. Fenn and Company Ltd., Mississauga, Ontario.

Typography by D&T/Bailey Typesetting, Inc.
Design by Harriette Bateman

Photographs on pages 6, 15, 24, 32, 37, 41, 47, 55, 62, 71, 86, 100, 104, 109, 110, 118, 128, 131, 144, 146, 155, 157, 181, 185, 192, 197, 205, 208, 213, 217, 219, 220, 221, 223, 225, 227, 228, 229, 232, 234, 237, 238, and 239 from the Sherwood Schwartz private collection and used with permission from Paramount Pictures.
Photographs on pages 224, 235, and 243 courtesy of Ann B. Davis.
Photographs on pages 16, 66, 81, 88, 93, 113, 116, 123, 136, 139, 151, 165, 168, 226, 230, and 233 courtesy of Howard Frank, Personality Photographs, P.O. Box 50, Brooklyn, NY 11230.

Library of Congress Cataloging-in-Publication Data

Davis, Ann B., 1926–
    Alice's Brady Bunch cookbook / Ann B. Davis, Ron Newcomer, and Diane Smolen.
        p.   cm.
    Includes index.
    ISBN 1-55853-307-9
    1. Brady bunch (Television program) 2. Cookery. I. Newcomer, Ron, 1946–   . II. Smolen, Diane, 1948–   . III. Title.
TX714.D39
641.5—dc20   94-29393
                                                                                                    CIP

Printed in the United States of America
1 2 3 4 5 6 7 8 — 99 98 97 96 95 94

Contents

Foreword by Sherwood Schwartz   7
Introduction by Ann B. Davis   9
Alice's Unspoken Rules   10
"The Brady Bunch" Cast and History   11

Breakfast at the Bradys   15
Noontime Specials   37
Brady Family Dinners   55
Second Time Around   113
The Great Brady Barbecue   123
On the Road   139
Family Treats   151
Brady Celebrations   165
Very Brady Holidays   177
Feel Good Foods   205
Personal Favorites   217

Ann B. Davis Biography   243
Books & Stuff   245
Acknowledgments   246
Index   247

The Brady Bunch

Foreword

’m often asked about the reason for the enormous and enduring popularity of "The Brady Bunch." One of the most frequent questions is, "How important was Ann B. Davis to the success of the show?" Fortunately, it's the easiest question to answer. She was indispensable!

In joining two separate families to form "The Brady Bunch," I knew many of the stories would involve problems between the two sets of children, and maybe between the parents as well. I needed a barometer who could sense storm warnings on the horizon, a barometer who was part of the family, one whom everyone could trust with their thoughts, their plans, and their secrets. The answer, of course, was a housekeeper. But it had to be someone with a comic talent to add to the humor and, at the same time, an acting ability to add to the reality of the Brady family life. Certain roles cry out for certain actors, and this one screamed for Ann B. Davis.

Unfortunately, Ann B. was unavailable. She was in Seattle doing a one-woman show. The studio told me to get someone else, someone like Ann B. Davis; but Ann B. Davises don't grow on trees. She's one of a kind. I advised Paramount to buy out the two remaining weeks of her contract in Seattle. When they told me that would be expensive, I replied, "Good things are often expensive."

Two days later, Ann B. put on her blue uniform for "The Brady Bunch" pilot film; and she kept it on for the next five years. Three years later, Ann B. put that blue uniform on again for "The Brady Bunch Variety Hour," seven years later for *The Brady Girls Get Married*, eight years later for *A Very Brady Christmas*, and two years later for "The Bradys." Ann B. and that blue uniform are like Superman and his cape. Both of them performed daily miracles. I'm happy to say Ann B. Davis performed her miracles for me and the "Bunch."

Sherwood Schwartz

"The Brady Bunch"

Here's the story
Of a lovely lady
Who was bringing up
Three very lovely girls.
All of them had hair of gold,
Like their mother,
The youngest one in curls.

It's the story
Of a man named Brady,
Who was busy with
Three boys of his own.
They were four men living all together,
Yet they were all alone.

Till the one day
When the lady met this fellow,
And they knew that it was
Much more than a hunch,
That this group must
Somehow form a family.
That's the way we all
Became the Brady Bunch.

The Brady Bunch!
The Brady Bunch!
That's the way we
Became the Brady Bunch!

Music by Frank DeVol
Lyrics by Sherwood Schwartz

Introduction

In the years and years that "The Brady Bunch" has appeared on television, I am more and more often asked the reason for its continued popularity.

At first I had a rather glib answer right at hand. The show first appeared when "slice of life" was the trend on TV (always an unattractive slice-of-life at that), and we were a welcome contrast to the (then) new grittiness in television series. When some of those shows hit syndication and started appearing on television right after school hours, the mothers of America rose in their wrath and demanded something more suitable that children just home from school could watch. This just about left us and "Gilligan's Island." Also, about then we all suddenly had about 85 new television channels to watch. All that hardware and not enough software!

Lately I have become convinced that something much deeper is involved. Every year a new set of children start to watch the show and find the family we all want to belong to: parents who love us, take care of us, and love us enough to correct and discipline us. Wouldn't we all love to have belonged to a perfect family, with brothers and sisters to lean on and where every problem is solved in 23½ minutes?

I believe our Creator made us with a God-shaped space in our hearts. We often spend our whole lives trying to fill that space with something other than God: money, family, possessions, career (that's mine), food, booze, drugs—all kinds of things. It is only when we start to fill that God-shaped space with God that we discover what it is to be whole.

I think that element of hope, that possibility of perfection, has carried the success of "The Brady Bunch" through the years. It is speaking to what we long for in a world that seems to be falling apart so rapidly.

Alice's Unspoken Rules

1 Wash up before you sit down at the table and try to comb your hair so everybody knows who they are talking to.

2 Attempt to be cheerful. Who knows, it might work.

3 Since everybody is half asleep at breakfast, it is no fair being grumpy or trying to settle an old argument from the night before.

4 For breakfast or lunch it is OK to read the newspaper or finish studying for a test. A pleasant "hello" is still required, and a nice word about the meal is always welcome.

5 Talk to everybody politely, and every once in a while give them a chance to speak.

6 Save all culinary criticism until after you eat. Who knows, you might be so full that you forget what you were going to say.

7 Meals are not a varsity sport, so don't play hockey with your food.

8 Finish chewing, then talk. It makes understanding you so much easier and looking at you so much more appealing.

9 If there is company, let them have first choice. More than likely they won't take the biggest piece anyway.

10 And always be thankful for a good hot meal.

"The Brady Bunch" Cast and History

Robert Reed	*Mike Brady*
Florence Henderson	*Carol Brady*
Barry Williams	*Greg Brady*
Maureen McCormick	*Marcia Brady*
Christopher Knight	*Peter Brady*
Eve Plumb	*Jan Brady*
Mike Lookinland	*Bobby Brady*
Susan Olsen	*Cindy Brady*
Ann B. Davis	*Alice Nelson*
Allan Melvin	*Sam ("The Butcher") Franklin*

The pilot telecast of "The Brady Bunch" was on September 26, 1969. Over the next five seasons, 117 half-hour episodes were aired on ABC's prime time schedule. The series was shot at Paramount Studios in Hollywood. The final episode was seen on March 8, 1974. Since then, "The Brady Bunch" has been in reruns five days a week somewhere in the world.

Sherwood Schwartz was the creator and executive producer. Howard Leeds and Lloyd J. Schwartz were the producers. "Brady" television spinoffs include twenty-two half-hour episodes of the animated series "The Brady Kids," which premiered on September 9, 1972, "The Brady Bunch Variety Hour" that aired on November 28, 1976, and was followed by eight shows of "The Brady Bunch Hour," which was seen at various times on various nights from January 23 to May 25, 1977.

Four years later, a two-hour television movie called *The Brady Girls Get Married* was made. At the last moment, NBC decided to edit it into four half-hour episodes to air weekly. Six more episodes were added, making a limited series called "The Brady Brides." It ran from February 6, 1981 to April 17, 1981.

Seven years later, on Sunday, December 18, 1988, CBS presented the TV movie, *A Very Brady Christmas*, which was a huge hit and gave the network its highest rated movie of the year. That was followed by "The Bradys," first as a two-hour show that aired on February 9, 1990, then four one-hour episodes.

The various Brady projects have the unique distinction of appearing on all three major networks.

Currently, there is a very successful stage show of "Brady" episodes called *The Real Live Brady Bunch*. There is also a feature motion picture in development at Paramount, which will arrive in theaters in 1994, the twenty-fifth anniversary of "The Brady Bunch" on television.

Twenty-five years of original Brady projects, and it's not over yet.

Alice's

**BRADY
BUNCH**™

Cookbook

Breakfast at The Bradys

The first of many, many photos on this staircase. I aged twenty-two years from the first shot to the last.

Freshly squeezed orange juice. What a perfect way to start the day. It's bright, it's cheery, and no Brady kid would leave home without it. In our household you're always one squeeze away from running out. But sometimes you're in the mood for something different. So I'm adding some choices.

Launch Pad Orange Juice

1 egg, optional   ½ cup milk
½ cup orange juice

In a blender combine all of the ingredients or plop that egg in a glass with juice and milk and stir.

   Alice's Note: This is a great pick-me-up for those times you can't sit down for breakfast.

One of the most famous weddings in all of television.

The World According to Alice

66Today I sat down for the first time in twenty-some-odd years and watched a 'Brady Bunch' episode from start to finish. It's really a strange sensation. I don't remember the lines or the plot or what happens next. Plus there is that much younger woman playing my part. And thinner, too!99

Kitty Karryall Cocoa _____

¾ cup cocoa
5 tablespoons sugar, or to taste

2 cups water
6 cups milk

In a large saucepan mix the cocoa and sugar. Add the water. Heat over medium heat, stirring until the mixture is smooth. Boil for a few seconds, and then slowly add the milk, stirring constantly. When the cocoa is hot, pour it into mugs and serve.

Alice's Note: This always got the kids going when the fog rolled off the ocean on those cool, southern California mornings.

Variation: For south of the border taste add a stick of cinnamon to each cup.

Makes 8 servings.

MIKE: (with a glass of milk): Ladies, I would like to propose a toast to the successful launch of project "Brady Bunch." Six happy kids, two lucky parents, and an interested bystander.

CAROL: Hear, hear!

ALICE: With all due respect, according to my calculations, you have only just blasted off the launching pad.

CAROL: Yes, but we are off to a good start.

ALICE: Oh, yes, ma'am. I only meant to say it would take time...lot's of it.

Jolly Green Garden
Tomato Juice

2 medium tomatoes, peeled
  and chopped

⅓ cup water
Salt and pepper to taste

In a blender combine all of the ingredients and blend on high for about 30 seconds.

Alice's Note: It's the fresh tomatoes that give it the zip. Mr. B. never started his day without his glass of T. juice.

Makes 1 serving.

ALICE: Okay, now, if the werewolf howls...if the vampire starts flapping his wings...don't come running to me. I'll be under the kitchen table.

Tutti Fruity Juice Food

1 large apple, cored and
  skinned
½ cup skim milk
1 tablespoon wheat germ

2 tablespoons bran
1 crushed ice cube
2 tablespoons honey

Combine all of the ingredients in a blender and blend on high until the mixture is smooth. Pour the drink into a glass.

Makes 1 serving.

Jungle Jim Banana Milk

1 ripe banana, peeled   ¾ cup milk
Pinch grated nutmeg

Put the banana, nutmeg, and milk in a blender and blend until the mixture is smooth.

Alice's Note: A superb muscle builder, or so the boys said.

Makes 1 serving.

> **ALICE:** This is a kitchen, not an emergency ward.

Groovy Old-fashioned Pancakes

2 eggs   1 tablespoon sugar
5 tablespoons melted butter   4 teaspoons baking powder
1 cup milk   ¾ teaspoon salt
1¼ cups all-purpose flour

In a mixing bowl beat the eggs until blended. Add the butter and milk, and mix well. In a separate bowl use a fork to combine the flour, sugar, baking powder, and salt. Slowly add the egg mixture just until the batter is thoroughly moistened.

Heat a skillet or griddle until drops of water sizzle on it. Lightly grease the hot griddle (if nonstick, no grease is needed). Drop 2 to 3 tablespoons of batter in the skillet for each pancake. Cook until bubbles form, turn, and cook until the bottom is lightly browned. Serve immediately.

Variations: For special occasions or just something different, try adding 2 cups of blueberries, raspberries, or strawberries to the batter. Or just add 2 to 3 tablespoons of berries to the top of each pancake when it starts to bubble. Turn over and finish as above. Peeled and trimmed fresh fruit such as bananas, peaches, oranges, or apricots may be used also.

Makes about 14 pancakes.

Bobby's Pool Hustler Pancakes _____

1 cup buttermilk	¾ cup all-purpose flour
1 egg, room temperature	2 teaspoons salt
3 tablespoons butter, melted	1 teaspoon baking soda

In a mixing bowl stir together the buttermilk, egg, and melted butter until smooth and blended.

In a separate bowl combine the flour, salt, and baking soda. Stir the dry ingredients into the buttermilk mixture just until the dry ingredients are moistened. Leave the lumps. Heat a skillet or griddle to medium hot. Lightly grease the hot griddle. Drop 3 tablespoons of batter in the skillet for each pancake.

Makes about 10 pancakes.

Cindy's Golden Apple Pancake ____

6 tablespoons butter	¼ cup confectioners' sugar
3 medium apples, peeled, cored, and sliced	3 eggs, room temperature
3 tablespoons lemon juice	¼ teaspoon salt
¼ teaspoon cinnamon	½ cup all-purpose flour
	½ cup milk

In a 10-inch skillet melt 4 tablespoons of butter. Remove the pan from the heat. Place the apple slices and lemon juice in a large bowl. Add the cinnamon and sugar, and toss to mix. Spoon the apple mixture into the skillet and heat to medium. Cook, stirring often, for about 3 or 4 minutes, or until the apples are tender but still hold their shape. Spread the apples evenly over the bottom of a buttered 9-inch round baking dish.

Combine the eggs, salt, flour, milk, and 2 tablespoons of melted butter in a mixing bowl. Beat until smooth. Pour the batter over the apples. Bake at 425° for about 20 minutes, or until golden and puffy. Turn the pancake onto a warm platter so the apples are on top. Dust with confectioners' sugar and serve.

Makes 1 apple pancake, or 6 to 8 servings.

Totally Mod Waffles _____

2 cups all-purpose flour
1 teaspoon salt
4 teaspoons baking powder
2 tablespoons sugar
2 eggs, room temperature

1½ cups milk, warmed
⅓ cup vegetable shortening,
  melted
⅓ cup butter, melted

In a large bowl mix the flour, salt, baking powder, and sugar together. Stir the mixture with a fork until blended. In a separate bowl beat the eggs well and stir in the milk. Pour the liquid mixture into the flour mixture, stirring until mixed. Add the shortening and butter and beat until blended. Heat a waffle iron until very hot. For each waffle, pour about ½ cup of batter into the hot waffle iron. Bake until golden and crisp.

Variations: Waffles with Fresh Fruit—sliced peaches, nectarines, apricots, bananas, and any berry—are great with waffles. Serve with waffles on the side. Strawberry Whipped Cream Waffles are so simple but make a very special breakfast. Just pile fresh whipped cream on the waffle and cover with fresh strawberries. The only problem I had with this was keeping the whipped cream away from Cindy long enough to use it.

Makes 8 waffles.

Confessions of a Graying Housekeeper

❝Well, I admit, my hair was gray all along, although the first year when the front office was obsessed with hair, it was a quite bright brown. About the third year I conspired with the hair department to let a few strands go gray every time I had it 'done' until the powers-that-be allowed me to be as gray as I really was.❞

Alice's Famous Whole Wheat Buttermilk Waffles _____

1 cup whole wheat flour	2½ tablespoons sugar
1 cup all-purpose flour	3 eggs
2¼ teaspoons baking powder	1¾ cups buttermilk
1 teaspoon baking soda	1 cup butter, melted
¾ teaspoon salt	½ cup milk, if needed

In a mixing bowl combine the flours, baking powder, baking soda, salt, and sugar. Stir with a fork to blend. In a separate mixing bowl beat the eggs until blended. Stir in the buttermilk and melted butter. Add the liquid ingredients to the flour mixture. Stir the mixture until well mixed. The batter should flow from the spoon, not plop. If the batter is too thick, add ¼ cup of milk to thin it. Grease and heat a waffle iron until hot. Cook the waffles until golden. Serve hot.

Makes 8 waffles.

Brady Trivia Quiz #1

Sit down with a glass of milk and see if you can answer the following questions.

a. In "The Slumber Caper" where is a rubber spider found lurking?

b. What is Alice preparing for Mr. Brady in "To Move or Not to Move"?

c. In "The Liberation of Marcia Brady" what does Peter have to sell dressed as a Girl Scout?

d. Under what does Jan hide a rubber spider in "The Practical Joker"?

e. Finish this bit of dialogue from "The Possible Dream":
ALICE: How about a cookie?
MARCIA: No, thanks. I'm not in the mood.
ALICE: Since when do you have to be in a special mood for _____?

Answers on Page 43.

Fluffy's Fab French Toast _____

8 eggs
1½ cups milk
Salt to taste

12 slices bread (use day-old
   bread the kids won't touch)
½ cup butter

In a large bowl combine the eggs, milk, and salt and stir with a fork until well blended. Pour the eggs into a wide, shallow bowl. In a skillet big enough to hold 3 slices of bread at once melt 2 tablespoons of the butter. Dip both sides of each slice of bread in the eggs. Fry the bread over medium heat until lightly browned on the bottom. Turn and repeat. Keep the cooked slices warm. Repeat with the remaining bread and butter. Serve warm sprinkled with confectioners' sugar, syrup, or your favorite jelly.

Makes 12 slices of toast.

> ALICE: It's my two-way stretch. I think it just went three ways.

Honey Bunch French Toast _____

4 eggs, slightly beaten
½ cup milk
½ cup honey
½ teaspoon salt
6 tablespoons butter

12 to 16 slices white or whole
   wheat bread
2 cups honey
¼ cup lemon juice
¼ cup butter

In a medium bowl combine the eggs, milk, ½ cup of honey, and salt. In a large skillet melt 6 tablespoons of butter over medium heat. Dip the bread slices in the egg mixture and fry in butter until golden brown. In a small saucepan mix together the remaining ingredients and heat until warm. Serve over toast.

Makes 12 to 16 slices of toast.

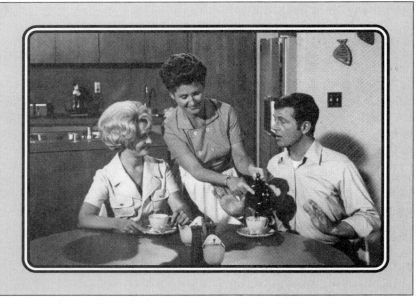

This might be the first coffee Alice ever poured for the newly married couple.

California Raised Doughnuts _____

1 package active dry yeast
1 cup warm water (110°)
¼ cup vegetable shortening
½ cup sugar
⅓ cup milk, warmed

2 eggs
4 cups all-purpose flour
½ teaspoon salt
1¼ teaspoons mace
Light oil for frying

Dissolve the yeast in ½ cup of warm water and let the mixture stand for about 5 minutes. In a small saucepan bring the remaining water to a boil. Add the shortening and sugar, and stir until the shortening has melted and the sugar has dissolved. Remove the pan from the heat. When the water is cooled, add the yeast and warm milk. Stir in the eggs and 2 cups of flour. Beat well. Add 2 more cups of flour and the salt and mace. Mix well. Add the flour slowly. Only add enough to make a soft and manageable dough. Turn the dough onto a lightly floured board and knead until smooth and elastic. Place the dough in a large greased bowl, cover, and let it rise until doubled in bulk.

Punch the dough down. On a lightly floured surface roll it out to ½-inch thickness. Cut out doughnuts with a 2-inch cutter. Place the doughnuts on waxed paper or a greased baking sheet about 1 inch apart. Let the doughnuts rise for 1 hour.

Heat the oil to 370°F in a skillet or deep fryer. Fry 3 doughnuts at a time—no crowding allowed. Fry until golden on each side. Remove and drain on paper towels. Prepare the glaze (recipe follows) or roll the doughnuts in sugar to coat.

Variation: For Jelly Doughnuts or Berlins roll out the dough to ¼-inch thickness. Cut out 2½-inch rounds. On one half put ½ teaspoon of jelly. Cover each round with a plain round, and seal together, pinching the edges. Coat with beaten egg whites. Fry as above. Dust with confectioners' sugar.

Makes about 30 doughnuts.

Doughnut Glaze for Raised Doughnuts

4 cups confectioners' sugar   ⅔ cup hot water

Mix the ingredients until smooth in a shallow bowl. While the doughnuts are hot, coat all sides of each doughnut in the glaze. If the glaze thickens, thin it with a little hot water.

And First Prize for Water Goes to . . .

❝I hope this doesn't destroy any illusions, but cooking on television usually has to be faked because of time and intercutting and camera angles and whatnot. However, one does like to make it look as legit as possible. Unless something specific was indicated in the script, I tried to be cooking something generic that would keep me in one place and give me something, like stirring, to do—I did a lot of stirring over 117 episodes!

"The stove was actually hooked up, so I liked to have something in a saucepan that would steam and that I could taste or add salt and pepper and stuff to. Dinty Moore stew worked I found. In later years, when my acting was less pure, boiling water worked just as well.❞

Sunshine Day Baked Eggs _____

½ cup chopped fresh parsley
½ cup minced ham
½ cup cubed Brie

6 eggs
¼ cup heavy cream
Salt and pepper to taste

In a greased 7x11-inch baking dish toss the parsley, ham, and Brie together. Break the eggs over the ham mixture evenly and drizzle the cream over the eggs. Season with salt and pepper to taste. Place the baking dish in a larger roasting pan. Fill the roasting pan with 1 inch of water. Bake at 400° for 15 to 20 minutes. Serve immediately.

ALICE: Me! Leave the Brady family? You couldn't get rid of me if you tried. I am a hundred-and-twenty-pound boomerang.
CAROL: A hundred-and-twenty pounds?
ALICE: Well, more or less.

Goofy Hole-in-One Eggs _____

8 slices white or wheat bread
½ cup butter
8 eggs
8 thin pieces of ham, pastrami,
  or corned beef

2 cups grated cheese (Swiss or
  Monterey Jack)

Make holes in the center of each slice of bread with a 1-inch round cutter. In a large skillet melt the butter over medium heat. Add the bread slices and cook until lightly browned on the bottom. Flip over and break an egg into the center of each slice. Cover and cook over medium low heat for about 2 minutes or until the eggs are almost done. Place a ham slice over each egg and sprinkle with cheese. Cover and cook over medium low heat for 1 to 2 minutes or until the cheese melts. Serve immediately.
    Makes 8 servings.

MIKE: Mind holdin' down the fort while we're gone?
ALICE: Oh, I don't mind holding down the fort. Bear in mind that those were the last words of General Custer.

B.B.'s French Omelet

3 eggs   1 tablespoon butter

In a small bowl beat the eggs with a whisk or fork until just blended. In an 8-inch skillet melt the butter over medium high heat. Make sure the bottom and sides of the pan are coated. Add the eggs when the butter just begins to brown. Slide the skillet back and forth over the heat, making sure the eggs are spread evenly over the bottom as the omelet cooks. Lightly brown the bottom of the omelet. Tilt the skillet, and run a fork under the edge of the omelet, giving a jerk to loosen it. Fold the omelet in half and turn it over onto a plate. Season as desired.

Variation: For filled omelets add desired ingredients just before folding and cook a little longer. (Swiss and Cheddar cheese, ham or bacon, and herbs are some popular additions. But kids love just plain old jelly.)

Makes 1 serving.

ALICE: I would like to introduce a subject for discussion.
MIKE: Feel free.
ALICE: What's the matter with the kids?
CAROL: We wish we knew!
MIKE: We were just talking about that. Did they say anything to you?
ALICE: Not a peep. But something is bugging them.
CAROL: I think I just have to ask them, that's all.
ALICE: Could you do it tomorrow? If there is anything I can't stand it's a perfect kid. Six of them! Yuck!
MIKE: I'll drink to that. Yuck!
CAROL: Yuck!

Not-So-Ugly Duckling Country Eggs _____

1 pound potatoes, peeled
½ cup butter
1 cup grated Gruyère cheese

8 eggs
1 cup heavy cream

Cut the potatoes into very thin rounds. In a saucepan melt the butter and sauté the potatoes, stirring occasionally so the potatoes do not stick. Season with salt and pepper. When the potatoes are soft transfer them to a 9-inch baking dish. Sprinkle with cheese. Break the eggs evenly over the potatoes and cheese. Cover with the cream. Bake at 425° until the egg whites have set but the yolks are soft.

A Peach of An Omelet _____

3 eggs, beaten
1 tablespoon water
⅛ teaspoon Worcestershire
   sauce
Salt and pepper to taste
2 tablespoons butter
1 cup grated Cheddar cheese

2 tablespoons diced green
   chilies
½ large peach, peeled and
   sliced
3 tablespoons sour cream
½ cup grated Swiss cheese
Fresh parsley

Blend together the eggs, water, Worcestershire sauce, salt, and pepper in a mixing bowl. In an 8-inch skillet or omelet pan over medium heat melt the butter until sizzling. Pour in the eggs while tilting skillet around so the eggs evenly cover the bottom. Continue shaking the skillet gently while cooking until the omelet is lightly set but still moist, about 2 to 3 minutes. Layer chilies and cheddar over half of the omelet. Top with the peaches and sour cream. Fold over the other half of the omelet and sprinkle with Swiss cheese. Cook until the cheese melts, about 3 minutes. Garnish with fresh parsley. Serve immediately.

Alice's Note: This goes great with the South of the Border Bread recipe that follows.

Makes 2 servings.

Gone with the Commercial

❝When we did 'The Brady Bunch,' each episode was 23 minutes and something. Now, I notice, they only take 20 minutes and 30 seconds. It has been much too long to remember what was cut, but like any actor I am sure that some of my greatest moments are in those 2 minutes and 30 seconds!❞

South of the Border Bread_____

2 packages active dry yeast
½ cup warm water (110°)
½ teaspoon baking soda
2 teaspoons salt
1 tablespoon sugar
1 cup cornmeal
2 eggs

1 cup milk
1 tablespoon lemon juice
½ cup vegetable oil
1 cup creamed corn
5 cups all-purpose flour
1½ cups grated Cheddar cheese
¼ cup chopped green chilies

In a large mixing bowl dissolve the yeast in the water. Let the mixture stand for 5 minutes. Add the baking soda, salt, sugar, and cornmeal, and beat until well mixed. Add the eggs, milk, lemon juice, oil, corn, and 2 cups of flour. Beat until blended. Add the cheese, chilies, and more flour (you may not use the full 5 cups) until the dough is easily kneaded. Knead until the cheese and chilies are thoroughly mixed. Let the dough stand for 10 minutes. Knead again until the dough is smooth and elastic. Place the dough in a greased bowl, cover, and set aside until doubled in bulk.

Grease two 9x5x3-inch loaf pans. Punch down the dough and divide it in half. Place each loaf in a greased pan. Cover the loaves and let them rise. Bake at 350° for 50 to 60 minutes. Remove the loaves from the pans and cool on racks.

Makes 2 loaves.

Brady Family Favorite Quiche_____

1½ cups grated Cheddar cheese
1½ cups grated Monterey Jack
  cheese
½ cup chopped cooked turkey
  breast
½ cup chopped baked ham

7 eggs
⅓ cup light cream
¼ teaspoon garlic salt
¼ teaspoon pepper
3 ounces diced green chilies
⅓ cup chopped red bell pepper

Butter a 9-inch round pie pan. Spread evenly with the cheeses, then turkey, then ham. Whisk together the eggs, milk, garlic salt, and pepper until thoroughly blended. Stir in the green chilies and red pepper. Pour the egg mixture over the turkey and cheeses. Bake uncovered at 375° for 35 to 40 minutes.

Makes 6 to 8 servings.

Très Cheesiest Quiche _____

Pastry for 9-inch pie
1 cup grated Swiss cheese
1 cup grated Cheddar cheese
1 cup grated Gruyère cheese
1 8-ounce package cream
  cheese, cubed

6 eggs
1½ cups light cream
¼ teaspoon salt
¼ teaspoon pepper

On a lightly floured surface roll the pastry to a circle 12½ inches in diameter. Fit the pastry into a 10-inch quiche pan. Make a rolled edge around the pastry with the tines of a fork or by hand. Layer the cheeses in the bottom of the pastry. Beat together the eggs and cream and pour the mixture over the cheeses. Season with salt and pepper to taste. Bake at 375° for 35 to 45 minutes or until the eggs are set.

Makes 6 servings.

ALICE: Oh yeah, I don't even tell my mother how old I am.

Woodland Park Potatoes —————

6 tablespoons butter
6 cups grated potatoes, raw or
  cooked

Salt and pepper to taste
½ cup heavy cream

In a large skillet melt the butter. Add the potatoes in one layer, pressing down with spatula. Season with salt and pepper to taste. Cook over medium heat for 6 minutes. Turn the potatoes over. Pour the cream evenly over the potatoes. Sprinkle again with salt and pepper. Cook for another 6 minutes, until the potatoes are crisp and brown on the bottom. Serve hot.

Makes 6 servings.

MIKE: There are two kids sitting in there watching television like nothing had ever happened.
ALICE: Be careful, Mr. Brady, they just might be recharging their batteries.

UFO Potatoes —————————————

4 large unpeeled russet
  potatoes, scrubbed and
  cubed

¼ cup butter
Salt and pepper to taste

Melt the butter in a skillet. Add the potatoes and season with salt and pepper to taste. Brown the potato cubes for about 4 minutes. Turn the potatoes over with a spatula, and season with salt and pepper again. Cook the potatoes another 3 minutes, until they are dark and brown. Serve with eggs or breakfast steak.

Makes 4 servings.

Sherwood Schwartz

In his long, stellar career in television, Sherwood Schwartz has written, rewritten, and/or produced more than 700 shows, starting with the "Joan Davis Show," "The Red Skelton Show," and "My Favorite Martian," before creating series of his own. He has won the highest honor in television, the Emmy Award, for which he was nominated two consecutive years, and he has the unique distinction of his scripts receiving five consecutive nominations from the Writers Guild of America in three different categories: comedy, variety, and play adaptation.

In 1963 Sherwood entered the Cult TV Hall of Fame when he created, wrote, and produced "Gilligan's Island," a very successful classic comedy series. "Gilligan's Island" holds the honor of having been rerun more than any other series in TV history.

His next television series was a bit more landlocked but just as successful: "The Brady Bunch," of course. Sherwood also created, wrote, and produced "The Brady Bunch" and all the many Brady spin-offs, including *The Brady Girls Get Married,* which he wrote and produced with his son, Lloyd J. Schwartz, as well as *A Very Brady Christmas,* which reunited the father-and-son team, and then the hour-long series "The Bradys." Recently, Sherwood and Lloyd finished the screenplay for a theatrical version of "The Brady Bunch," called naturally, *The Brady Bunch Movie.* They are producing it at Paramount for a 1994 release, which, as everyone who grew up with the show knows, is the twenty-fifth anniversary of "The Brady Bunch" series.

Sherwood wrote a biography, *Inside Gilligan's Island,* which is probably the first biography of a television show from concept to syndication. In a broader sense, *Inside Gilligan's Island* is a backstairs look at the television industry. Published as a film studies textbook by McFarland & Company, it will be published shortly in a more commercial edition by St. Martin's Press.

Sherwood's play *Rockers,* which starred some actress named Ann B. Davis, was produced in June 1993 at the Flat Rock Playhouse in North Carolina, where *Gilligan's Island: The Musical* was first launched. Sherwood also wrote the theme songs for "The Brady Bunch" and "Gilligan's Island," which are two of the biggest hits in televisionland, allowing him to be a member of the Writers Guild of America, the Dramatists Guild, and A.S.C.A.P.

All of this, plus he is a heck of a good guy and a dear friend.

Great Scots' Breakfast Baps (Breakfast Rolls) _____

3 packages active dry yeast
1½ teaspoons sugar
½ cup warm water
4 cups all-purpose flour

1½ teaspoons salt
½ cup shortening
½ cup milk, warmed
⅓ cup warm water

In a small bowl dissolve the yeast and sugar in ½ cup of warm water. Let the mixture stand for 5 minutes. In a separate bowl mix the flour and salt. Cut in the shortening with a pastry blender or a fork. Add the yeast mixture, milk, and ⅓ cup of water, and stir to mix. Mix by hand until the dough is soft. Cover the dough and let it rise for about 1 hour or until doubled in bulk. Turn the dough onto a floured board and knead until smooth. Slice the dough into 16 pieces and form each into a small ball. Place the balls on a greased baking sheet. Allow the baps to rise for 30 minutes. Bake at 400° for 20 to 25 minutes or until golden brown. Serve hot.

Makes 16 baps.

I'm So Blueberry Coffee Cake _____

2 cups sifted all-purpose flour
2 teaspoons baking powder
¼ teaspoon salt
¼ cup butter
¾ cup sugar
1 egg

½ cup milk
2 cups blueberries
½ cup sugar
¼ cup all-purpose flour
½ teaspoon cinnamon
¼ cup butter

Grease and flour an 8-inch square pan. In a large bowl sift together 2 cups of flour, the baking powder, and salt. In a separate bowl cream ¼ cup of butter and beat in ¾ cup of sugar. Add the egg and milk and beat well. Add the dry ingredients. Fold the blueberries into the batter. Pour the batter into the prepared pan.

For the crumb topping, mix ½ cup of sugar, ¼ cup of flour, and the cinnamon. Cut in ¼ cup of butter until the mixture makes coarse crumbs. Sprinkle the topping over the batter. Bake at 350° for about 35 minutes or until a toothpick inserted in the center comes out clean.

Makes 9 servings.

Marcia, Marcia, Marcia Muffins

2 cups whole wheat flour
2 teaspoons baking powder
½ teaspoon salt
1 egg, beaten

¼ cup oil
½ cup honey
1½ cups milk

In a medium bowl mix the flour, baking powder, and salt. Add the egg, oil, honey, and milk, and mix with fork just until moistened. Do not overbeat. Spoon the batter into 12 large greased muffin cups. Bake at 400° for 20 minutes.

Makes 12 large muffins.

CAROL: Which part did you think was the saddest?
ALICE: Well, the part where Romeo dies is sad. The part where Juliet dies is sad, too. But I think the saddest part of all is when Jan said, "Who goes there?" before Peter said, "Hark!"
CAROL: Good night, Alice.
ALICE: Good night. See ya in the morning.

Mellow Out Orange Muffins

2 cups sifted pastry flour
3 tablespoons sugar
3 teaspoons baking powder
1 teaspoon salt

2 eggs, separated
¾ cup orange juice
Grated rind of 1 orange
¾ cup melted butter

Sift the flour, sugar, baking powder, and salt together. Beat the egg yolks until thick and add the orange juice and orange rind. Blend in the dry ingredients. Add the melted butter and beat well. Beat the egg whites until fluffy and fold them into the batter. Spoon into well-greased muffin cups. Bake at 425° for 15 minutes.

The Sunshine Sisters

66Our prop men were something else again. Two guys named Irving and Joe had been in the business for years and were about to retire. They were not too anxious to do anything not called for in the script. Once I asked them to put some more air in a basketball, and they didn't want to because the basketball had already been established! In fact, these two used to bother me a lot. I've always been able to make people smile eventually, given enough time and motivation, but not those two.

"Finally it got to bothering me so much I went to Lloyd Schwartz, our producer, and asked him how to handle the problem. Lloyd thought a moment, then said, 'Just call them the Sunshine Sisters.' So from then on I did, both in and out of their presence. This amused them, and from then on we got along just fine.99

Country Custard Corny Corn Bread

4 egg yolks
3 tablespoons melted butter
¼ cup sugar
½ teaspoon salt
2 cups milk
4 teaspoons lemon juice

1 cup all-purpose flour
¾ cup cornmeal
½ teaspoon baking soda
1 teaspoon baking powder
1 cup heavy cream

Grease an 8-inch square baking dish. Warm the dish in the oven while making the batter.

In a large bowl beat the egg yolks and butter until blended. Add the sugar, salt, milk, and lemon juice, and beat well. Sift together the flour, cornmeal, baking soda, and baking powder. Add the dry ingredients to the eggs and mix until there are no lumps. Pour the batter into the heated dish. Without stirring, pour the cream into the center of the dish. Bake at 350° for 1 hour or until lightly browned. Serve warm with fresh fruit.

Brady Cowboy Breakfast Steak ___

8 small ¼-inch thick tenderloins

Trim the fat from the tenderloins. Drop about 1 tablespoon of the fat into a large skillet and and let it slowly melt over medium-low heat. Move the fat around the skillet until completely filmed. Increase the heat until the skillet is very hot. Put the steaks in the skillet, season with salt and pepper to taste, and fry about 1 minute on each side.

Makes 8 small steaks.

MIKE: Alice, you are marvelous, absolutely the greatest...
CAROL: Oh, honey, stop it. You are embarrassing her.
ALICE: Are you kidding? I love it! Go on, you can say it some more!
MIKE: Sensational. Unforgettable. Terrific...

Honeymoon Heavenly Hash _____

**8 cups cooked and diced
  corned beef
6 cups cooked and diced
  potatoes
2 cups chopped onions**

**Salt and pepper to taste
6 tablespoons butter
¼ cup oil
1 cup heavy cream**

In a large bowl toss the corned beef, potatoes, and onions together. Season with salt and pepper. Heat the butter and oil in a large skillet that has a cover. Add the corned beef mixture and press down with a spatula, spreading the mixture evenly over the bottom of the skillet. Pour the cream evenly over the hash. Cover and cook over medium-low heat for 10 minutes, until the bottom of hash is light brown. Turn over and cook an additional 5 minutes. Serve with sunny-side-up eggs on top if desired.

Makes 8 servings.

Noontime Specials

Are my ears really that big? Artist: Dave Woodman

Juliet Is the Sun Julep _____

2 cups cold water
½ cup sugar
⅓ cup fresh mint leaves

7 cups English breakfast tea,
  brewed and chilled
Mint sprigs for garnish

In a small saucepan combine the water, sugar, and mint. Cook over low heat, stirring constantly, until the sugar is dissolved. Increase the heat and bring the mixture to a boil. Boil for 5 minutes, until the liquid becomes syrup. Remove the pan from the heat and allow it to cool. Strain the syrup into a pitcher and stir in the tea. Pour into serving glasses and garnish with mint sprigs. Y'all enjoy.

Makes 8 servings.

Even a Frog's Got Feelings

66 One of the very few times I did a 'star thing' involved a frog wrangler. Yes, that's right. I went to my dressing room and refused to come out until he stopped using an electric prod to move the frogs. When I came out, the trainer moved the little beasties with some kind of spring (like a mouse-trap in reverse) tucked under the ground cloth. One big hop for 'frogkind.' That's why I decided against frog pizza as one of my recommended recipes. 99

Lovely Lady Lemonade _____

½ cup sugar
½ cup hot water
½ cup freshly squeezed lemon
  juice

7½ cups water

Dissolve the sugar in the hot water and allow to cool. Pour the lemon juice, water, and sugar mix into to a pitcher and stir. Add ice for the best drink on a hot summer day.

Makes 8 servings.

Great White Whale Bread _____

2 packages active dry yeast
½ cup warm water (110°)
2¾ cups warm water (110°)
¼ cup sugar

1 tablespoon salt
3 tablespoons shortening
9 to 10 cups all-purpose flour
Butter

In a large mixing bowl dissolve the yeast in ½ cup of warm water and set aside for 5 minutes to soften. Stir in the remaining water, sugar, salt, shortening, and 5 cups of flour. Beat until smooth. Add the remaining flour until dough is easy to knead. Turn the dough onto a lightly floured board and knead until smooth and elastic. Place the dough in a greased bowl and cover. When dough has doubled in bulk, punch down. Divide in half. Place in 2 greased 9x5x3 loaf pans. Brush with butter. Let rise until double. Place the loaves in the center of the oven. Bake at 425° until golden brown, about 30 to 35 minutes. The loaves will sound hollow when tapped. Remove the loaves from the pans and place on wire racks to cool. Brush with butter while still warm if desired.

Makes 2 loaves.

St. Paddy's Whole Wheat Oatmeal Bread _____

¾ cup buttermilk
1 beaten egg
1 tablespoon melted butter
2 cups whole wheat flour
1 cup quick cooking oats (not instant)

⅓ cup firmly packed light brown sugar
1½ teaspoons baking powder
½ teaspoon baking soda
½ teaspoon salt

In a small bowl combine the buttermilk, egg, and melted butter, and mix well. In a large bowl mix together the remaining ingredients. Make a hole in the dry ingredients and pour the buttermilk mixture into the hole. Fold the flour into the buttermilk until completely blended. Place the dough on a floured board and knead gently for 3 minutes. Shape the dough into a round loaf and place it on a greased baking sheet. Make an X in the top of the loaf. Bake at 350° for 40 to 50 minutes. Serve warm.

Makes 1 loaf.

Head Cheerleader Ham Loaf _____

5 cups ground ham
4 pounds ground pork
1 teaspoon coarsely ground
pepper
4 teaspoons finely chopped
fresh thyme

2 whole bay leaves, crumbled
2 cups fresh bread crumbs
(I prefer dark pumpernickel)
2 eggs, lightly beaten
1 cup milk

Butter 2 medium loaf pans. In a large bowl mix all of the ingredients together. Lightly pack the mixture into the loaf pan. Bake at 350° for 40 to 50 minutes or until the loaf is bubbling around the edges. Remove and pour off the excess fat. Allow the loaf to cool for 10 minutes in the pan before turning out. Slice at once or refrigerate and use for sandwiches later.

Makes 8 servings.

MIKE: You have been here with me and the boys for a long time.
ALICE: Seven years, four months, thirteen days, and nine-and-a half hours.

Grandma Connie's Curried Chicken Spread _____

3 cups cooked ground chicken
1 cup minced celery
4 hard-boiled eggs, chopped
1 4-ounce jar pimiento, drained
and chopped
2 tablespoons minced onions
2 garlic cloves, minced

1 teaspoon fresh lemon juice
1 teaspoon curry powder
1 teaspoon salt
½ teaspoon nutmeg
¼ teaspoon cayenne
1½ cups mayonnaise

In a large bowl mix all of the ingredients thoroughly. Cover and chill for at least 8 hours. Spread on toasted, buttered white bread. Garnish with parsley.

Makes 5 cups, or 10 to 12 servings.

Was there ever a better looking group of kids? The casting was perfect.

S.S. Brady Tuna Fish Spread_____

1 7-ounce can water-packed
   tuna, drained
5 tablespoons mayonnaise
1 tablespoon fresh lemon juice

1 teaspoon capers, finely
   chopped
Salt and pepper to taste

In a medium bowl combine all of the ingredients thoroughly and mix with a fork until mashed. Use immediately or cover and refrigerate. Best if used within 1 day.

Variation: For a different taste, instead of lemon juice and capers use 2 tablespoons of pickle relish.

Tattletale Tuna Sandwich _____

1 7-ounce can white tuna,
  drained
1¼ cups diced Swiss cheese
¾ cup chopped green bell
  peppers

½ cup mayonnaise
2 teaspoons minced onion
¾ teaspoon dillweed
1½ tablespoons lemon juice

In a large bowl combine all of the ingredients and mix well with a fork. Serve with St. Paddy's Whole Wheat Oatmeal Bread (recipe on page 43) for a truly wholesome take-with-you lunch.

Makes about 3 cups, or 6 to 8 servings.

MIKE: Hey, did you enjoy your day off?
ALICE: Well, I took my aunt to the dentist...then we went to the hopsital to visit her next door neighbor...then we went home and played mah jong until ten and went to bed. It may not have been exciting but, on the other hand, it sure was dull.

Zacchariah T. Brown's
Golden Chicken Sandwich _____

3 hard-boiled egg yolks
1½ teaspoons butter, melted
1 teaspoon lemon juice

1½ cups minced cooked
  chicken
Salt and pepper to taste

In a large bowl mash the egg yolks with a fork. Stir in the butter and lemon juice. Add the chicken, salt, and pepper. Mash the mixture to a smooth paste.

Alice's Note: I like this best with fresh white bread.

Makes 1½ cups, or about 4 to 6 servings.

Florence Henderson Remembers Ann B.

"Ann B. is not a woman of many words. She is not given to trivia. She doesn't like to sit around and just shoot the breeze. When she has something to say, she talks. I admire that in people more than I can tell you because I tend to be kind of a motormouth. I learned a lot from Ann B. Not that she can't be fun, because Ann B. can loosen up and have a ball and you can have more fun with her than anybody. But she's who she is, and she doesn't want to be anyone else—she doesn't pretend to be anyone else. You know how some performers all of a sudden become other people and put on airs. Ann B. is just Ann B. That's why she is so wonderful with the characters she plays.

"Alice was very real because that's the way Ann is. Alice worked for the Bradys because she loved them and was forever loyal to them. Ann B. is the same way, and audiences see that. She makes everybody else believable without any nonsense. I have so many memories of Ann B., like taking a mule ride down the Grand Canyon or screaming our heads off on the roller coaster on King's Island. But my best memories are of her quietly doing her needlework, waiting for her next scene while complete havoc was going on around her. I would love to do another series with her sometime. I know that the experience would be creative and professional, and a whole lot of fun.**"**

Answers to Trivia Quiz #1

a. Chocolate chip cookies.
b. Chocolate chip cookies.
c. Chocolate chip cookies.
d. Chocolate chip cookies.
e. Chocolate chip cookies.

Davy Jones' Fan Club Sandwich ___

2 slices bread (white or egg
  bread)
Butter
2 slices cooked chicken breast
Salt

1 tomato, sliced
1 tablespoon mayonnaise
2 slices bacon, cooked and
  drained
Lettuce leaves

Toast and butter the bread. Lay the slices of chicken on one slice of toast and season to taste with salt. Arrange the tomato slices over the chicken, spread the mayonnaise on them, and crumble the bacon over that. Top with the lettuce and cover with a second piece of toast. For school lunches leave out the tomato—no one likes soggy toast.

Makes 1 sandwich.

CAROL: What are you doing home from school?
PETER: They sent me home. Measles.
ALICE: It is either measles or a strange case of red freckles.
CAROL: You have got a temperature.
PETER: They told me. A hundred-and-one-point-one. What's the record?
CAROL: Never mind. That's one record you don't want to break.
ALICE: Right. You don't get to hold the title very long.

Melancholy Danish Prince _____

1 hard-boiled egg, chopped
1½ teaspoons chopped scallions
  (green onion)
2 radishes, sliced
Salt and pepper

1 tablespoon grated sharp
  Cheddar cheese
1½ tablespoons mayonnaise
1 crusty French bread roll

In a medium bowl mix the egg, scallions, and radishes, and season with salt and pepper to taste. Add the Cheddar cheese and mayonnaise and mix lightly with the egg mixture. Spread on the roll.

Sunflower Girls' Sunflower Seed Spread

1 14-ounce can tuna, drained
¾ cup shelled sunflower seeds
1 red onion, chopped

¾ teaspoon chopped fresh basil
¾ cup mayonnaise

In a mixing bowl combine all of the ingredients, mixing well. Serve on the bread of choice.

Alice's Note: This spread is great on crackers for those impromptu sleepovers.

Makes 3 cups, or 6 to 8 servings.

ALICE: You know, Mrs. Brady, I don't know how you do it.
CAROL: Do what?
ALICE: Take a tiny seed, some dirt and a little water, and get a beautiful flower. Whenever I try it, all I get is a muddy seed.

Big River Salmon Spread

1 cup flaked cooked salmon
¼ teaspoon salt
¼ teaspoon pepper
⅓ cup finely chopped green bell pepper
¼ cup finely chopped scallions (green onions)

2 to 3 tablespoons mayonnaise
1 tablespoon lemon juice
1 cucumber, thinly sliced
Dark or rye bread

In a medium bowl combine the salmon, salt, pepper, green pepper, scallions, lemon juice, and mayonnaise. Spread the salmon mixture on the bread and top with one layer of sliced cucumbers per sandwich.

Alice's Note: For dip, omit the cucumbers and serve with chunks of crusty French bread.

Makes about 1½ cups, or 6 sandwiches.

Slumber Party Sub

1 12-inch loaf crusty French
  bread
5 tablespoons soft butter
1 teaspoon garlic salt
4 slices bologna, halved
4 slices Swiss cheese, halved
4 slices Cheddar cheese,
  halved

4 slices Italian salami, halved
4 slices ham, halved
6 slices cucumber
½ green bell pepper, seeded
  and sliced
½ teaspoon dried basil
Salt

Cut the French bread in half lengthwise and spread both halves with the butter. Season with garlic salt. Arrange the halves of meat and cheeses on half the bread so that they overlap and cover the surface. Top with cucumber and strips of green pepper. Sprinkle with basil and salt. Cover with the remaining half of the bread. Wrap the whole sandwich in foil and take off to enjoy the best of southern California— the beach!

Makes 1 sub.

Clinton Avenue Homemade Corned Beef

6 pounds corned brisket of
  beef
8 peppercorns
1 large bay leaf

¾ cup firmly packed brown
  sugar
3 carrots, chopped
1½ large onions, chopped

Trim the fat from the corned beef and place it in a large pot with enough cold water to cover. Cover the pot and simmer slowly. Skim the foam. Add the peppercorns, bay leaf, and brown sugar. Cover and cook slowly for 2 hours and 45 minutes. Then, for flavoring only, add the carrots and onion. Cover and simmer for another hour, until the meat is tender. Pour off the juice. Chill until needed. Slice what you need.

Alice's Note: Watch out! Kids and Mr B. have a tendency to pick at this before it ever leaves the pot.

Makes about 12 to 16 servings.

A hard day of playing Mrs. Dad.

Broadway Joe's Corned Beef Special

½ cup butter
4 teaspoons horseradish
2 cups shredded cabbage
¼ cup mayonnaise
16 slices rye bread

8 slices homemade corned beef, cut ½-inch thick
¼ cup country Dijon mustard
8 slices Swiss cheese

In a mixing bowl cream the butter with the horseradish. Spread the mixture on the bread. Blanch the shredded cabbage in boiling water until slightly wilted. Drain and combine with the mayonnaise. On 8 slices of the bread place 1 slice of corned beef and spread mustard on the meat. Top each with 2 tablespoons of shredded cabbage and a slice of Swiss cheese. Cover with the remaining bread slices. Be sure the cabbage is between the corned beef and the cheese so the bread doesn't get soggy.

Makes 8 sandwiches.

Raquel the Goat's Greek Sandwiches

1 cup sour cream
2 tablespoons prepared
   horseradish
1 teaspoon dill
8 pita breads

2 pounds thinly sliced roast
   beef
2 cups crumbled feta cheese
2 small tomatoes sliced and cut
   in strips

In a small bowl mix the sour cream, horseradish, and dill. Warm the pita bread. Open the pockets of each pita and stuff in the beef, cheese, and tomatoes, dividing evenly among all eight. Spoon some of the sour cream mixture into each pocket.

Makes 8 pitas.

ALICE: Okay! That's enough of small talk. Come on you two, front and center. Sit down over here. Come on. Keeping your room spotless...washing behind your ears...eating everything on your plate...That's bad enough. But this doing chores around the house without being asked is too much! You do-gooders are driving me right up the wall. Either you tell me what is going on around here, or I'll tell all the kids at school the way you are behaving.

GREG: Alice, you wouldn't!

ALICE: Wouldn't I?

Fried Ham and Cheese Hot Rod Sandwich

16 slices firm-textured white
   bread, crusts removed
Butter, softened
16 slices Gruyère cheese
8 slices boiled ham
Ground allspice

Pepper
4 eggs
¼ cup water
6 tablespoons butter
6 tablespoons vegetable oil

Spread butter on one side of each slice of bread. On 8 bread slices, arrange 1 slice of Gruyère, 1 slice of ham, and then another slice of Gruyère. Sprinkle with allspice and a little pepper. Cover with the remaining 8 slices of bread. In a shallow dish beat the egg with the water and dip both sides of each sandwich in the mixture.

In a skillet heat some of the butter and some of the oil. Brown the sandwiches on each side for five minutes, or until golden, adding butter and oil as needed. Serve warm.

Makes 8 sandwiches.

What's in a Name?

66The pilot film was called 'The Brady Brood.' Sherwood came on the set taking a poll on what was better, brood or bunch. I certainly thought bunch was a funnier word. I guess others agreed with me.**99**

Millicent's Meatball Sandwich _____

1 egg	1 clove garlic, minced
1 cup bread crumbs	½ teaspoon leaf oregano
1 pound ground lamb	All-purpose flour
1 large onion, finely minced	2 tablespoons olive oil
1 tablespoon tomato paste	10 long crusty French rolls
¼ cup dry white wine	Sour cream

Beat the egg lightly, add the bread crumbs, and mix well. Add the lamb and mix well. Add the onion, tomato paste, wine, garlic, and oregano, and work the mixture together until it is well blended. Cover and refrigerate for about 1 hour.

Cut the rolls lengthwise without cutting all the way through. Pull out part of the soft centers to create pockets. In a skillet heat the oil. Form the meat mixture into 1-inch balls, and roll them in flour. Fry the meatballs, a small batch at a time, in the oil until they are nicely browned all over. Put 4 meatballs into each roll along with some of the pan drippings. Serve immediately with sour cream on the side.

Makes 10 large sandwiches.

Santa Monica Corn Dogs _____

¾ cup yellow cornmeal
¾ cup all-purpose flour
1½ tablespoons sugar
1¼ teaspoons dry mustard
1 teaspoon baking powder
¾ teaspoon salt

¾ cup milk
1 egg
1 tablespoon oil
8 skewers
8 frankfurters

In a mixing bowl combine the cornmeal, flour, sugar, mustard, baking powder, and salt. Add the milk, egg, and oil, and mix until smooth. Pour the mixture into a shallow pan. Insert a skewer into each frankfurter. Roll the frankfurters in the batter to coat. Deep fry in oil at 375° for 2 minutes, until golden brown. Drain on paper towels.

   Alice's Note: Great eat-and-run food.

   Makes 8 corn dogs.

Mike's Top Secret Shrimp and Celery Salad _____

4 quarts water
1 tablespoon salt
36 medium shrimp, shelled and deveined
6 stalks celery, cut diagonally into 1-inch pieces
3 tablespoons white wine vinegar
2 tablespoons country Dijon mustard

1 teaspoon sugar
Pinch salt
⅓ cup whipping cream
¼ cup minced dill
⅓ cup oil
1 head lettuce
1 medium red onion, thinly sliced

In a large pot bring the water and salt to a boil. Add the shrimp and celery, and cook for 1 minute. Drain and cool to room temperature. In a small saucepan blend the vinegar, mustard, sugar, and salt. Whisk in the cream. Cook over medium heat just to simmering, stirring constantly. Remove the pan from the heat and mix in the dill. Slowly whisk in the oil. Arrange the lettuce leaves on plates and divide the shrimp mixture among them. Top with onion slices and then drizzle dill dressing over each serving. Offer fresh ground pepper at the table.

   Makes 6 servings.

Newton's Applesauce

6 large green apples, peeled,   ¼ cup sugar
  cored, and cubed   ¼ cup lemon juice
¾ cup water

In a saucepan heat the apples and water over medium heat. Cook until the apples are tender, about 5 minutes, stirring constantly. Blend in the sugar and lemon juice. Cook for another 1 or 2 minutes. Remove the pan from the heat and mash with a fork. Chill and serve with sandwiches.

Makes 4 cups.

Brady-riffic Black Bean Soup

4 cups black beans, soaked in   3 leeks, thinly sliced
  cold water overnight and   2 bay leaves
  drained   1 tablespoon salt
5 quarts cold water   ¼ teaspoon freshly ground
¼ cup butter   black pepper
3 large onions, finely chopped   1 cup dry Madeira wine
2½ tablespoons all-purpose   2 hard-boiled eggs, finely
  flour   chopped
½ cup parsley, finely chopped   3 lemons, thinly sliced
3 ham hocks

In a large pot cover the beans with the cold water. Cook over low heat for 1 hour and 30 minutes. In a large skillet melt the butter and sauté the onions for 8 minutes or until tender. Stir in the flour and parsley, cooking and stirring for about 1 minute. Add this mixture to the beans a little at time. Add the ham hocks, leeks, bay leaves, salt, and pepper. Simmer for 4 hours. Add the Madeira wine, stirring until blended. Simmer for 5 minutes. Remove the pan from the heat and stir in the eggs. Serve in bowls with a lemon slice on top of each serving.

Makes 8 servings.

California Dreamin' Shellfish Stew

6 tablespoons olive oil
3 cups finely chopped onions
3 red bell peppers, seeded and diced
1 green bell pepper, seeded and diced
8 garlic cloves, finely chopped
2 cups water
3 cups Zinfandel wine
1 35-ounce can peeled plum tomatoes, drained
1½ tablespoons leaf basil
1½ teaspoons leaf thyme

2 bay leaves
Salt and black pepper to taste
Red pepper flakes
10 large shrimp, peeled and deveined
1¼ pounds bay scallops, rinsed and patted dry
10 small clams, cleaned and steamed open
10 mussels, cleaned and steamed open
1½ cup chopped Italian parsley

In a large soup pot heat the oil over low heat. Add the onions, peppers, and garlic. Cover and cook until the vegetables are tender, about 25 minutes. Increase the heat to medium and add the water, Zinfandel, and tomatoes. Stir in the basil, thyme, and bay leaves, and season to taste with salt, pepper, and red pepper flakes. Bring the mixture to a boil. Reduce the heat and simmer for 30 minutes, stirring occasionally. Increase the heat and quickly bring to a boil. Drop in the shrimp and scallops, then the clams and mussels in their shells. Add the parsley, stir well, and remove the pan from the heat. Let the stew stand, covered, for 1 minute. Remove the bay leaves. Serve immediately with good, crusty white bread or rolls.

Makes 8 servings.

CAROL: Measles.
ALICE: Let's hope all the others don't start coming down with it.
CAROL: Oh, that would be terrible.
ALICE: Right. As the warden of the state prison once said, "I sure would hate to see them all break out at once."

ALICE: Aren't you famished, too?
CAROL: Yeah, but I think I'll wait. I don't want to spoil my appetite for that delicious fresh fish.
ALICE: Oh, well, if you can wait, I can wait. I'll just use a little psychology. I took psychology in school.
CAROL: You did, Alice?
ALICE: Yeah, if you don't think about food, you won't get hungry. So I just won't think about food...Come to think of it, I flunked psychology.

Aunt Jenny's Minestrone With Sausage

⅓ cup olive oil
1 large onion, thinly sliced
4 large carrots, peeled and sliced
1 bulb fennel, chopped
2 large potatoes, peeled and diced
1 green bell pepper, diced
3 medium zucchini, diced
1½ cups green beans, sliced
1 medium cabbage, shredded
5 cups beef stock
5 cups water

1 20-ounce can plum tomatoes
2 tablespoons leaf oregano
1 tablespoon leaf basil
Salt and pepper to taste
¼ cup grated Parmesan cheese
1 8-ounce package small shell pasta
1 14-ounce can white kidney beans, drained
1½ pounds sweet Italian sausage, cooked and sliced

In large stock pot heat the oil and sauté the onion for 10 minutes. Add the carrots and sauté for 2 to 3 minutes. Add the fennel, potatoes, green peppers, zucchini, and green beens, cooking each 2 to 3 minutes before adding the next ingredient. Add the cabbage and cook for 5 minutes. Add the beef stock, water, tomatoes with juice, oregano, basil, salt, and pepper. Stir in the Parmesan cheese and heat to boiling. Reduce the heat and simmer for 2½ to 3 hours. The soup will be thick.

About 15 minutes before the soup is done increase the heat and add the pasta and kidney beans. Stir occasionally until the pasta is cooked. Just before serving add the sausage and heat it through. Serve in shallow bowls.

Makes 8 servings.

A Picture in Time

66Certain moments stick in your mind forever. I remember one from the first year on the set. Barry was often particularly understanding and nice to the younger kids, and once Susan, who couldn't have been more than six or seven at the time, fell asleep with her head on his shoulder. He was probably twelve or thirteen. He was very careful and didn't move until she woke up. It was a pretty good nap, too. A small moment, but one I recall with great affection.99

Brady Family Dinners

Susan Olsen on the warpath.

ALICE: You got to watch egg whites pretty close, because if they get too stiff you can't unstiff 'em.

Secret Admirer Caesar Salad _____

1 egg, lightly beaten
2 cloves garlic, crushed
¼ cup fresh lemon juice
¾ cup olive oil
1 head romaine lettuce, washed, dried, and chilled
5 anchovy fillets, drained and chopped

3 hard-boiled eggs, peeled and crumbled
¾ cup freshly grated Parmesan cheese
1 cup fresh garlic croutons

In a small bowl whisk the egg, garlic, lemon juice, and oil together. Pour the mixture into a large salad bowl. Add the lettuce, anchovies, and hard-boiled eggs, and toss well.

Add the cheese and toss again. Sprinkle with croutons and serve immediately. Season with pepper to taste at table.

Makes 4 servings.

That's Not Schultzy

66 I still remember how I got my first demographic report on the future popularity of 'The Brady Bunch.' At a USO function, a friend of mine introduced me to her young daughter (about six, I guess). 'Honey,' my friend said, 'You remember Schultzy.' Her daughter said, with lisping indignation, 'That's not Schultzy, that's Alice!' And this was shortly after we'd gone on the air. 99

Vote for Brady Vegetable Salad ____

½ cup white wine vinegar
¼ cup minced parsley
4 garlic cloves, minced
2 fresh jalepeño chilies, seeded
  and minced
½ cup light oil
6 tablespoons olive oil
Salt and pepper
1 bunch carrots, peeled and cut
  into sticks

5 large zucchini, sliced
  diagonally
1 head cauliflower, cut into
  florets
1 head broccoli, cut into florets
2 boxes cherry tomatoes,
  stemmed

In a large bowl mix the vinegar, parsley, garlic, and chilies. Add the oils and season to taste with salt and pepper.

Blanch the carrots in boiling salt water for 6 minutes. Drain, rinse under cold water, and drain again. Blanch the zucchini, cauliflower, and broccoli, each for 1 minute. Rinse and drain. Add the vegetables to the dressing and toss to coat. Refrigerate for 1 hour. Arrange the vegetables on a platter to serve.

Makes 6 to 8 servings.

Thyme to Change Vinaigrette _____

1 shallot, minced
1 teaspoon chopped fresh
  thyme
2½ teaspoons fresh lemon juice
¾ teaspoon country Dijon
  mustard

¼ teaspoon freshly ground
  pepper
¼ teaspoon salt
2 tablespoons olive oil

In a small bowl combine all of the ingredients with a fork. Let the dressing stand for 30 minutes. Use this dressing the day you make it.

Makes ¼ cup.

Dr. Cameron's Vinaigrette Dressing

1 tablespoon wine vinegar	Freshly ground black pepper
1 teaspoon salt	¼ cup good olive oil

In a small bowl or container with a lid combine the vinegar, salt, and pepper to taste. Mix well. Add the olive oil, mixing well.

Makes ¼ cup.

MARCIA: If I was to tell you something in secret, would you promise to keep it a secret?

ALICE: They don't call me Alice Clam-Up for nothin'.

Father of the Year French Dressing

2 teaspoons white wine vinegar	Freshly ground black pepper
1 teaspoon salt	¼ cup heavy cream

In a small bowl or container with a lid combine the vinegar, salt, and pepper. Mix well. Add the cream gradually, until well blended. Refrigerate.

Makes ¼ cup.

Lost Locket Lentil Soup _____

¼ pound slab bacon, cubed
2 cups finely chopped yellow
  onions
2 carrots, peeled and finely
  chopped
2 cups finely chopped celery
3 large cloves garlic, peeled
  and chopped

7 cups chicken stock
1 teaspoon leaf thyme
2 bay leaves
Salt and freshly ground black
  pepper to taste
1½ cups brown lentils

In a soup pot sauté the bacon over medium heat until crisp. Remove the bacon with a slotted spoon and set it aside. Add the onions, carrots, celery, and garlic to the skillet. Cover and sauté in the bacon fat over low heat until tender and golden, about 25 minutes.

Add the chicken stock, thyme, bay leaves, salt, pepper, and lentils, and bring the stock to a boil. Reduce the heat and cover the pan. Simmer until the lentils are very tender, about 40 minutes.

Discard the bay leaves. Taste and add salt if necessary. Stir in the reserved bacon and simmer about 1 minute before serving.

Makes 6 to 8 servings.

Alice's No Tears Onion Soup _____

6 tablespoons butter
3 cups minced yellow onion
6 leeks, white part only, thinly
  sliced
¾ cup chopped shallots
6 cloves garlic, minced
4 cups chicken broth

1½ teaspoons leaf thyme
1 bay leaf
Salt and pepper to taste
1½ cups cream
4 scallions (or green onions),
  sliced
Fresh toasted croutons

In a large covered pot melt the butter and cook the onions, leeks, shallots, and garlic over low heat until tender, about 25 minutes. Add the broth, thyme, and bay leaf, and season to taste with salt and pepper. Bring the soup to a boil. Reduce the heat, cover, and simmer for 20 minutes, stirring occasionally. Whisk in the cream and bring the soup to a simmer. Add the scallions and simmer for another 5 minutes. Sprinkle croutons over the soup in bowls before serving.

Makes 6 servings.

Brady Trivia Quiz #2

a. In "Kitty Karryall Is Missing" Alice is recruited to play the judge for the kid's trial. During the proceedings, something burns in the oven, to which Alice sadly observes, "Now I know why judges get paid so much, they gotta keep buying new _____!"

b. What was Alice carefully making in "A Camping We Will Go" that looked perfect one second and like the remains of the Hindenburg the next?

c. In "The Big Sprain," what was the name of the annual event that Sam invited Alice to attend?

d. In "Lost Locket, Found Locket" we find out that Alice, like Jan, is a middle child. What is the name of Alice's oldest sister? And what is the name of her baby sister?

e. What is the name of the bowling league that Sam and Alice belong to?

Answers on Page 69.

Dr. Vogel's Vegetable Soup _____

¼ cup butter or margarine
½ cup peeled and diced carrots
½ cup diced onion
½ cup diced celery
¼ teaspoon leaf oregano
⅛ teaspoon leaf basil
⅛ teaspoon leaf thyme
⅛ teaspoon leaf rosemary
1 clove garlic, minced
1 bay leaf
7 cups beef stock
1 cup canned whole tomatoes, drained

⅔ cup peeled and diced potato
⅓ cup peeled and diced turnip
¼ cup cooked kidney beans
¼ cup cooked navy beans
1 tablespoon chopped fresh parsley
1 tablespoon barley
1 tablespoon split peas
1 tablespoon lentils
Salt and pepper to taste
1 cup chopped turnip greens
½ cabbage, chopped

In a large pot melt the butter over medium heat. Add the carrots, onion, celery, oregano, basil, thyme, rosemary, garlic, and bay leaf. Cook for about 8 minutes, until the vegetables soften. Add the beef stock, tomatoes, potato, turnip, kidney beans, navy beans, parsley, barley, split peas, and lentils. Season with salt and pepper to taste. Cover and cook for 40 minutes. Add the greens and cabbage, and cook an additional 10 minutes. Serve immediately.

Makes 8 servings.

ALICE: How was the ballet lesson?
CAROL: Wonderful. You ought to come sometime.
ALICE: Yeah, in my tu-tu. In my case you better make that a two-two by a four-four.

Meat Cutters' Ball
Beef Tenderloin

1 4-pound beef tenderloin
¼ cup country Dijon mustard
2 tablespoons green
 peppercorns, drained
3½ tablespoons coarsely ground
 black pepper

8 fresh large sage leaves
3 tablespoons unsalted butter
4 bay leaves
Salt to taste

Make a cut lengthwise down the center of the tenderloin through ⅔ thickness. Spread the meat open and flatten slightly. Spread mustard thinly over the open portion. Cover evenly with green peppercorns and lightly press into the meat. Sprinkle 1½ tablespoons of the black pepper over the open portion. Arrange the sage leaves down the center fold. Fold the tenderloin back to its orginal shape and tie shut. Rub the outside with butter and sprinkle with the remaining pepper. Salt to taste. Place seam side down in a shallow roasting pan. Place the bay leaves on top. Roast at 425° for 45 to 55 minutes, longer if you prefer well-done. Let the tenderloin stand for 10 minutes before carving. Spoon the pan juices over the slices.

Makes 8 servings.

Florence Henderson

To list all of Florence Henderson's credits would require a book about the size of a telephone directory. In three decades of extraordinary work on stage, screen, and television, Florence Henderson has earned millions of fans the world over. Her enormous talent has given her a thriving career as a television performer, nightclub entertainer, popular recording artist, stage and motion picture actress, and, most recently, an author. What gets me is that she still looks like she did when we made "The Brady Bunch"!

As you might expect, she got started at the tender age of two when, as the youngest of ten children, she learned to sing a repertoire of fifty songs. Her career officially began at seventeen when she entered New York's prestigious American Academy of Dramatic Arts. Shortly afterward she landed a part in *Wish You Were Here,* a musical from the acclaimed Joshua Logan. In the blink of a Broadway eye, Rodgers & Hammerstein hired her for the lead in the last national company of *Oklahoma.*

Since then Florence has performed nonstop. She was enchanting as Maria in the national company of *The Sound of Music* and as the lead in *The Girl Who Came to Supper,* Noel Coward's last show on Broadway. Her drawing power was so strong that she was chosen to inaugurate the Los Angeles Music Center with a standing-room-only run as Anna in *The King and I* with Ricardo Montalban, followed by the lead in Rodgers & Hammerstein's *South Pacific* at the New York State Theatre in Lincoln Center. From there she spent eight months in Europe making her first feature film, *The Song of Norway.*

Florence was the first woman ever to host the "Tonight Show." She followed this feat by becoming the mother every young child wished for—and still wishes for in 122 countries throughout the world—on "The Brady Bunch" and all the Brady specials, including *A Very Brady Christmas,* which was the highest rated movie-of-the-week in the 1988–89 television season.

Florence's regular appearances on such hit series as "Murder, She Wrote," "The Love Boat," "Fantasy Island," "It's Garry Shandling's Show," "Dave's World," and "Roseanne" attest to her marvelous range and versatility. On top of all this, she was on "Country Kitchen" for nine seasons, which generated her own cookbook, *A Little Cooking, A Little Talking and A Whole Lot of Fun.* For fifteen years she has been the national host of the United Cerebral Palsy Telethon and has helped such charitable activities as the City of Hope and many more.

She has been urged to write her autobiography, but she is just too busy living to get started.

Sam's Cold Tenderloin with Horseradish Sauce

1 4-pound beef tenderloin
Olive oil
Salt
Freshly ground white pepper
6 tomatoes, puréed
4 medium cucumbers, diced
2 medium green bell peppers, diced
2 medium red bell peppers, diced
2 medium red onions, diced

½ cup grated horseradish root
½ cup red wine vinegar
6 teaspoons minced fresh basil
6 teaspoons minced fresh thyme
¾ teaspoon cayenne pepper
¾ teaspoon ground white pepper
¾ teaspoon ground black pepper
¾ teaspoon salt

Rub the tenderloin with oil, salt, and pepper. Set on rack in shallow roasting pan. Roast at 425° until a meat themometer reads 140° F for rare. Allow the tenderloin to cool and then refrigerate until chilled.

In a large bowl combine all of the remaining ingredients. Refrigerate for 8 hours. To serve, slice the tenderloin thinly and serve the sauce on the side. A great hot summer evening meal.

Makes 8 to 12 servings.

Never too Busy to Listen

66 I see myself trying to find little bits of business to make me look occupied and legitimate and maid-like, even though they usually had to be stationary and small, not calling for any extra props. Like feeling a coffee pot with the back of my hand before Carol carries it away—making sure it's hot enough. Or I would mop with minimal movement so as not to interfere with camera placement or cause any of the kids present to move out of position. I made sure that Alice was always busy, always in a bit of a hurry, but not too busy to listen.**99**

Silver Platters Steak _____

½ cup butter
8 4-ounce fillet steaks
Salt and coarsely ground black
   pepper
¼ cup shallots, finely chopped

1 cup mushrooms, sliced
2 cups heavy cream
1 cup Irish whiskey
Fresh parsley for garnish

In a large frying pan melt the butter over medium heat. Add the steaks and sauté for 1 minute on each side. Season with salt and pepper. Remove the steaks to a serving platter and keep them warm. Add the shallots and mushrooms to the pan, and sauté until tender and lightly browned. Add the cream and whiskey. Cook over medium heat until the sauce is reduced by half. Pour the sauce over the steaks. Garnish with fresh parsley and serve immediately.

Makes 8 servings.

Fast and Easy Rider
Pepper Steak _____

2 pounds boneless sirloin
   steak, ½-inch thick
¾ teaspoon salt
3 medium onions, chopped
1¼ cups beef broth
3¼ tablespoons soy sauce
2 cloves garlic, minced

3 green bell peppers, chopped
¼ cup all-purpose flour
½ cup cold water
2 tomatoes, peeled and cut into
   eighths
3 to 4 cups hot cooked rice

Trim the fat from the meat. Cut the meat into 8 serving pieces. Grease a large skillet lightly with the fat from the meat. Brown the meat thoroughly on one side; turn and season with half of the salt. Brown the other side of the meat; turn, and season with the remaining salt. Push the meat to one side of the skillet. Add the onion and cook until tender. Stir in the broth, soy sauce, and garlic. Cover and simmer for 10 minutes. Add the green pepper. Cover and simmer for 5 minutes. In a small bowl mix together the flour and water until blended. Stir the flour mixture gradually into the meat mixture. Bring the mixture to a boil, stirring constantly. Boil for 1 minute. Add the tomatoes and cook until heated through. Serve over rice.

Makes 8 servings.

Fillmore Flank Steak with Garlic-Ginger Sauce _____

1 cup olive oil
8 cloves garlic, minced
¼ cup chopped fresh ginger
 root
5 large carrots, peeled and
 diced
1 white onion, minced

1¼ cups dry white wine
¾ cup water
1 tablespoon leaf oregano
¾ cup fresh parsley, chopped
Salt and pepper to taste
1 tablespoon sesame oil
1 2½-pound flank steak

In a medium-size skillet heat the oil over medium heat. Add the garlic, ginger, and carrots, and sauté for 10 minutes. Stir in the onion and sauté 2 minutes more. Add the wine, water, and oregano, and simmer over low heat for 30 minutes. Stir in the parsley and season to taste with salt and pepper. Rub sesame oil into both sides of the steak. Broil for 5 minutes per side. Cut the steak diagonally into thin slices. Arrange the steak on a platter and spoon the sauce over.

Makes about 6 servings.

Banquet Night Hostess London Broil _____

1 tablespoon butter or
 margarine
2 medium onions, thinly sliced
½ teaspoon salt
2 tablespoons vegetable oil
1 teaspoon lemon juice

2 cloves garlic, crushed
¼ teaspoon salt
¼ teaspoon pepper
1 2-pound flank steak, scored
 diagonally

In a large skillet melt the butter. Add the onions and ½ teaspoon of salt. Cook and stir until the onions are tender. Keep warm over low heat. In a small bowl mix together the oil, lemon juice, garlic, and the remaining salt and pepper. Brush the top side of the meat with half of the oil mixture. Broil the meat 2 to 3 inches from the heat for about 5 minutes or until brown. Turn the meat over, brush with the oil mixture, and broil 5 minutes longer. Cut the meat into thin slices and serve on a platter with the onions.

Makes 4 servings.

The Swiss Family Brady.

Professor Whitehead's Beef Teriyaki

3 cups sake
1 cup sugar
3 cups soy sauce

1 8½-pound rib steak with bone removed

In a saucepan mix the sake and sugar and cook over low heat until the sugar has dissolved. Turn off the heat and ignite the sake mixture with a match, shaking the pan until the flame dies. Add the soy sauce and bring the mixture to a boil. Continue boiling until the mixture thickens and becomes syrupy. Pour the sauce into a shallow bowl large enough to dip the steaks.

Preheat the broiler or if using barbecue grill, be sure the coals are white hot. Dip the steak into the teriyaki sauce, coating the meat thoroughly. Broil or barbecue to the desired doneness, dipping the meat into the sauce again when it is turned. Reheat the remaining sauce. To serve, slice the steaks into ½-inch slices and arrange the slices on a warmed plate. Pour some of the remaining sauce over the steaks and garnish with parsley. Serve with hot rice and the remaining sauce on the side.

Makes 8 servings.

Out of this World Round Steak And Gravy

1 3½-pound beef round steak,
  1-inch thick
½ cup all-purpose flour
3 tablespoons oil

1 envelope dry onion soup mix
½ cup water
1 10-ounce can condensed
  cream of mushroom soup

Coat one side of the meat with half the flour and pound it in. Turn and repeat with the other side. Cut the meat into 8 serving pieces. In a large skillet heat the oil and brown the meat over medium heat, about 15 minutes. Sprinkle the onion soup mix over the meat. In a small bowl mix the water and cream of mushroom soup and pour the mixture over the meat. Cover and simmer for 1½ hours or until tender.

Place the meat on a warm platter. Heat the remaining gravy mixture to boiling, stirring constantly, and pour the mixture over the meat.

Makes 8 servings.

Et Tu, Pot Roast

66 I have to confess that at the beginning I dabbled in method acting for the character of Alice, just to get into the part. One afternoon, I was taking a pot roast out of an oven that wasn't on—the roast had been prepared at 5:00 A.M. that morning—when I realized I did not have a mitten on one of my hands. Instead of reacting naturally, since the metal pan was cold, I let out a scream like I was about to be burnt and dropped the roast, pan and all. As they mopped up the mess, I realized that too much realism could be an untidy thing. **99**

Judge Alice's Pot Roast _____

1 3½-pound chuck roast
1 teaspoon pepper
3 tablespoons olive oil
2½ cups dry red wine
1 bunch parsley, chopped
1 teaspoon salt
2½ cups chopped onions

2½ cups peeled carrot chunks
8 medium potatoes, cut in thirds
2 cups canned plum tomatoes with juice
1 cup diced celery

Rub the roast with pepper. In a large heavy pot heat the olive oil and sear the roast on both sides until well browned. Pour in the wine and add the parsley, salt, and pepper. Stir in the onions, carrots, potatoes, tomatoes, and celery. The liquid should not cover the meat completely. Cover and cook over low heat for 3 to 3½ hours. Serve immediately.

Makes about 8 servings.

CAROL: Listen, Sam is a very romantic fellow.
ALICE: Mrs. Brady, Sam's idea of romance is two pounds of liver—heart shaped!

Black Forest Spiced German Pot Roast _____

2½ tablespoons butter	¼ cup all-purpose flour
5 pound beef chuck pot roast (arm, blade, chuck eye, or cross rib)	2 cloves garlic, crushed
	1¾ teaspoons salt
	½ teaspoon pepper
1¼ teaspoons salt	½ teaspoon ginger
¾ teaspoon pepper	¼ cup tomato sauce
1¼ cups water	2 tablespoons vinegar

In a large skillet or Dutch oven melt the butter over medium heat and brown the meat for about 15 minutes. Season with 1¼ teaspoons of salt and ¾ teaspoon of pepper.

Reduce the heat. Add the water to the skillet and cover tightly. Simmer or bake at 325° for 3 hours or until tender. Remove the meat and keep the pan warm while making gravy.

Pour the drippings in a bowl, leaving the brown particles in the pan. Skim off the fat, reserving ¼ cup. Return the reserved fat to the pan. Blend in the flour. Cook over low heat, stirring constantly, until the mixture is smooth and bubbly. Remove the pan from the heat. Pour the meat juice into a large measuring cup and add enough water to measure 2¼ cups of liquid. Stir the liquid slowly into the flour mixture. Heat to boiling, stirring constantly. Stir in the garlic, 1¾ teaspoons of salt, ½ teaspoon of pepper, ginger, tomato sauce, and vinegar. Reduce the heat and simmer for 10 minutes, stirring occasionally. Serve the meat on a platter with gravy on the side.

Makes 6 to 8 servings.

Answers to Trivia Quiz #2

a. Pot roast.
b. Cheese soufflé.
c. The Meat Cutters Ball.
d. Emily (who did the bossing) and Myrtle.
e. The Meat Packers and the Meat Cutters.

Carol Brady's Spiced Beef And Vegetables _____

1 12-ounce bottle dark beer
2 cups beef broth
½ cup brandy
1 tablespoon Worcestershire
  sauce
½ cup all-purpose flour
1 teaspoon ground cinnamon
½ teaspoon ground allspice
½ teaspoon ground ginger
3 tablespoons orange
  marmalade
1 teaspoon salt

½ teaspoon pepper
2 large onions, sliced
3 large baking potatoes, peeled
  and sliced
3 carrots, peeled and sliced
  ½-inch thick
½ cup pitted prunes
½ cup raisins
½ cup dried apricots
2½ pounds boneless beef chuck
  steaks, 1-inch thick

In a deep 6-quart ovenproof casserole or Dutch oven mix together the beer, broth, brandy, Worcestershire sauce, flour, cinnamon, allspice, ginger, marmalade, salt, and pepper. Pour 2 cups of the mixture into a measuring cup. In a 2-quart casserole dish layer half of the onions, potatoes, carrots, prunes, raisins, and apricots. Place the steaks on top and repeat with a second layer. Pour 2 cups of the reserved broth mixture over all. Cover and bake at 325° for 2 hours.

Uncover and spoon the gravy from the bottom of the pan over the top. Cover, return the dish to the oven, and bake 1 hour longer.

Makes 6 to 8 servings.

Safety Monitor Stroganoff _____

3 cups sour cream
1½ tablespoons country Dijon
  mustard
3 tablespoons tomato paste
3 tablespoons Worcestershire
  sauce
2 teaspoons paprika
Salt
Freshly ground black pepper
½ cup plus 3 tablespoons
  unsalted butter

1 pound medium white
  mushrooms, thinly sliced
20 medium white pearl onions,
  peeled
3 pounds beef tips, thinly
  sliced diagonally
3 cups cooked wide noodles,
  buttered

Wouldn't everybody want parents like these?

In a medium saucepan combine the sour cream, mustard, tomato paste, Worcestershire sauce, paprika, and salt and pepper to taste and simmer slowly for 20 minutes. Remove the pan from the heat, cover, and let it stand.

In a medium skillet melt 3 tablespoons of butter and sauté the mushrooms until tender, about 10 minutes. Transfer the mushrooms to a bowl and reserve.

In the same skillet heat another 2 tablespoons of butter and sauté the onions, stirring often, until they are lightly browned, about 10 minutes. Transfer the onions to the bowl with the mushrooms.

In the same skillet heat the remaining butter and sauté the sliced beef over high heat until lightly browned, about 3 minutes. Transfer the meat to a platter and keep it warm.

Return the sour cream mixture to a simmer over medium heat. Add the mushrooms, onions, and juices from the sautéed vegetables and simmer for 5 minutes. Add the beef and juices and cook until the meat is heated through, about 2 minutes. Serve immediately over cooked noodles.

Makes 6 servings.

Stage Fright
Swedish Meatballs

1½ pounds ground beef
1 pound ground lean pork
¾ cup minced onion
1 cup dry bread crumbs
4 teaspoons minced parsley
2 teaspoons salt
¼ teaspoon pepper
1 teaspoon Worcestershire
sauce

1 large egg
¾ cup milk
½ cup oil
⅓ cup all-purpose flour
½ teaspoon salt
¼ teaspoon pepper
2¼ cups water
1 cup sour cream

In a large bowl mix together the beef, pork, onion, bread crumbs, parsley, 2 teaspoons of salt, ¼ teaspoon of pepper, Worcestershire sauce, egg, and milk. Chill. Shape the mixture by hand into 1-inch balls. In a large skillet heat the oil and slowly brown the meatballs. Remove the meatballs and keep them warm.

In the skillet blend the flour, ½ teaspoon of salt, and ¼ teaspoon of pepper into the oil in the skillet. Cook over low heat, stirring constantly, until the mixture is smooth and bubbly. Remove the pan from the heat and stir in the water. Heat to boiling, stirring constantly, about 1 minute. Reduce the heat and slowly stir in the sour cream, mixing until smooth. Add the meatballs and heat through, about 2 minutes. Serve with rice or noodles.

Makes 6 to 8 servings.

CAROL: As to manner of payment, we refer you to Section 12, Article C, Paragraph 42 of contract. Now what do you suppose they mean by "manner of payment"?

ALICE: Sorry. Hungarian goulash I understand. Legal goulash I don't.

Far Out Hungarian Goulash _____

¼ cup butter
2 pounds beef chuck or round,
  in 1-inch cubes
1 cup sliced onion
1 small clove garlic, minced
¾ cup tomato sauce
2 tablespoons Worcestershire
  sauce
1 tablespoon packed brown
  sugar

2 teaspoons salt
2 teaspoons paprika
½ teaspoon dry mustard
⅛ teaspoon cayenne pepper
1½ cups water
2 tablespoons all-purpose flour
¼ cup red wine
3 cups hot cooked noodles

In a large skillet melt the butter. Add the beef, onion, and garlic. Cook, stirring until the meat is brown and the onion is tender. Stir in the tomato sauce, Worcestershire sauce, sugar, salt, paprika, mustard, cayenne, wine, and 1¼ cups of water. Cover and simmer for 2 to 2½ hours.

Blend the flour and ¼ cup of water until smooth. Stir the mixture slowly into the meat mixture. Heat to boiling, stirring constantly, about 1 minute. Serve over the hot noodles.

Makes 6 servings.

Alice's Ever Popular Meat Loaf _____

2 pounds ground beef
1 pound lean ground pork
2 cups dry bread crumbs
2½ cups milk
2 eggs, beaten
½ cup minced onion
2 teaspoons salt

½ teaspoon pepper
½ teaspoon celery salt
1 clove garlic, finely minced
1 teaspoon dry mustard
1 teaspoon leaf sage
1 tablespoon Worcestershire
  sauce

In a large bowl combine all of the ingredients. Divide the mixture in half and spread into 2 ungreased 9x5-inch loaf pans. Bake at 350° for 1 hour and 30 minutes.

Alice's Note: Double loaves are great because whatever isn't eaten at dinner becomes lunch tomorrow.

Makes 8 servings.

CAROL: Alice, you can put the hamburgers on any time you're ready.
ALICE: All right, Mrs. Brady, that's rare for you and Mr. Brady...medium rare for Jan and Peter...well-done for Marcia...could be a lot simpler if I just pounded this whole thing together into a meat loaf.

Skip Farnum's Spanish Meat Loaf

1 8-ounce can tomato sauce
1½ pounds ground beef
8 large black olives, sliced
1 medium onion, chopped
1 egg

2 tablespoons olive oil
1 teaspoon salt
¼ teaspoon pepper
½ cup oats

In a large bowl combine half of the tomato sauce and the remaining ingredients. Spread the mixture in an ungreased 9x5-inch loaf pan. Spread the remaining tomato sauce over the loaf. Bake at 350° for 1 hour and 15 minutes.

Makes 6 servings.

ALICE: She already did, Mr. Brady. But there would be no point in her snooping in here again. Once she already snooped it, it's snooped-out.
MIKE: Alice, you are talking a little bit like your meat loaf. A little bit of everything and all mixed up.

Drysdale's Home Run Stuffed Green Peppers _____

5 cups water	2 tablespoons chopped onion
Salt to taste	1 teaspoon salt
6 large green bell peppers,	1 clove garlic, finely minced
cleaned, cored, and seeded	1 cup cooked rice
1 pound ground beef	1 15-ounce can tomato sauce

In a large saucepan bring the water to a boil. Add salt to taste. Cook the peppers in the boiling salted water for 5 minutes. Drain.

In a medium skillet brown the ground beef. Add the onion and cook until tender. Drain the fat. Stir in the salt, garlic, rice, and 1 cup of the tomato sauce, and heat through. Lightly stuff each pepper evenly with meat mixture. Stand the peppers upright in an ungreased 8-inch square baking dish. Pour the remaining tomato sauce over the peppers. Cover and bake at 350° for 45 minutes. Uncover and bake 15 minutes longer.

Makes 6 servings.

Old Dutch Oven Beef Stew _____

3 pounds lean beef stew meat	5 medium baking potatoes,
1 10½-ounce can condensed	peeled and cut into eighths
cream of celery soup	8 carrots, peeled and halved
½ envelope onion soup mix	crosswise
1 cup dry red wine	1 cup broccoli florets
1 onion, coarsely chopped	1 cup cauliflower florets

In a 5-quart Dutch oven combine the beef, soup, soup mix, wine, and onion, and mix well. Stir in the potatoes and carrots. Cover and bake at 350° for 2 hours. Stir in the broccoli and cauliflower. Cover and bake 15 more minutes. Uncover and bake 15 minutes longer.

Alice's Note: You can get all your housework done while this recipe cooks along.

Makes 6 to 8 servings.

Sam Loves Alice Lamb Chops _____

1 cup honey
1 cup country Dijon mustard
½ small white onion, finely
   chopped

¼ teaspoon pepper
16 lamb ribs (or loin or sirloin
   chops), 1-inch thick

In a saucepan combine the honey, mustard, onion, and pepper and heat, stirring occasionally. Keep warm over low heat.

Arrange the chops on a broiler pan. Broil the chops 3 inches from the heat for 7 minutes. Brush with the honey mustard. Turn the chops and broil for 5 minutes more. Brush again. Serve the remaining honey mustard with the chops.

Makes 8 servings.

The Egg and Bob

66Bob Reed could be difficult, but there were times when he would do something so engaging that you'd have to give him another chance. In one show he and Carol were doing a role reversal thing—he was cooking while she was teaching baseball. Bob was asked to play 'slipping and falling down' (that's an old acting term) because of a dropped egg on the kitchen floor. There was quite a scene until Bob reluctantly agreed to at least rehearse it once. In the process, he actually did drop an egg and actually did slip and fall down—so fast I would have sworn he hit the floor before the egg did. After ascertaining that he hadn't really hurt himself, I asked him if he thought he could play the scene, and he said, 'You know, Ann, all the way down I was thinking, I deserve this!' He had his moments.99

Fighting Irish Beef Casserole _____

2 tablespoons butter
2 pounds stew meat, cubed
2 tablespoons all-purpose flour
1 bottle Guiness stout
1 clove garlic

1 teaspoon dry mustard
1 green pepper, sliced
1 large onion, sliced
½ cup sliced mushrooms

In a skillet heat the butter and brown the stew meat. Stir in the flour. Add the Guiness, garlic, and mustard. Bring the stew slowly to a boil. Pour the mixture into a 1½-quart ovenproof casserole. Bake at 300° for 2 hours and 30 minutes. Add the green pepper, onion, and mushrooms, and cook another 30 minutes.

Makes 6 servings.

Do-it-Yourself Flour Tortillas _____

4 cups all-purpose flour
2 teaspoons salt

⅓ cup shortening
1½ cups warm water

In a large bowl combine the flour and salt. Cut in the shortening until the mixture resembles coarse meal. Add the water and mix until doughlike. Knead the dough in the bowl for 1 minute. Turn the dough onto a floured surface. Cover and set aside for 30 minutes. Divide the dough into 18 balls. Roll each ball between both hands until smooth, then flatten into discs. Wrap in plastic and set aside for 1 hour. Roll out each disc to a 10-inch round.

Heat a skillet or griddle. Place each round on a griddle and count to 10, then turn over. Keep counting and turning until each tortilla has golden spots and has stopped bubbling. Wrap in a kitchen towel, cool, and then wrap individually in foil and store in a plastic bag until ready to use. May be refrigerated for one week or frozen.

Makes 18 tortillas.

Outer Space Chimichangas _____

1 quart water
1 pound lean steak, cut in
  2-inch cubes
1½ teaspoons salt
2 tablespoons oil
1 small onion, sliced
1 clove garlic, minced
¾ pound tomatoes, seeded and
  chopped
1½ green bell peppers, seeded
  and sliced
1½ teaspoons pepper

8 12-inch flour tortillas (see
  recipe, page 81)
Oil
Green Chili Salsa (see recipe,
  page 83)
2 cups grated Cheddar cheese
2 cups grated Monterey Jack
  cheese
Sour cream
3 tomatoes, diced
Minced green onion tops

In a heavy saucepan combine the water, beef, and salt and bring the mixture to a boil. Skim. Reduce the heat to simmer and cook for about 2 hours or until the meat is tender. Cool and drain, retaining 1½ cups of liquid.

Shred the meat. Heat the oil in a large skillet over medium heat. Add the onion and garlic, and cook until soft. Mix in the beef and ¾ pound of tomatoes, and simmer for 5 minutes. Add the bell pepper, pepper, and ½ cup of the reserved liquid. Cover and simmer until the liquid is almost absorbed. Heat a separate skillet over medium heat. Cook 1 tortilla at a time until soft, about 10 seconds per side. Place ½ cup of beef mixture on a tortilla and fold the lower half over the beef. Fold in the sides and roll up. Repeat with each tortilla. Heat the oil in a large skillet to 375°. Add the chimichangas and cook until golden brown, about 3 minutes on each side. Do not crowd. Drain on a paper towel.

Spoon Green Chili Salsa (see next page) over the chimichangas. Top with the cheeses and sour cream. Sprinkle with the diced tomatoes and minced green onion tops.

Makes 8 servings.

Green Chili Salsa

1 8-ounce can chopped
  tomatoes
1 cup beef broth
1 small habanero (yellow) chili,
  seeded and minced
½ green bell pepper, minced
2 ounces canned whole green
  chilies, seeded and cut in
  strips

¼ cup diced green onion
1 teaspoon oregano
1 garlic clove, minced
Salt
3 tablespoons butter
1¼ tablespoons all-purpose
  flour

In a medium saucepan mix all of the ingredients except the flour and butter, and bring the mixture to a boil. Melt butter in small skillet over low heat. Add flour and stir 3 minutes. While stirring gradually add the flour mixture to the salsa mixture. Simmer for 15 minutes. Spoon over the chimichangas.

Young Pros

66The kids acted like real pros right from the start. That was due primarily to the way they were treated when we first started filming. John Rich directed the pilot and the first five episodes, a very good director who knew exactly what he was doing. He graciously dismissed the parents and guardians from the rehearsal stage, then proceeded to treat the youngsters as if they were professional adult actors. So that was how they responded. They always knew their lines and were present when and where they were expected, sometimes better than the rest of us! Sherwood did a remarkable job casting the youngsters. Each had a likable personality and plenty of charm. They were the kind of kids you would enjoy having in a family, which is why the show worked.99

Elopement Enchilada Casserole _____

1 10½-ounce can condensed
   creamy chicken mushroom
   soup
¾ cup sour cream
2 tablespoons milk
1 4-ounce can diced green
   chilies
2 scallions, chopped

9 5-inch corn tortillas
2 cups chopped cooked beef
½ red bell pepper, chopped
2 cups shredded Cheddar
   cheese
1 5¾-ounce can ripe olives,
   drained

In a medium bowl combine the soup, sour cream, milk, chilies, and scallions. Arrange 3 tortillas in the bottom of an 11x7-inch baking dish. Layer with half the beef, half the red pepper, and a third of the cheese, then top with a third of the soup mixture, spreading evenly. Repeat the layers. Top with the remaining 3 tortillas, the olives, and the remaining soup mixture, and then sprinkle with remaining cheese. Bake at 350° for 30 to 35 minutes, or until heated through and bubbly.
   Makes 6 to 8 servings.

Italian Spaghetti Western _____

2 pounds ground beef
2 onions, finely chopped
¼ cup butter
8 pounds plum tomatoes,
   skinned and finely chopped
4 large cloves garlic, chopped
3 teaspoons sugar
Salt and pepper to taste

8 fresh basil leaves, finely
   chopped
¼ cup red wine
16 ounces spaghetti, cooked
   and hot
Freshly grated Parmesan
   cheese

In a large skillet cook the ground beef and onion, stirring frequently, until the meat is brown and the onion is tender. Drain. Set aside and keep warm. In a separate saucepan heat the oil and butter, and add the remaining ingredients except the spaghetti and Parmesan. Simmer for 40 minutes or until the sauce is thick. Add the meat and cook until heated through, about 5 minutes. Serve with spaghetti and Parmesan cheese.
   Makes 6 to 8 servings.

The subtle art of the curve ball.

Peter's Volcanic Mushroom Sauce

¼ cup butter
2 medium onions, sliced
½ pound fresh mushrooms, sliced
1 cup cooked peas

1½ cups heavy cream
¼ cup grated Parmesan cheese
1 pound pasta (your choice), cooked
Salt and pepper

In a large skillet melt the butter. Sauté the onions and mushrooms until tender. Stir in the peas, cream, and Parmesan, and heat through. Pour over hot pasta and toss. Season with salt and pepper to taste.
   Makes 6 to 8 servings.

MIKE: Hi, Sam.
   SAM: Hi, Mr. Brady.
MIKE: Hey, that was a great roast we had the other night.
   SAM (hugs Alice): Thanks. This ain't a bad little lamp chop right here, either.

Most Popular Girl Pine Nut Pasta Sauce

½ cup butter
2 tablespoons toasted pine
  nuts, chopped
1 tablespoon chopped fresh
  marjoram

1 pound pasta (any shape),
  cooked
Salt and fresh pepper to taste
1 cup freshly grated Parmesan
  cheese

In a small saucepan melt the butter. Add the nuts and marjoram and cook for 3 minutes. Pour the sauce over the pasta and season with salt and pepper to taste. Sprinkle with Parmesan.

Note: To toast pine nuts, arrange the pine nuts on a baking sheet and bake at 350° for 10 minutes.

Makes 6 servings.

Warren Mulaney Mushroom Sauce

½ cup butter
4 medium onions, thinly sliced
1 cup sliced fresh mushrooms
1 cup cooked peas
3 cups heavy cream

½ cup freshly grated Parmesan
  cheese
2 cups cooked pasta
Salt and freshly grated pepper
  to taste

In a large skillet melt the butter. Add the onions and mushrooms, and cook until the mushrooms are tender. Stir in the peas, cream, and Parmesan, and cook until heated through. Pour the sauce over the hot pasta and toss. Season with salt and pepper. Serve with more Parmesan on the side.

Makes 2 servings.

Peter the Great Pesto _____

1½ cups fresh basil leaves
¾ cup olive oil
¼ cup soft butter
¾ cup freshly grated Parmesan
  cheese

2 tablespoons chopped flat leaf
  parsley
2 garlic cloves, chopped
Salt and fresh pepper to taste

In a food processor combine all of the ingredients except the salt and pepper, and purée. Season with salt and pepper. To use as a sauce, thin with a few tablespoons of warm water. For seasoning, don't dilute.

Serving Suggestion: For special occasions, split a Brie wedge through the center, spread pesto on the bottom half, and sprinkle with minced toasted pine nuts. Cover with the top of the Brie and serve with chunks of French bread.

Mrs. Desi Arnaz, Jr., Lasagna _____

1 pound lean ground beef
6 ounces lean ground pork
¾ cup chopped onion
1 clove garlic, minced
1 16-ounce can tomatoes
1 15-ounce can tomato sauce
3 tablespoons chopped parsley
2 tablespoons sugar
2½ teaspoons salt

1 teaspoon chopped fresh basil
3 cups ricotta cheese
1 cup grated Parmesan cheese
1 teaspoon oregano
8 ounces lasagna noodles,
  cooked
¾ pound mozzarella cheese,
  shredded

In a large saucepan brown the beef, pork, onion, and garlic. Drain. Stir in the tomatoes and tomato sauce. Add 2 tablespoons of parsley, the sugar, 1 teaspoon of salt, and the basil. Bring the mixture to a boil, stirring constantly. Reduce the heat and simmer for 1 hour. Reserve ½ cup of sauce.

In a medium bowl mix the ricotta, ½ cup of Parmesan, 1 tablespoon of parsley, 1½ teaspoons of salt, and the oregano. In an ungreased 13x9-inch baking pan layer ¼ each of pasta, meat sauce, mozzarella, and ricotta mixture. Repeat the layers 3 times. Spread the reserved sauce over the top. Cover with ½ cup of Parmesan. Bake at 350° for 45 minutes. Let the lasagna stand for 10 minutes before cutting. Serve immediately.

Makes 9 servings.

I Lived the Simple Life

66Of course, I didn't get too caught up in the mod styles of the day, like flaired pants and mad plaid shirts. My uniform, of which I had several, just kept rolling along. Once in a while I'd get a dress or a sweater or something. Fine with me—give me the simple life. On 'The Bob Cummings Show,' back in the 50s, I wore one skirt and I00 different blouses. **99**

Everybody's Smiling Beef and Eggplant Casserole

1 pound lean ground beef
2 cloves garlic, minced
1 teaspoon salt
½ teaspoon pepper
½ cup long grain white rice
2 pounds eggplant, cut in
  1-inch cubes

2 tablespoons olive oil
2 teaspoons leaf oregano
1 medium onion, sliced
4 cups tomatoes, finely minced
2 eggs, lightly beaten
1 tablespoon heavy cream

In a 4-quart Dutch oven cook the beef with the garlic, salt, and pepper over medium-high heat until brown, stirring constantly, 5 to 7 minutes. Drain.

Stir in the rice and cook for 1½ minutes, until translucent. Remove the pan from the heat. Place the eggplant over the meat mixture. Drizzle 1 tablespoon of oil over the eggplant. Sprinkle with 1 teaspoon of oregano. Arrange a layer of onion on top of the eggplant. Add the tomatoes. Drizzle with the remaining oil and sprinkle with the remaining oregano. Cover. Bake at 350° for 1 hour.

Beat the eggs with the cream. Pour the mixture over the casserole. Return the pan to the oven and bake for 5 to 10 minutes, until the custard is set.

Makes 4 servings.

Personality Kid Roast Pork _____

2 teaspoons chopped fresh
basil
2 tablespoons chopped fresh
parsley
3 cloves garlic, crushed
4 teaspoons finely chopped
onions

1 tablespoon lemon juice
1 4-pound pork loin
¼ cup olive oil
¾ cup red wine

A day in advance, in a small bowl combine the basil, parsley, garlic, onion, and lemon juice. Score the skin of the loin with a sharp knife. Rub the herb mixture into the skin of the loin. Wrap the loin and refrigerate overnight.

Remove the loin from the refrigerator 1 hour before starting to cook and brush the skin well with olive oil. Place the meat on a rack in a roasting pan. Roast at 375° for 2 hours. When cooked, skim off the excess fat from the juice in the pan and add the wine for gravy.

Serve with baked potatoes.

Makes 8 servings.

SAM: Isn't Alice with you anymore?
MIKE: Oh, that's right, you didn't know. No, Alice is in bed. You see she had a fall.
SAM: Oh, bad?
MIKE: Well, sprained her ankle.
SAM: Gee, that's a shame.
MIKE: Yeah.
SAM: But it could be worse. At least it wasn't her short ribs. I'll take a dime for that last joke.
MIKE: Could you take a quarter?

Maureen McCormick

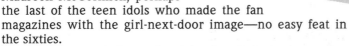

Her friends and family call her Mo, a nickname that is straight-forward, implying a bit of a tomboy and certainly down-playing the image of a Holly-wood starlet. All these are qualities of Marcia Brady, at least partly because they are the very real qualities of Maureen McCormick, perhaps the last of the teen idols who made the fan magazines with the girl-next-door image—no easy feat in the sixties.

Maureen made her acting debut in a little-theater production of *Wind It Up and It Breaks* at the La Jolla Playhouse. She made dozens of commercials, including one as Peppermint Patty from "Peanuts." Maureen also recorded about twenty-five soundtracks for talking toys and dolls; so go find your old Chatty Cathy, pull the string, and listen very closely. This led to her first major television exposure on "Camp Runamuck," followed by bit parts on "Bewitched," "I Dream of Jeannie," and "My Three Sons," her prelude to the larger Brady family.

Maureen appeared in all "The Brady Bunch" spin-offs except the hour-long "The Bradys." During the series, she became so popular with fans that she was asked to write an advice column, "Dear Maureen," for 16 SPEC magazines. One year she won 16 magazine's Female Star of the Year award.

Putting her Marcia Brady image aside, Maureen continued to make television appearances in such hit series as "Harry O," "Fantasy Island," "The Love Boat," and "Streets of San Francisco." She made several motion pictures including *Moonshine County*, *Take Down*, a well received drama of high school wrestlers, also starring Edward Herrmann and Lorenzo Lamas, *Staketown U.S.A.*, and *Texas Lightning*, for which she composed and sang the theme song, "It's A Typical Day." She also had a serious role in *The Idolmaker*, a tour de force about the music business.

Maureen is happily married and raising her daughter, Natalie. Lately she has been very busy working on a country album in Nashville, involved with a children's video for Warner Brothers, making guest appearances on television series, like "Herman's Head," and planning a new series. It's been a busy life for a teen legend named Mo.

Greg Gets Grounded Grilled Lamb

½ cup raspberry vinegar
⅓ cup olive oil
¼ cup firmly packed dark
  brown sugar
½ cup chopped fresh mint
½ teaspoon coarse black pepper

¼ teaspoon salt
16 large mushrooms, cleaned
16 small green tomatoes
4 pounds leg of lamb, cut into
  1½-inch cubes

In a large bowl mix the vinegar, oil, brown sugar, mint, pepper, and salt. Add the mushrooms, tomatoes, and lamb, and toss to combine. Cover and refrigerate, stirring occasionally, 3 to 4 hours.

Prepare hot coals for grilling. The coals should be white hot.

Thread the mushrooms, tomatoes, and meat alternately on 8 long thin metal skewers. Reserve the marinade. Place the skewers on a grill and cook about 12 minutes, turning and basting with the marinade frequently. Serve immediately.

Makes 8 servings.

Shove It in the Oven Fried Chicken

½ cup butter
½ cup oil
1 cup all-purpose flour
1 teaspoon salt
2 teaspoons red cayenne
  pepper

1 teaspoon garlic salt
½ teaspoon pepper
2 3-pound broiler-fryers,
  cleaned and sectioned

In a large baking pan melt the butter and oil in the oven. In a medium bowl mix together the flour, salt, cayenne pepper, garlic salt, and pepper. Coat the chicken pieces with the flour mixture. Place the chicken skin-side down in the melted butter. Bake at 350° for 30 minutes. Turn over and cook 30 minutes longer or until the thickest pieces are fork-tender.

Makes 6 to 8 servings.

The Brady ladies built their own clubhouse.

ALICE: I've never been in court myself, but I'm what you might call an amateur expert anyway.

CINDY: How come?

ALICE: From watching television. I've learned a lot from "The Bold Ones" and "Owen Marshall." I expect to pass the bar on "Perry Mason" reruns.

The Funky Chicken au Gratin _____

1½ cups butter
2 3-pound chickens, skinned
  and sectioned
2 onions, chopped
Salt and freshly ground black
  pepper
¼ cup tomato paste
½ cup red wine
4 carrots
10 stalks celery, julienned

2 small red bell peppers,
  julienned
2 small green bell peppers,
  julienned
2 teaspoons chopped fresh
  parsley
1 teaspoon minced fresh basil
1 teaspoon leaf oregano
¼ cup Parmesan cheese, grated

In a Dutch oven melt the butter and add the chicken, onion, salt, and black pepper. Cook until the chicken is lightly golden. Add the tomato paste, wine, carrots, celery, peppers, parsley, basil, and oregano. Simmer for 1 hour.

Arrange the chicken and vegetables on a serving platter and top with Parmesan cheese. Serve with rice and a green salad.

Makes 6 to 8 servings.

Divine Decadence
Baked Chicken _____

½ cup butter
1 cup plus 2 tablespoons all-
  purpose flour
2½ cups chicken broth
1⅓ cups milk
1 teaspoon lemon juice

Salt and pepper to taste
Grated nutmeg
1 pound egg noodles, cooked
2 4-pound chickens, poached
  and sectioned
⅔ cup Parmesan cheese

In a saucepan melt the butter over medium heat. Blend in the flour. Whisk in 1 cup of broth and all of the milk. Increase the heat and bring the mixture to a boil. Reduce the heat to simmer and cook until thick, about 10 minutes. Blend in the lemon juice and season to taste with salt, pepper, and nutmeg. Moisten the bottoms of 8 individual casseroles with the remaining broth. Divide the noodles among the casseroles. Place 2 pieces of chicken in each. Top each with sauce. Bake at 350° for 30 minutes. Sprinkle with cheese. Serve hot.

Makes 8 servings.

The Orange Blossom Roasted Chicken Special _____

5 medium oranges	2 4-pound chickens
2½ tablespoons olive oil	1½ teaspoons salt
5 cloves garlic, minced	¾ teaspoon pepper
2½ bay leaves, crumbled	1¼ cups chicken stock
¼ cup butter	2 tablespoons red wine vinegar

With a vegetable peeler remove the colored part of the rind from the oranges. Cut the peel into slivers. Squeeze the juice from the oranges and set it aside. Brush a large roasting pan with oil. In a small bowl combine the garlic, bay leaves, and butter, and rub the chicken inside and out with the mixture. Season with salt and pepper. Place the chicken on a rack in the pan. Dot with butter. Bake at 325° for 30 minutes.

Baste with ½ of the orange juice and sprinkle with ½ of the orange slivers. Bake for 15 more minutes.

Cover the remaining peel with water and simmer for 10 minutes. Drain. Transfer the chicken to a platter. In the pan used for cooking the chicken stir together the chicken stock, peel, remaining orange juice, and vinegar. Boil gently until the sauce is thick, about 15 minutes. Spoon the sauce over the chicken. Garnish with orange sections if desired.

Serve with I'm Just Wild about Saffron Rice (recipe follows).

Nice Is as Nice Does

66The crew seemed to get really involved with us, more than I've ever run into, before or since. Both on the show and on the various reunions. They seemed to take a personal interest above and beyond their jobs, offering helpful suggestions and volunteering assistance. I remember a grip once waving at me frantically just before an entrance, telling me I'd forgotten to remove my glasses. Not world-shaking perhaps, but boy, when that kind of an attitude prevails, it sure makes the job a whole lot more fun.99

I'm Just Wild about Saffron Rice __

¼ cup butter
1½ cups long grain rice
2 tablespoons minced green
  onions
2 cloves garlic, minced

2½ cups chicken broth
⅛ teaspoons saffron threads,
  crushed
3 tablespoons butter
Salt and pepper to taste

In a large skillet melt ¼ cup of butter over medium heat. Add the rice, onion, and garlic, and cook, stirring constantly, until the rice is golden. Add the broth and bring the mixture to a boil. Add the saffron and stir until dissolved. Reduce the heat, cover, and simmer until the rice is done, about 20 minutes. Season with salt and pepper to taste.

The Real McCoy Cider Chicken __

2 3-pound chickens, quartered
2 cups apple cider
1 cup all-purpose flour
1 tablespoon ground ginger
2 teaspoons ground cinnamon
Salt and freshly ground black
  pepper, to taste

3 tablespoons molasses
⅓ cup sweet white wine
2 apples, cored and cut into
  thin wedges

Place the chicken pieces in a shallow dish and pour the cider over them. Marinate overnight in the refrigerator, turning the pieces occasionally. Remove the chicken from the cider and reserve the liquid. In a shallow bowl mix the flour, ginger, cinnamon, and salt and pepper to taste. Coat the chicken with the flour mixture and place skin-side up in a shallow baking pan. Bake the chicken at 350° for 40 minutes.

Combine the reserved liquid, molasses, wine, and apple slices, and pour the mixture over the chicken. Bake for 25 minutes more, basting occasionally with the pan juices. Serve immediately.

Makes 6 to 8 servings.

Incident at Vermicelli with Chicken and Roasted Peppers _____

3½ tablespoons olive oil
3 large cloves garlic, minced
1½ onions, sliced
1½ cups roasted red bell
　pepper strips
1½ cups roasted green bell
　pepper strips
1½ cups whipping cream
¼ cup tomato paste

3 tablespoons chopped fresh
　parsley
1 teaspoon red pepper flakes
Salt and pepper to taste
4 cups chopped cooked
　chicken breasts
1 pound vermicelli, freshly
　cooked

In a large saucepan heat the oil over medium heat. Add the garlic and sauté for 2 minutes. Add the onions and cook for 3 minutes. Stir in the pepper strips and cook for 5 minutes. Add the cream and tomato paste, and season with parsley, red pepper, salt, and pepper. Cook until the sauce thickens, about 10 minutes. Add the chicken and cook until heated through. Toss the vermicelli with the chicken mixture.

Makes 8 servings.

The World's Shortest Signature

66 This must have been one of the early years because I remember how tiny Susan looked next to the uniformed policeman who was working security. We had been signing autographs at some outdoor affair for the longest time, and she was getting more and more tired. But she was a trouper right from the start and insisted on working as long as the rest of us. But as she wore down, her signature got shorter and shorter. From Susan Olson to Susan O to Susan and finally just S. She was a neat lady right from the start. 99

The Roaring Twenties never looked better.

CAROL: Well, Alice, they served us weak coffee and stale donuts. Then they threw us to the lions. With a smile, of course.

ALICE: Oh, of course. You can't be a politician nowadays without a perma-press smile.

Psychedelic Bachelor Pad Paella

1 tablespoon oil
8 chicken pieces (thighs, wings, and breasts)
8 small pork chops
2 medium onions, chopped
1 red bell pepper, cut in chunks
1 green bell pepper, cut in chunks
1½ cups converted rice
¾ teaspoon leaf oregano

¼ teaspoon saffron threads
2 cloves garlic, crushed
3 cups chicken broth
1 16-ounce package frozen peas, thawed
½ pound medium shrimp, deveined, tails left on
½ cup canned artichoke hearts, drained and quartered
2 tomatoes, cut into wedges

In a 5-quart Dutch oven heat the oil until hot. Add the chicken pieces and cook over medium-high heat until brown on both sides. Remove the chicken to a plate. Add the pork chops to the drippings and cook until lightly browned, about 5 minutes. Remove the pork to a plate. Reserve 1 tablespoon of pan drippings and drain the rest. Add the onions, red and green peppers, and rice. Cook over medium heat, stirring constantly, for 5 to 6 minutes, until the onions are tender. Stir in the oregano, saffron, garlic, and chicken broth. Heat to boiling. Arrange the chicken pieces and pork chops on top of the rice mixture. Reduce the heat to low, cover, and simmer for 30 minutes, or until most of the liquid is absorbed. Stir in the peas, shrimp, and artichoke hearts. Cook until the shrimp are pink, loosely curled, and opaque throughout, about 10 minutes longer. Gently stir in the tomatoes. Serve hot in a large bowl or paella dish. Let the folks serve themselves. Muy continental.

Makes 8 servings.

CAROL: Oh, Alice, you know something, I bet when I go to sleep tonight I am going to dream about bells.
ALICE: I always dream about bells. They are always the same kind: wedding bells. Then I wake up.

Evil Stepmother Sour Cream Enchiladas

2 large chicken breasts
2 10½-ounce cans cream of chicken soup
2 16-ounce cartons sour cream
2 6-ounce cans diced green chilies

2 cups milk
2 packages small corn tortillas
1 cup grated sharp longhorn cheese
2 bunches scallions (or green onions), chopped

In a saucepan cover the chicken in water and boil for 20 to 25 minutes. Cool. Shred the chicken into small pieces.

In a large bowl combine the soup, sour cream, chilies, and milk. Refrigerate the mixture for 1 hour to allow the flavors to blend.

In a skillet heat a small amount of oil and fry the tortillas for just a flash to soften. Place 2 tablespoons of the sour cream mixture, some cheese, scallions, and chicken inside each tortilla. Wrap each tortilla around the filling. Arrange the enchiladas in a 9x13-inch pan. Cover the enchiladas lightly with the sour cream mixture, more cheese, and the scallions. Bake at 350° for 20 to 25 minutes.

Makes 8 servings.

Leapin' Salmon Fish Cakes

1 pound fresh salmon, cooked and flaked
1 pound potatoes, freshly cooked and mashed
Salt and pepper to taste

½ cup butter, melted
4 eggs
Bread crumbs
Oil

In a large bowl blend the salmon and potatoes. Season with salt and pepper. Add the butter and 2 eggs to the mixture. Roll the mixture to 1-inch thickness and cut into the desired shapes. In a small bowl beat the remaining eggs. Dip the salmon cakes into the beaten eggs and then in the bread crumbs. Shake off any surplus. In a skillet heat about ½ inch of oil. Fry the salmon cakes on both sides until golden brown. Drain on a paper towel and serve hot.

Makes 4 servings.

Sweet Salmon Pie

4 cups milk
2 pounds fresh salmon
½ cup grated Romano cheese
1 clove garlic, crushed

¼ cup butter
¼ cup all-purpose flour
Salt and pepper

In a saucepan warm the milk over medium heat until hot but not boiling. Poach the salmon in the milk for 15 minutes. Remove the salmon and flake it into a bowl. Add ¾ of the Romano and all of the garlic.

In a separate saucepan melt the butter. Blend in the flour. Gradually blend in 2 cups of the milk used for poaching and cook over medium heat until smooth and thickened to a sauce consistency.

Add sauce to the fish until just moist. Season with salt and pepper to taste. Transfer the mixture to a greased 2-quart baking dish and sprinkle with the remaining grated cheese. Bake at 350° for 30 minutes.

Makes 6 servings.

What America Means to Me Mountain Trout

4 celery stalks, thinly sliced
  diagonally
½ cup oil
½ cup sliced red onion
¼ cup minced parsley
3 tablespoons Worcestershire
  sauce
2½ tablespoons sugar
Salt and pepper to taste
Oil

8 trout filets
3 cups all-purpose flour
8 eggs, beaten
4 cups bread crumbs
1 cup butter
1 cup firmly packed light
  brown sugar
½ cup Amaretto liqueur
½ pound lightly salted almonds

In a medium bowl combine the first 6 ingredients. Season with salt and pepper to taste. Cover and refrigerate until well chilled.

Heat the oil in deep fryer to 375°. Open each trout and flatten completely. Coat with flour. Dip in egg. Let the excess drip back into the bowl. Coat with bread crumbs. Lower the trout into the oil in batches. Don't crowd. Fry until golden brown, 4 to 6 minutes. Drain on paper towels. Set aside and keep warm.

In a saucepan over medium heat melt ½ cup of butter. Add the brown sugar and Amaretto, and stir until the sugar dissolves. Add the almonds and bring them to a simmer, stirring constantly. Remove the pan from the heat and whisk in the remaining butter.

Place the trout on plates and spoon some of the celery mixture down the center of each. Surround with sauce.

Makes 8 servings.

CAROL: And just have a nice vacation.
ALICE: I will. I really will. You know, it just broke my heart saying good-bye to the children. It's going to seem like a year before I see them again.
MIKE: Alice, you are only going to be gone a week.
ALICE: So, I'm three-hundred-and-fifty-eight days off.

Soleful Cabbage

2 small green cabbages, cored and cut into 8 wedges
½ cup water
¼ cup dry white wine
1 clove garlic, finely minced
1 teaspoon leaf thyme
1 cup butter, cut into tablespoons
Salt and freshly ground pepper
16 sole filets
1 small red bell pepper, blanched and thinly sliced
Fresh parsley

Steam the cabbage until tender. In a saucepan bring the water, wine, garlic, and thyme just to a boil. Remove the pan from the heat and whisk in 2 tablespoons of butter. Return to low heat and whisk in the remaining butter 1 tablespoon at a time. Season with salt and pepper. Cover and keep warm.

Steam the sole until just tender, about 8 minutes. Arrange the cabbage wedges on a platter and place the filets between each. Surround with sauce. Garnish with red bell pepper and parsley.

Makes 8 servings.

Fringed Vest Flounder _____

¾ cup chopped tomatoes
¾ cup chopped green bell
  pepper
½ cup lemon juice
1⅓ tablespoons oil
2½ teaspoons salt

1 tablespoon minced onion
2 teaspoons minced fresh basil
½ teaspoon black pepper
4 teaspoons red cayenne
  pepper
2½ pounds flounder

In a large bowl combine all of the ingredients except the fish. Let the mixture stand for 30 minutes. Place the fish in a greased baking dish in 1 layer. Spoon the tomato mixture over the fish. Bake at 500° for 5 minutes or until the fish flakes with a fork. Serve immediately.
  Makes about 6 servings.

Sunday Barbecue Grilled Shrimp With Green Salsa _____

¼ cup oil
¼ cup butter
2 tablespoons chili powder
¼ cup lemon juice
1 pound large shrimp, peeled
  and deveined, tails left on
3 medium green tomatoes,
  cored and finely chopped

2 cloves garlic, minced
1 avocado, cut into 1-inch
  cubes
1 jalapeño pepper, seeded and
  chopped
4 cilantro sprigs, chopped
Salt

Prepare a barbecue grill. The coals should be white-hot. In a small saucepan combine the oil, butter, chili powder, and 2 tablespoons of lemon juice. Stir until the butter melts. Allow the mixture to cool slightly. In a medium bowl combine the shrimp and cooled marinade. Marinate at least 15 minutes. Thread the shrimp on skewers. Grill until the shrimp turn opaque, about 1½ minutes on each side. In a medium bowl combine the remaining ingredients, stirring until completely blended. Serve the salsa on the side with the shrimp.
  Makes 4 servings.

Scoop Brady's Crab Saint Barts ___

1 cup milk
2 jalapeño chilies, minced
1 teaspoon minced fresh thyme
2 bay leaves, crumbled
2 tablespoons minced fresh
   parsley
Salt and pepper to taste

2 cups fresh bread crumbs
1 pound crab meat, patted dry
3 tablespoons minced onion
3 tablespoons minced fresh
   chives
¼ cup butter
2 tablespoons lime juice

In a small saucepan combine the milk, chilies, 1 teaspoon of thyme, bay leaves, 2 tablespoons of parsley, and salt and pepper to taste. Bring the mixture to a boil. Reduce the heat and simmer for 15 minutes. Cool. Strain into a bowl. Add the bread crumbs and soak for 15 minutes. Squeeze dry. Stir the crab into the bread crumbs. In a medium skillet melt the butter over medium heat. Add the crab mixture and sauté until brown. Blend in the lime juice.

Pour the sautéed crab into a large casserole. Bake at 300° for about 10 to 15 minutes. Serve immediately.

Mushroom and Barley Casserole On Broadway ___

½ cup plus 2 tablespoons butter
4 medium onions, diced
8 cups water
1 teaspoon salt
1½ teaspoons leaf thyme

½ teaspoon leaf sage
Freshly ground pepper
9 cups fresh mushrooms, sliced
3 cups barley

In a large saucepan melt ¼ cup of butter and sauté the onion until translucent. Add the water, salt, thyme, sage, and pepper to taste. Bring the mixture to a boil. In a separate skillet melt the remaining butter and add the mushrooms and barley. Sauté until the mushrooms begin to brown, stirring constantly. Transfer the mushroom mixture into a 4-quart baking dish and pour the water mixture over all. Cover tightly. Bake at 350° for 1 hour and 15 minutes, or until the liquid is absorbed. Serve immediately.

Makes 8 to 12 servings.

Susan after a hard day of signing autographs.

Alice Doesn't Shop Here Anymore

❝ I recall an incident that took place in a supermarket in a small town I've forgotten. I was on the road a lot in those days, doing dinner theater and summer stock, and would pop into unexpected places to pick up dog food or a Coke or whatever. A smallish child walked by me, looked up and said casually, 'Hi, Alice!' and went on her way. A few minutes later she returned dragging her reluctant mother, who protested, 'But darling, she wouldn't be *here*!' Small kids are seldomly surprised to see me in person. After all, I'm in their living rooms— why wouldn't I be in their supermarkets? ❞

Bubbles' Cheesy Bubbling Potatoes

8 baking potatoes, scrubbed
2 tablespoons butter
1 cup sour cream
2 cups grated Swiss cheese

1 cup grated Cheddar cheese
1 tablespoon minced fresh
parsley

Prick the potatoes and bake at 400° for 1 hour or until easily pierced with a fork. Set aside until cool enough to handle. Slit lengthwise and scoop out without tearing the skin, leaving ¼ inch of flesh inside. Divide the butter in 8 bits and place 1 in each shell. Mash together the scooped potato, sour cream, cheeses, and parsley. Spoon back evenly into the shells. Place the stuffed potatoes on a baking sheet and bake an additional 20 minutes, until the cheese is bubbling.

Alice's Note: Kids will always eat these potatoes.

Makes 8 servings.

Jan's Crusty Cauliflower Casserole

3 tablespoons olive oil
3 cloves garlic, minced
¾ cup tomatoes, finely diced
8 cups cauliflower florets
4 large eggs
1 cup cottage cheese
1 cup milk

1 cup grated Parmesan cheese
1½ tablespoons minced fresh
parsley
Dash cayenne pepper
Coarse black pepper
1 cup grated Muenster cheese
½ cup bread crumbs

In a large skillet heat the oil over medium heat. Add the garlic and cook for 30 seconds. Add the tomatoes and cook for 5 minutes. Stir in the cauliflower. Add 2 tablespoons of water and cover. Cook until the cauliflower is tender, about 8 minutes. Remove the pan from the heat and allow the cauliflower to cool to room temperature.

In a large bowl beat the eggs. Add the cottage cheese, milk, Parmesan, parsley, cayenne pepper, black pepper, and Muenster. Stir in the cauliflower mixture. Transfer the cauliflower mixture to a buttered baking dish and sprinkle with bread crumbs. Bake at 375° for 20 minutes or until bubbly.

Makes 9 servings.

Attack of the
Eggplant Parmigiana _____

3 small eggplants, sliced in ½-inch slices
2½ cups cottage cheese
2 large eggs
½ cup grated Parmesan cheese
1½ cups chopped parsley
Salt and black pepper to taste
¾ cup olive oil
2¼ cups tomato sauce
3 cups grated mozzarella cheese

Salt the eggplant and let it stand for 30 minutes. In a large bowl mix together the cottage cheese, eggs, Parmesan, and parsley. Season to taste with salt and pepper. Rinse the eggplant and pat it dry on paper towels. In a large skillet heat 2 tablespoons of olive oil over medium heat. Add 1 layer of eggplant slices. Do not crowd. Turn the slices quickly to coat both sides lightly with oil, and reduce the heat slightly. Fry the eggplant until lightly browned on both sides. When the slices are browned, drain on paper towels. Repeat with more oil and eggplant until all eggplant pieces are done.

Spread ¾ cup of tomato sauce over the bottom of a 3-quart square baking dish. Arrange a layer of eggplant slices over the sauce. Top each eggplant slice with 1 tablespoon of the cottage cheese mixture and sprinkle ⅓ of the mozzarella over all. Repeat, arranging eggplant slices to cover the gaps between the slices in the first layer, like laying bricks. When all ingredients have been used, cover the layers well with the remaining tomato sauce, and spoon the remaining cottage cheese mixture down the center of the dish. Sprinkle the remaining mozzarella over the tomato sauce. Bake at 400° for 25 to 30 minutes, or until bubbling. Let the mixture stand for 10 minutes before slicing.

Makes 8 servings.

The Long Good Bye

66 I recently found a clipping of an article by Cynthia Lowry of the AP that said, '...and despite the valiant efforts of Ann and stars Robert Reed and Florence Henderson, it is highly unlikely "The Brady Bunch" will see a second season.' But, to be honest, who would have ever guessed! 99

Here's the Story Soufflé du Potato

8 medium potatoes, cleaned
  and peeled
½ cup hot milk
½ cup butter

Salt and pepper to taste
4 egg yolks, beaten
4 egg whites, stiffly beaten

Cook the potatoes in water until soft. Drain and mash. Beat in the milk and butter, and season with salt and pepper to taste. Add the egg yolks and mix well. Fold in the egg whites. Pour the mixture into a buttered soufflé dish and bake at 425° for 25 minutes or until golden brown.

Makes 6 to 8 servings.

Twice Married Potatoes with Cheese and Chilies

8 large baking potatoes,
  cleaned and dried
1 cup mild green chili peppers,
  diced
½ cup heavy cream

1¼ cups grated sharp Cheddar
  cheese
Salt and pepper to taste
1 cup sour cream

Cut a deep small slit in the top of each potato. Bake at 375° for 1 hour or until easily pierced with a fork.

Let the potatoes cool slightly. Slit open and scoop out the pulp without tearing the skin. In a large bowl mash the pulp and stir in the chilies, cream, and 1 cup of Cheddar. Season with salt and pepper to taste. Spoon the mixture back into the skins, carefully mounding the extra mixture on top. Sprinkle with the remaining cheese. Place the potatoes on a baking sheet. Bake at 400° until the potatoes are hot and the cheese bubbles. Top each with sour cream and serve immediately.

Makes 8 servings.

I don't know what I said, but it must have been a lulu.

Garlic (No Vampire) Potatoes _____

5½ pounds new red potatoes,
 scrubbed and pricked
8 cloves garlic, minced
1½ cups olive oil

¾ cup chopped fresh basil
2 tablespoons salt
Freshly ground pepper to taste

Arrange the potatoes in a shallow roasting pan. Bake at 350° for 2 hours.

Cut each potato in half. In a large bowl combine the garlic, oil, basil, salt, and pepper. Toss the potatoes in the mixture. Let the potatoes stand for 15 minutes before serving.

Makes about 8 servings.

Bugs' Sweet and Sour Carrots _____

2 teaspoons oil
½ teaspoon grated ginger (or powdered)
4 teaspoons cornstarch
2 teaspoons sherry
2 teaspoons tomato sauce

2 teaspoons vinegar
2 tablespoons firmly packed brown sugar
1 cup cold water
2 large carrots, finely sliced

In a saucepan heat the oil and fry the ginger briefly. In a small bowl mix the cornstarch, sherry, tomato sauce, vinegar, brown sugar, and water. Add the mixture to the ginger and cook, stirring constantly, until the sauce thickens. Add the carrots and heat to boiling. Cook until tender. Serve hot.

Makes 4 to 6 servings.

Cousin Emma's Military Tomatoes And Green Beans _____

½ cup olive oil
2 pounds green beans
2 large cloves garlic, chopped
2 onions, sliced into rings
5 small tomatoes, chopped

½ cup chopped fresh parsley
5 tablespoons red wine vinegar
2 teaspoons leaf oregano
Salt and pepper to taste

In a large skillet heat the olive oil and sauté the beans until just beginning to soften, stirring constantly. Reduce the heat to low and add the garlic and onion. Cook for 1 minute. Add the remaining ingredients and cook an additional 5 minutes. May be served hot or at room temperature.

Makes 8 servings.

Peter's Perfect Peas

2 tablespoons olive oil
1 clove garlic, minced
1 white onion, sliced
2 tablespoons minced fresh
  parsley

2 ½ cups fresh peas
Salt and pepper to taste
¼ cup water

In a saucepan heat the olive oil over medium high heat. Sauté the garlic, onion, and parsley until brown. Add the peas and season with salt and pepper to taste. Cook for 1 minute, stirring constantly. Add the water, reduce the heat to low, and simmer for 10 minutes. Serve hot.
  Makes 6 servings.

GREG: It's no use, Alice. All the evidence points to me, even
      If I'm not guilty.
ALICE: Sometimes evidence just looks like real evidence
      when it's really circumstantial. Or partly
      circumstantial, thereby being unsupported or hearsay.
GREG: What does that mean?
ALICE: I don't know, but it saved some guy's life last night on
      TV.

Beebe Gallini's Brussels Sprouts And Red Bell Peppers

1 ½ pounds Brussels sprouts,
  trimmed
3 tablespoons safflower oil
3 tablespoons sesame oil

4 medium red bell peppers,
  seeded and cut in strips
1 small hot red chili, minced
1 teaspoon salt

Cook the Brussels sprouts in salted boiling water until just tender. Drain and rinse. Then drain again. When cool enough, cut each in half lengthwise. In a 12-inch skillet heat the safflower and sesame oils. Add the bell peppers, chili, and salt, and cook until the peppers begin to soften, about 6 minutes. Mix in the Brussels sprouts and cook until heated through. Serve immediately.
  Makes 6 servings.

Veni, Vidi, Vici Veggy Vermicelli____

1 tablespoon olive oil
3 strips bacon
1 onion, chopped
1 cup fresh peas
1 cup lightly blanched
asparagus tips

1 artichoke, cooked, tough
leaves removed, leaves
sliced, and heart wedged
1 cup fresh spinach
3 cups cooked vermicelli

In a large skillet heat the oil over medium heat. Add the chopped bacon and onion. As soon as the onion begins to brown add the peas. Cook for 3 minutes, stirring constantly. Add the asparagus, spinach, and artichokes. Cook until heated through. Toss with the vermicelli.

Makes 6 to 8 servings.

Maureen McCormick on Ann B.

66Let's see, what do I remember about Ann B. Davis? To start with, she had the greatest Halloween parties of all time. In fact, I think they were the best parties ever. She would go all out with her wild, creative imagination, and the parties would be fantastic. Ann taught me needlepoint. She made me a small pillow once with a heart on it. I still have it.

"What I remember most about Ann is that it was a treat to work with her. She made it so easy for me to give my lines. I was always very aware of her amazing talent. To make comedy seem simple takes real talent. Timing-wise there was no one better. Even when I was young, I had a sense that no matter how wacky or silly things became, Ann made it all seem perfectly real. And today I admire Ann for all she does to help people. Everyone talks about making a difference, but Ann is really doing something. She works with the homeless and spreads a lot of love. I admire her a lot for that. I think the best thing about Ann is that I respected her when I was a kid, and now I respect her even more for all the good she is doing. There are not many people you can say that about.99

Whole Wheat Sunny Buns _____

2 packages active dry yeast
1½ cups warm water (110°)
1 teaspoon salt
1 tablespoon sugar
1 tablespoon packed brown
  sugar

2 cups whole wheat flour
1½ cups all-purpose flour
Yellow cornmeal

In a large bowl dissolve the yeast in the water. Set aside for 5 minutes.

Add the salt, sugar, brown sugar, and whole wheat flour. Beat for 1 minute. Add the all-purpose flour and mix until smooth. Cover the bowl and let the dough rise until doubled.

Punch down and turn onto a floured surface. With floured hands shape into 12 buns. Sprinkle a baking sheet with cornmeal. Place the buns on the baking sheet. Set the buns aside to rise for 15 minutes. Mist the buns with water. Bake at 400° for 15 minutes. Mist with water again and bake an additional 10 minutes. (Water makes the crust crispy.)

Makes 12 buns.

MIKE: Well, you're the director. Who do you want to be? Priscilla?

GREG: Jan. But Marcia won't be in the movie if she's not Priscilla.

ALICE: Jan? Do you think she's ready for such a romantic role?

CAROL: Well, I would think Marcia...

ALICE: Well, I was thinking about myself.

GREG: You?

ALICE: Sure. Speak for yourself, Alice. After all, I played the part of Pilgram Cecil at PS-34 in '43. Or was that PS-43 in '34?

Maureen McCormick

Cyrano de Brady Breadsticks _____

3 cups all-purpose flour
1 package active dry yeast
1 tablespoon sugar
1 teaspoon salt

¼ cup oil
1¼ cups hot water (125°)
1 egg white, beaten
Coarse salt

In a large bowl combine 1 cup of flour, the yeast, sugar, and salt. Add the oil and water, and mix until well blended. While still mixing, add additional flour until the dough is no longer sticky. Turn onto a floured surface and knead until smooth. Divide the dough in half. Roll each half into a 10-inch log. Cut each log into ½-inch pieces. Roll each piece into a 14-inch stick. Place the dough sticks on a baking sheet and set aside to rise for about 25 minutes.

Brush with egg white and sprinkle with salt. Bake at 300° until golden brown, about 40 minutes. Serve warm or room temperature.

Makes 40 breadsticks.

It's amazing how little Maureen's looks change. Her beauty was very adult even when she was young.

Baked Bananas à la Brady_____

6 tablespoons all-purpose flour	10 bananas
¾ cup sugar	½ cup butter
1 teaspoon cinnamon	1 cup heavy cream
¼ teaspoon nutmeg	1 tablespoon almond extract

In a shallow bowl combine the flour, sugar, cinnamon, and nutmeg. Peel the bananas and split them lengthwise. Roll the bananas in the dry mixture. Place the bananas in a baking dish. Add the melted butter. Blend together the cream and almond extract, and pour the mixture over the bananas. Bake at 350° for 15 minutes.

Oahu Pineapple Spice Cake _____

1¼ cups oil
¼ cup firmly packed brown
  sugar
1 cup sugar
3 eggs
1 cup pineapple, chopped
1½ cups whole wheat flour
1½ cups all-purpose flour
1 tablespoon baking powder
1 teaspoon salt
1 teaspoon cinnamon

½ teaspoon nutmeg
¼ teaspoon ginger
¼ teaspoon allspice
1 teaspoon cloves
1 cup chopped pecans
⅓ cup pineapple juice
¼ cup butter
¼ cup sugar
¼ cup packed brown sugar
¼ cup rum

In a medium bowl whisk together the oil, ¼ cup of brown sugar, and 1 cup sugar. Add the eggs one at a time. In a separate bowl combine the flour and spices. Blend the dry ingredients into the egg mixture, then add the pineapple and pecans. Pour the batter into a buttered and floured 10-inch ring pan. Bake at 350° for 50 minutes, or until the cake pulls away from the sides of the pan. Cool for 10 minutes. Turn the cake out onto a cake platter. Cool.

In a saucepan combine the juice, ¼ cup of butter, ¼ cup of sugar, ¼ cup of brown sugar, and rum. Bring the mixture to a boil, sirring constantly. Reduce the heat and simmer for 7 minutes. Cool and drizzle over the cake.

Makes 12 servings.

Snow White Apple Crisp _____

7 firm green apples, peeled,
  cored, and thinly sliced
2 tablespoons fresh lemon juice
1⅓ cups all-purpose flour

1⅓ cups sugar
2 teaspoons cinnamon
1 teaspoon salt
¾ cup butter

In a greased 9-inch square pan layer the apples, sprinkling each layer with lemon juice. Press lightly down on the apples. Combine the dry ingredients and cut in the butter until crumbly. Press the mixture over the apples, sealing the edges. Bake at 350° until the top is golden, about 1 hour. Serve with homemade vanilla ice cream.

Makes about 9 servings.

Color Television Coffee Cake _____

6 ounces ground oatmeal
  cookies
1 tablespoon firmly packed
  sugar
3½ tablespoons butter
3 8-ounce packages cream
  cheese
1⅛ cups firmly packed brown
  sugar
4 eggs

2½ tablespoons coffee liqueur
½ teaspoon vanilla extract
6 teaspoons Irish whiskey
6 tablespoons cocoa
1 tablespoon whipping cream
¾ teaspoon cocoa
1½ cups whipping cream
2 tablespoons sugar
½ teaspoon espresso powder
Cocoa

In a medium bowl combine the cookies, 1 tablespoon of brown sugar, and the 3½ tablespoons butter until thoroughly moistened. Press the mixture into a buttered 9-inch springform pan, covering the bottom and 1½ inches up the side. Bake at 325° for 8 minutes. Cool.

Blend the cream cheese and 1⅛ cups of brown sugar until smooth. Mix in 1 egg, the coffee liqueur, and vanilla. In a small bowl dissolve 6 tablespoons of cocoa in the whiskey. Fold the whiskey mixture and remaining beaten eggs into the cream cheese mixture. Pour the filling into the cooled crust. Bake at 325° for 45 minutes. The outer edges should be firm. Cool, and then chill for 24 hours.

In a small bowl blend ¾ teaspoon of cocoa in 1 tablespoon of cream. Beat the remaining 1½ cups of cream and 2 tablespoons sugar until stiff. Fold in the cocoa mixture and espresso powder. Spread the icing over the cheesecake and sprinkle with cocoa.

Makes 12 servings.

Second Time Around

I think Florence is about to ride past the studio gates and up into the Hollywood Hills.

Brady Six Spinach and Egg Casserole

1½ cups cooked spinach
2 tablespoons minced onion
1 clove garlic, finely minced
2 tablespoons vinegar
¼ cup grated Swiss cheese
¼ cup grated Cheddar cheese
4 hard-boiled eggs, peeled and
  sliced

3 tablespoons olive oil
3 tablespoons all-purpose flour
½ teaspoon salt
¼ teaspoon pepper
½ teaspoon Dijon mustard
2¼ cups milk
½ cup bread crumbs
1 tablespoon melted butter

In an ungreased 8-inch square baking dish stir together the spinach, onion, garlic, and vinegar. Spread the spinach mixture evenly over the botton of the dish, sprinkle with the cheeses, and top with egg slices. In a saucepan heat the oil over low heat and stir in the flour, salt, pepper, and mustard, stirring until smooth. Add the milk and bring the mixture to a boil, stirring constantly. Boil for 1 minute, then pour the mixture over the spinach. Toss the bread crumbs in the melted butter and sprinkle them over all. Bake at 400° for 20 minutes.

Alice's Note: A spectacular breakfast in which you may cleverly use up that odd bit of cheese, the unwanted spinach, and the eggs left over from yesterday.

Makes 6 to 8 servings.

Headed West Best Sandwich

1 tablespoon butter
2 teaspoons blue cheese
½ cup steak sauce
1 French roll
¼ to ½ pound cooked sirloin
  (you know, last night's doggy
  bag)

1 slice red onion
Salt and pepper to taste

In a small bowl cream the butter and blue cheese, and mix in the steak sauce. Slit the roll lengthwise and spread with the steak sauce mixture. Thinly slice the steak and layer it on the bread. Top with the onion, separating the rings to cover. Sprinkle with salt and pepper. Slap the bread together and there you have a sandwich.

Alice's Note: The boys like this better than the original sirloin.

Makes 1 sandwich.

Two-handed Stuffed French Bread

2 cups leftover pot roast, finely chopped
3 tablespoons minced onions
3 tablespoons minced parsley
2 mild chilies, minced
2 hard-boiled eggs, chopped
Dash Tabasco sauce
1 tablespoon Worcestershire sauce
Mayonnaise
1 large loaf French bread
Softened butter

In a large bowl combine all of the ingredients except the bread and butter. Mix until throughly blended. Cut off both ends of the bread and hollow out the loaf. The shell should be ½-inch thick. Brush the inside with softened butter. Stuff with the meat mixture. Place the ends back on and wrap tightly in foil. Chill. Slice to the desired amounts.

Alice's Note: This is a great treat when the kids bring friends home.
Makes 6 to 8 servings.

In Between Takes

66There's a lot of time to kill on a set. The first year I was doing paint-by-numbers pictures for my dressing room. That palled quickly. Too many numbers, too little patience. So I started doing needlepoint. I was delighted to learn that I could. I'm not too dexterous, not at all. But no matter how clumsy you look handling the needle, if you get it in the right hole you have a perfect stitch! Very soon I was doing it all the time, on the set and off. I got Florence and Maureen started, too—three generations of stitchers filling in the time between shots. I did a director's chair with the help of Sherwood's daughter Hope (she did the design), which I still have. I even got my picture with it in a book called *Celebrity Needlepoint.*99

When Broadway Joe Namath arrived on the set, all the ladies' hearts were a'flutter.

Brady Trivia Quiz #3

Alice used to complain about the high prices Sam charged for his quality meats. Think back twenty-some years and see if you remember the price tags on these prime cuts (per pound).

a. Beef tongue.
b. Triangle tip roast.
c. Chicken livers.
d. Beef ribs.
e. Lean ground sirloin.

Answers on Page 171.

The Count of Monte Cristo Sandwiches

4 eggs
¼ cup all-purpose flour
1 cup milk
2 teaspoons salt
½ teaspoon pepper
¼ teaspoon paprika

16 slices whole wheat bread
Softened butter
8 slices cooked ham
8 slices cooked chicken breast
8 slices Swiss cheese
Sour cream

In a medium bowl combine the eggs, flour, milk, salt, pepper, and paprika, and mix until smooth. Spread the butter on the bread slices. Place a slice of ham, chicken, and cheese on each of 8 slices of bread. Cover the sandwiches with the remaining bread. Dip the sandwiches in the egg mixture, turning to coat both sides. In a large skillet melt 3 tablespoons of butter and brown the sandwiches on both sides. Repeat until all sandwiches have been grilled. Serve with sour cream on the side.

Makes 8 sandwiches.

Dear Libby's Chicken Loves Broccoli Salad

4 cups chopped cooked
  chicken
2 cups chopped cooked
  broccoli
1 cup walnuts, chopped
1½ cups apples, cored and
  chopped

1 tablespoon lemon juice
1¼ cups mayonnaise
½ cup sour cream
Salt and pepper to taste
Lettuce

In a large bowl mix the chicken, broccoli, walnuts, and apples. In a separate bowl combine the mayonnaise, lemon juice, and sour cream. Season with salt and pepper. Add the mayonnaise mixture to the chicken mixture and toss until well coated. Chill at least 1 hour. Serve on lettuce leaves.

Makes 6 to 8 servings.

Sometimes I had to play sheriff on the Brady homeplace.

Greg's Chicken Surprise Salad ____

2 hard-boiled eggs, chopped
1 teaspoon salt
⅛ teaspoon cayenne pepper
½ cup olive oil
½ cup vegetable oil
1 3¾-ounce can sardines,
   drained
Mayonnaise
2 tablespoons lemon juice

2 tablespoons chopped fresh
   parsley
2 cups diced cooked chicken
3 cups cooked rice
3 tablespoons white wine
   vinegar
¾ cup cooked peas, chilled
Salt and pepper to taste

In a medium bowl blend the eggs, salt, cayenne, olive oil, and vegetable oil. Mash the sardines and add them to the egg mixture. Mix in the mayonnaise. Stir in 1 tablespoon of lemon juice and the parsley. Add the chicken and toss well. Chill. In a separate bowl combine the rice, vinegar, peas, and remaining lemon juice. Season with salt and pepper to taste. Press the rice mixture into a greased 1-quart ring mold. Chill at least 1 hour. Turn the rice mold onto a platter and spoon the chicken mixture into the center.

Alice's Note: The sardines are the surprise.

Makes 6 to 8 servings.

Trading Stamps Turkey Florentine

2 cups cooked turnip greens, finely chopped
1 tablespoon sherry
3 tablespoons olive oil
¼ cup all-purpose flour
1½ cups turkey giblet broth
⅓ cup heavy cream
¼ teaspoon black pepper
½ teaspoon nutmeg

Salt to taste
2½ tablespoons grated Parmesan cheese
2½ tablespoons grated Swiss cheese
2 cups diced cooked turkey
4 teaspoons bread crumbs
Butter

In a medium bowl combine the greens and sherry. In a saucepan heat the oil over medium heat and whisk in the flour until smooth. Add the broth, stirring constantly, and bring the sauce to a boil. Reduce the heat and simmer for 5 minutes. Stir in the cream, pepper, nutmeg, and salt, and heat through. Mix 3 tablespoons of the sauce with the greens. Set the mixture aside. To the remaining sauce add 2 tablespoons each of the cheeses and cook for 1 minute, until melted. Brush a 1½-quart casserole dish with butter. Spread the turnip green mixture in the dish. Top with turkey and spoon the sauce over all. Sprinkle with bread crumbs and the remaining cheeses. Dot with butter. Bake at 375° for 15 minutes or until the edges bubble.

Makes 6 servings.

MIKE: The roast we were going to have has been burnt to a crisp.

SAM: Oh, how about some chops? I have, ah, lamb chops, pork chops, veal chops...Or you can take some of each and have chop suey!

Tiki Cave Turkey Casserole _____

2 green bell peppers, seeded
  and chopped
2 onions, chopped
1 4-ounce can pimientos,
  drained
4 tomatoes, chopped
¼ cup oil
2 jalapeño chilies, chopped

1 teaspoon salt
1 tablespoon hot salsa
⅛ teaspoon cinnamon
⅛ teaspoon ground cloves
¼ cup dry bread crumbs
1 ounce unsweetened
  chocolate, grated
8 large slices cooked turkey

In a large bowl combine the green peppers, onions, pimientos, and tomatoes until well blended. In a large skillet heat the oil over medium heat. Add the green pepper mix, chilies, salt, salsa, cinnamon, and cloves, and bring the mixture to a boil. Reduce the heat, cover, and simmer for 20 minutes. Stir in the bread crumbs and chocolate, and cook until the chocolate is melted. Alternate layers of turkey and sauce in a 2½-quart casserole dish. Bake at 350° for 20 minutes.

Makes 8 to 10 servings.

Johnny Bravo's Turkey au Gratin ___

6 tablespoons butter
1 cup chopped onion
1 teaspoon finely minced garlic
2 tablespoons lemon juice
1 cup chopped tomato
1½ cups turkey giblet broth or
  chicken broth

2 teaspoons catsup
1 bay leaf
Salt and pepper to taste
2 tablespoons turkey gravy
8 large pieces roast turkey
1 cup bread crumbs
2 tablespoons chopped basil

In a large skillet melt 2 tablespoons of butter. Brown the onions and garlic. Add the lemon juice, stirring constantly for 2 minutes. Add the tomatoes and broth and bring the mixture to a boil. Reduce the heat to very low and simmer gently. Add the catsup, bay leaf, and salt and pepper, and cook uncovered for 20 minutes. Stir in the gravy. Add the turkey slices and continue simmering for 5 minutes. Place the turkey slices in a shallow 2½-quart baking dish and cover with sauce. Sprinkle with bread crumbs and dot with the remaining butter. Brown lightly under a preheated broiler. Sprinkle with basil.

Makes 8 servings.

Marcia's Croissant French Toast ___

6 eggs
1 cup heavy cream
⅓ cup sweet vermouth
2½ tablespoons sugar
2 teaspoons cinnamon

8 croissants (stale ones from
  last night)
7 tablespoons butter
Confectioners' sugar
Warmed honey

In a medium bowl whisk together the eggs and cream. Add the vermouth, sugar, and cinnamon, and whisk until well blended. Pour the mixture into a shallow bowl. Dip the croissants in the egg mixture and coat both sides. Melt 2 tablespoons of butter in the skillet over medium heat and cook 2 croissants at a time until golden on both sides. Repeat until done.

Arrange the toasted croissants on a platter and sift confectioners' sugar over them. Serve with warm honey on the side.

Alice's Note: You'll wonder why you have been tossing those old croissants to the birds.

Makes 8 servings.

Take Two Laughing Pills and See Me In the Morning

❝Florence and I always had to shoot our scenes after the kids were gone, because of their restricted hours. We were usually tired and a tad cranky. Unfortunately, the form it usually took was an advanced case of the giggles. Have you ever tried to stop giggling when you were edging toward hysteria? The dumbest things would set you off. They never were as funny as they appeared—especially when the clock was moving toward time-and-a-half. But we had a lot of good laughs this way.❞

Naturally Curly Bob

❝Bob Reed and his curly hair. There are two Bob's—
Before Hawaii and After Hawaii. After our return from
location shooting in Hawaii and the havoc the humidity
played on his naturally curly hair, he gave up trying to
tame it. That's why in later episodes he looks like he
had gone the hippie route, but that was Bob's real
hair.❞

Monster Mashed Potato Cakes ____

2 cups cold mashed potatoes   1 teaspoon salt
¼ cup butter, melted   ¼ cup all-purpose flour

In a medium bowl blend the potatoes and butter. Add the salt and
blend in the flour. On a floured surface roll out to ⅛-inch thickness.
Cut out in rounds or fun shapes. Heat a nonstick griddle and fry for 3
minutes on each side. Serve with melted butter.
    Makes 6 servings.

ALICE: Step right up, folks. Right out of the oven. I got your
favorite goodies. Brownies!
PETER: No thanks, Alice. I'm not hungry.
ALICE: He turned down brownies? That's like Bob Hope
turning down laughs.

The Great Brady Barbecue

After they got out of jail, the Bradys hightailed it to the Grand Canyon. It sure was fun getting away from the studio.

Let's start with those iced teas you sip while swinging on the old porch swing. You know the ones. So cool and refreshing, just rolling the glass across your forehead makes you feel better. I know, I've seen the same commercials, but they're real.

Exact Words Ice Tea

12 teaspoons black tea leaves
  (strong teas hold taste when
  ice melts)
2 quarts water

10 teaspoons sugar
Ice
Lemon slices

In a clear glass jar or tea container combine the tea leaves and water. Place the jar on the back porch in the sun. (This is southern California.) Let the tea sit until the water becomes tea brown. Strain into a large pitcher and add the sugar and ice. Stir and serve with lemon slices.

There are many fruit teas (raspberry, blackberry, melon, etc.) that can be made in the same fashion for a nice change. Adding soda or sparkling water makes a nice spritzer.

Makes 2 quarts.

ALICE: Appeal to their vanity.
PETER: Vanity? What's vanity?
ALICE: Vanity is what makes women with size 12 feet wear
     size 8 shoes.

Johnny Apple Juice Tea _____

8 teaspoons English breakfast
  tea
8 cups apple juice

Sugar
Cinnamon sticks

In a stock pot or saucepan bring the apple juice to a boil. Remove the pan from the heat and add the tea. Cover and set aside for 5 minutes. Strain out the leaves. Refrigerate until chilled. Serve with sugar and cinnamon sticks.

Makes 8 servings.

Over the Rainbow Pepper Salad ___

3 cups water
2 teaspoons salt
2 cups long grain white rice
½ cup peanut oil
3 tablespoons white wine
  vinegar
2 teaspoons country Dijon
  mustard
Pepper to taste

1 large green bell pepper,
  thinly sliced
1 large red bell pepper, thinly
  sliced
1 large yellow bell pepper,
  thinly sliced
6 scallions, sliced
¼ cup minced parsley
1 tablespoon minced cilantro

In a large pot bring the water and 1½ teaspoons of salt to a boil. Add the rice and 2 tablespoons of oil. Reduce the heat, cover, and simmer for about 20 minutes or until the water is absorbed. In a small bowl whisk together the remaining oil, vinegar, mustard, pepper, and salt. In a large bowl toss the rice, bell peppers, and scallions together. Add the dressing, parsley, and cilantro, and toss again. Serve at room temperature or chilled.

Makes 12 servings.

Mike's Favorite Potato Salad_____

2½ pounds potatoes boiled just
    until soft, cut in 1-inch cubes
3½ tablespoons white wine
    vinegar
3½ tablespoons oil
2 teaspoons dill
Salt and pepper to taste

4 hard-boiled eggs, sliced
¾ cup sliced celery
¾ cup chopped red onion
¼ cup chopped parsley
1 cup mayonnaise
2 tablespoons milk

In a medium bowl toss the potatoes with the vinegar, oil, and dill. Season with salt and pepper. Set the bowl aside for 10 minutes.

Add the eggs, celery, onion, and parsley, and gently mix. In a separate bowl mix together the mayonnaise and milk. Pour the mixture over the potatoes and toss gently. Chill. Toss again just before serving.

Makes 4 to 6 servings.

A Sign of the Times

66I see why everybody makes such fun of the Brady clothes now, but you must remember that at the time we were on the cutting edge of style. My only consolation is that twenty-five years from now, today's youthful fashions are going to look just as silly, if not more so. Baggy shorts with the crotch down to the knees?99

Surfin' Greg's Coconut Cabbage Salad _____

1 head cabbage, shredded
½ head red cabbage, shredded
1 cup flaked coconut
1 cup sour cream
3 tablespoons lemon juice

1 tablespoon orange juice
Salt and pepper to taste
1½ tablespoons sugar
¼ cup toasted almonds,
    chopped

In a large bowl combine the cabbages and coconut. In a small bowl blend together the sour cream, lemon juice, orange juice, salt, and pepper. Stir the sour cream mixture into the cabbage mixture. Sprinkle with sugar and almonds and fold them in lightly.

Makes 6 to 8 servings.

Meet the Bradys Macaroni Salad

1 cup mayonnaise
2 tablespoons white wine vinegar
1 tablespoon cream
1 tablespoon country Dijon mustard
Salt and pepper to taste
1 8-ounce package elbow macaroni, cooked, drained, and cooled

½ cup very thinly sliced red cabbage
1 cup diced celery
½ cup shredded carrots
½ cup diced red bell pepper
¾ cup sliced scallions
¼ cup chopped parsley

In a medium bowl combine the mayonnaise, vinegar, cream, and mustard, and season with salt and pepper. In a large bowl combine the macaroni and the mayonnaise mixture. Chill for 1 hour and 30 minutes. Add the remaining ingredients and toss gently. Serve immediately.

Makes 6 servings.

Swingset Sour Green Pea Salad

3 pounds frozen green peas, defrosted
8 scallions (green onions), sliced

1 cucumber, sliced
1 cup sour cream
Salt and pepper to taste

In a medium bowl toss the peas, scallions, cucumber, sour cream, and salt and pepper. Chill for 1 hour. Serve over lettuce.

Makes 8 servings.

Barry Williams

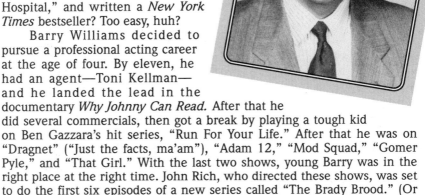

O.K., which smiling Brady has appeared on Broadway, played a dance teacher on "General Hospital," and written a *New York Times* bestseller? Too easy, huh?

Barry Williams decided to pursue a professional acting career at the age of four. By eleven, he had an agent—Toni Kellman— and he landed the lead in the documentary *Why Johnny Can Read.* After that he did several commercials, then got a break by playing a tough kid on Ben Gazzara's hit series, "Run For Your Life." After that he was on "Dragnet" ("Just the facts, ma'am"), "Adam 12," "Mod Squad," "Gomer Pyle," and "That Girl." With the last two shows, young Barry was in the right place at the right time. John Rich, who directed these shows, was set to do the first six episodes of a new series called "The Brady Brood." (Or was it "Bunch?") Barry got the part, and one of the most respected older brothers in television history was born—Greg Brady. He stayed with the role for the next twenty-some years. Judging by his book, he must have kept an incredible journal.

Barry tested the waters of his musical career during "The Brady Bunch" (remember "Adios Johnny Bravo?"), and he played the title role in *Pippin* on Broadway and in the first touring company. He returned to Broadway recently in the musical *Romance/Romance* at the Helen Hayes Theater. Most recently he completed a successful run in the first National Touring Company of *City of Angels.*

Besides "General Hospital" (which he has been on twice) Barry has been on "Murder She Wrote" and a two-part episode of "Highway To Heaven." Theater has become his first love, and he has starred in numerous productions including *They're Playing Our Song, Oklahoma!, I Love My Wife, Born Yesterday, West Side Story, I Do! I Do!,* and, a role he was born to play, *The Music Man.*

Then one dark and stormy night he sat down and started writing *Growing Up Brady/I Was A Teenage Greg.* Who would have ever thought a behind-the-scenes book about the Bradys and the challenges of a showbiz childhood would leap to the *New York Times* bestseller list for more than three months? But it sure did.

An avid tennis player, he hosts the Barry Williams Tennis Classic, which benefits the Adam Walsh Child Resource Center for missing and abused children. He is married to Diane Martin, who is a model and former Miss Arizona.

A remarkable career for a Teenage Greg who had Day-Glo orange hair on the last episode of "The Brady Bunch."

Jesse James' T-bone Steak _____

¼ cup Worcestershire sauce
2 teaspoons Tabasco sauce
¼ cup firmly packed brown
   sugar
¼ cup lemon juice

1 small onion, finely minced
1 clove garlic, finely minced
½ cup tomato sauce
8 T-bone steaks

In a medium bowl blend all of the ingredients except the steaks. Set the mixture aside for 20 minutes. Pour the mixture into a shallow pan. Add the steaks and marinate in the refrigerator for at least 2 hours, turning the steaks to make sure both sides are coated. Remove the steaks from the marinade. In a saucepan bring the marinade to a boil, and then allow it to cool.

Prepare the grill. The coals should be white hot. Place the steaks on the grill 4 inches above the coals. Cook for about 2½ minutes on each side for rare; add another minute each side for medium, and so on. Check for doneness by slicing close to the bone. Serve immediately. Serve the remaining marinade on the side.

Makes 8 servings.

Bell Bottoms
Barbecued Short Ribs _____

1 cup olive oil
1 cup red wine vinegar
10 large cloves garlic, crushed
1 cup chopped fresh basil
¼ cup chopped fresh oregano

2 tablespoons chopped fresh
   thyme
Salt and pepper to taste
8 pounds short ribs

In a medium bowl combine all the ingredients except the ribs and pour them into a deep pan. Add the ribs and turn until all are completely covered. Cover and refrigerate for 5 hours. Turn the ribs every hour.

Prepare the grill. The coals should be white hot. Brown the ribs on the grill 4 inches above the coals. Cover and cook for 20 minutes, checking frequently for doneness. The meat should be very tender. Cook longer if necessary.

Makes 8 servings.

Frankly, My Dear, I Don't Give a Darn

66Everybody on the set was so nice to those kids. There were sixty-five instant grandfathers present at all times. If anyone ventured so much as a 'damn,' he was immediately told that such language was not allowed on this set!99

House of Cards Hamburgers _____

1 slice bread
1 egg
3 pounds lean ground beef

3 tablespoons minced onion
Salt and pepper to taste

In a large bowl shred the bread in tiny pieces and add the egg. (The egg and bread help hold the burger together.) Mix in the beef, onion, salt, and pepper by hand. Form into 12 large burgers. Flatten each slightly.

Prepare the grill. The coals should be white hot. Cook for about 5 minutes on each side. If adding cheese, place a slice on top of each burger for the last minute of cooking. Serve on buns.

Alice's Note: For a great sauce try cooking 1 sliced onion and ½ cup of sliced mushrooms in 2 tablespoons of butter until the onion just starts to brown. Salt and pepper to taste.

ALICE: Oh, boy, now I know where those calories went. I've been sittin' on 'em.

Barry loved sporty cars. For a long time, he and I even owned the same model Porsche. Hollywood was never the same afterward.

Figaro, Figaro, Figaro Burgers —

2 pounds ground sirloin
2½ tablespoons chilled red
  wine
2 teaspoons salt
¾ teaspoon leaf basil

1 teaspoon leaf oregano
¾ teaspoon pepper
⅓ cup tomato sauce
8 slices mozzarella cheese

In a large bowl hand mix the sirloin, wine, salt, basil, oregano, pepper, and tomato sauce. Divide into 16 balls and flatten each. Place the mozzarella cheese on half of the patties and cover each with another half. Press firmly together. Grill over white hot coals for about 5 minutes a side or until the burgers are cooked to taste.

Makes 8 burgers.

Quarterback Sneak Hot Dogs _____

3 tablespoons butter
½ cup minced onions
3 teaspoons firmly packed
  brown sugar
1½ teaspoons Dijon mustard
Salt and pepper to taste

¼ cup lemon juice
7 tablespoons water
8 frankfurters
3 tablespoons Worcestershire
  sauce
1 teaspoon Tabasco sauce

In a skillet melt the butter and sauté the onions. Add the remaining ingredients except the frankfurters and simmer for 15 minutes. Prick the franks with a fork and arrange them in a shallow dish. Pour the marinade over the franks and refrigerate for 2 hours. Grill over hot coals until lightly singed on all sides. Serve with buns.
    Makes 8 servings.

Outstanding Citizen
Rosemary Chicken _____

1 cup olive oil
1 cup melted butter
1 cup dry white wine
2 tablespoons lemon juice
Salt and pepper to taste
2 teaspoons fresh rosemary,
  crushed

1½ teaspoons leaf sage
2 cloves garlic, finely minced
4 2-pound fryer chickens,
  cleaned, patted dry, and
  halved

In a saucepan combine all of the ingredients except the chicken and simmer for 15 minutes over very low heat. Brush the chicken all over with the sauce.
    Prepare the grill. Place the chicken on the grill cavity-side down. Cover and cook for about 50 minutes, basting and turning the chicken every 10 minutes. Cook until the chicken is no longer red inside against the bone.
    Makes 10 to 12 servings.

En Guarde! Barbecued Swordfish

¾ cup butter, melted and still
  warm
½ cup lemon juice

Salt to taste
8 swordfish steaks
Parsley

In a small bowl mix together the butter, lemon juice, and salt. Coat both sides of the steaks. Cook on a hot grill 8 inches above the coals for about 6 minutes on each side. Arrange the steaks on a platter and pour the remaining butter sauce over them. Garnish with parsley.
  Makes 8 servings.

Benedict Arnold's Best Baked Beans

1 tablespoon butter
1 onion, chopped
1 clove garlic, chopped
½ cup maple syrup
½ cup firmly packed dark
  brown sugar
¼ cup molasses
3 tablespoons rum
1 tablespoon cider vinegar
2 teaspoons Worcestershire
  sauce

1 tablespoon dry mustard
½ teaspoon curry powder
¼ teaspoon salt
⅛ teaspoon pepper
2 ham hocks
1 16-ounce can white beans,
  drained
1 16-ounce can kidney beans,
  drained
1 16-ounce can lima beans,
  drained

In a saucepan melt the butter and sauté the onion and garlic over medium heat until soft. Add the syrup, brown sugar, molasses, rum, vinegar, Worcestershire sauce, dry mustard, curry, salt, and pepper, and simmer for 2 minutes. Place the ham hocks in a deep 2-quart casserole and add the beans. Pour the sauce over and stir gently. Bake at 350° for 1 hour or until bubbly.
  Makes 8 servings.

Ah, But He Had Panache

66At first Chris couldn't be given line readings, mostly because he had a tin ear, which was put to good use in the episode in which Greg writes a song, rents a sound studio, and Peter's voice suddenly changes. On the other hand, Chris could give a certain pixie quality to lines that would sound rude coming from anybody else.99

Summer Picnic Watermelon Basket _____

1 watermelon
1 bunch red or green grapes, stems removed
1 cantaloupe, rind removed and cubed
1 honey melon, rind removed and cubed
4 oranges, peeled and sectioned
4 apples, cored and sliced in wedges
1 cup fresh pineapple chunks
1 cup fresh cherries, seeded and halved
Fresh lemon juice

Cut off a quarter of the watermelon lengthwise. Scoop out the fruit and cut it into chunks. Toss the watermelon with the remaining fruits and sprinkle lemon juice over all to prevent discoloration. Arrange the fruit mixture in the watermelon. Store any extra fruit in an airtight plastic container so the watermelon basket can be refilled as the fruit is served.

Alice's Note: Most any fruit can be used for basket, but I don't like to use bananas because they discolor so easily.

Makes 8 servings.

Marcia Gets Peachy Peach Ice Creamed

2 tablespoons all-purpose flour
1 cup sugar
1 cup half and half
6 fresh peaches peeled and
  pitted

2 tablespoons fresh lemon juice
1 cup cream, stiffly whipped

In a saucepan combine the flour, sugar, and half and half, and cook over medium heat until the mixture thickens. Cool.

Chop the peaches and mash them in a bowl. Add the mashed peaches and lemon juice to the thickened sauce. Fold in the whipped cream. Pour the mixture into an ice cream freezer and freeze according to the manufacturer's directions.

Makes 2 quarts.

GREG: Alice, what's this?
ALICE: Leftovers.
GREG: Leftover what?
ALICE: This (has) been left over so long I forgot.

Bobster's Perfect Almond Torte

3 eggs
1 cup sugar
1 cup crushed graham crackers

½ cup chopped almonds
Lemon curd
Whipped cream

Grease and flour a 9-inch cake pan. In a medium bowl beat the eggs until thick and lemon-colored. Add the sugar, crumbs, and almonds, and mix well. Pour the batter into the prepared pan. Bake at 350° for 25 minutes or until a toothpick inserted in the center comes out clean. Cool in the pan. Turn onto a cake platter and top with a layer of lemon curd. Cut in wedges and serve with whipped cream.

Makes 8 servings.

I bet Clint Eastwood never did dangerous stunts like this!

Everybody Can't Be George Washington's Apple Crumble

2 pounds tart green apples,
  cored and sliced
¼ cup apple cider
¾ cup all-purpose flour
½ cup sugar
½ cup firmly packed light
  brown sugar

1 teaspoon cinnamon
¾ teaspoon allspice
½ teaspoon salt
½ cup butter

In a shallow greased 2-quart baking dish spread the apples around the bottom and pour the cider over them. In a medium bowl mix together the flour, sugar, brown sugar, cinnamon, allspice, and salt. Cut in the butter until the mixture is crumbly. Spread the topping over the apples. Bake at 350° for 40 minutes or until the topping is golden brown. Serve warm.

Makes 8 servings.

Sunshine Sisters' Sour Cream Pound Cake

1 cup soft butter
2¾ cups sugar
6 eggs
3 cups all-purpose flour

½ teaspoon salt
¼ teaspoon baking soda
1¼ cups sour cream
1 teaspoon almond extract

In a large bowl cream together the butter and sugar. Beat in the eggs one at a time. Sift together the flour, salt, and soda. Add the dry ingredients to the butter mixture. Blend in the sour cream and almond extract. Pour the batter into a greased and floured 10-inch tube pan. Bake at 350° for 1 hour and 15 minutes or until a toothpick inserted in the center comes out clean. Cool in the pan.

Makes 12 servings.

Barry Williams Talks Turkey

66 A special meal around the Brady table would normally take two days to shoot. That meant two different turkeys: the fresh one that Robert Reed would ceremoniously cut into at the end of day two, the one that had just been removed from the hot oven. Then there was the prop turkey, the one that the Sunshine Sisters stuffed and slapped together at 4:00 A.M. on the first day of shooting. At 8:00 A.M. the prop turkey smelled delicious when the camera started rolling, but as the morning turned into afternoon the hot lights on the set began to take their toll on the old bird. The next day the turkey was removed from the refrigerator and put back on the Brady table, adding a new challenge for us actors. By high noon on the second day, the bird began to swell from internal gases. If anyone had been foolish enough to stick a fork into the decomposing carcass, the bird would have flown around the sound stage like a punctured basketball. Thus, the happy faces on the Brady family when the fresh turkey was finally sliced into was in part a sigh of relief from not having to stare at the Sunshine Sisters' holiday time bomb any longer. 99

Dreamy Dentist Delicious Strawberry Shortcake _____

2 cups all-purpose flour
2 tablespoons sugar
1 teaspoon salt
1 tablespoon baking powder
¼ cup butter
½ cup milk
1 egg

Softened butter
6 cups strawberries, sliced and
   very lightly sugared
1½ cups heavy cream, chilled
12 strawberries, cleaned and
   drained, stems on

In a medium bowl sift together the flour, sugar, salt, and baking powder. Cut in ¼ cup of butter until crumbly. Add the milk and egg, and mix until just blended. Turn onto a floured surface and roll out to ⅝-inch thickness. Cut with a 3-inch cookie cutter. Gather the scraps, roll out, and cut again until there are 12 cakes. Bake the cakes on a greased baking sheet for 10 minutes or until lightly browned. Cool and split. Butter the split sides. Place the bottoms on dessert plates and spoon in sliced strawberries. Top with the remaining shortcake halves and cover with whipped cream. Top each serving with a whole strawberry.

Makes 12 servings.

Fruit of the Gods Crumble_____

3 pounds nectarines, peeled,
   pitted and sliced
2 tablespoons kirsch or peach
   brandy
⅓ cup honey
1 cup rolled oats
½ cup all-purpose flour
⅓ cup firmly packed brown
   sugar

¼ cup sugar
¼ teaspoon allspice
¼ teaspoon salt
¼ cup butter
1 cup plain yogurt
1 tablespoon honey

In a large bowl toss the peaches with the kirsch and ⅓ cup of honey. Spoon into a shallow, greased baking dish. In a separate bowl mix the oats, flour, brown sugar, sugar, allspice, and salt. Cut in the butter until crumbly. Sprinkle the oat mixture over the nectarines. Bake at 350° for 45 minutes, until light brown and bubbly. Mix the yogurt and 1 tablespoon of honey and serve on the side.

Makes 8 servings.

On The Road

Fortunately for me, the gun wasn't loaded.

> *I'm going to start on the beach because that's the nearest excursion in Southern California.*

Frontier Scouts' Fabulous Fish Fry

Oil
12 perch, cleaned
3 cups bread crumbs

Salt and pepper to taste
3 eggs, beaten

Place a grill over the fire to hold a large pot. Pour the oil in the pot and place it on the grill. In a shallow dish season the bread crumbs with salt and pepper. When the oil is hot, dip the fish in the eggs and then coat with bread crumbs. Fry the fish until golden brown. Drain on paper towels.

Alice's Note: You are allowed to eat with your fingers. (Pour cooled, used oil back in the bottle and take it home. Don't leave nature to take care of it.)

Makes 12 servings.

Rattle Proof Bags

66 Paper lunch bags had to be treated so they would not rattle when handled, which is no easy trick when you have to hand out six of them right in a row to six rushing kids while all of you are saying lines.
Otherwise, if they rattle, it sounds like the place is on fire. Sound men hate sound: paper bags, running down the stairs, pots and pans. I think it's a control thing. 99

Tiger's Hush Puppies

Prepare the batter ahead to take with you.

1½ cups cornmeal
1 cup water
¾ cup milk
1 tablespoon melted butter

2 teaspoons grated onion
2 eggs, beaten
1 cup all-purpose flour
3 teaspoons baking powder
1 teaspoon salt
2 teaspoons sugar
Oil

In a saucepan combine the cornmeal, water, and ½ cup of milk. Cook over medium heat until the cornmeal becomes dry enough to roll into a ball, about 6 minutes. Blend in the remaining milk, butter, onion, and eggs. In a medium bowl sift together the flour, baking powder, salt, and sugar. Add the dry ingredients to the batter. At this point, the batter may be stored in an airtight container for travel.

When ready to fry, drop 1 tablespoon of batter at a time into hot oil and cook until golden brown. Drain on paper towels. If using the same oil as for the fish, cook the hush puppies first.

Makes 8 servings.

Easy Steaming Clams

How easy can it get? Just spread them out on a rack over steaming water, cover, and wait until they open.

ALICE: Sam, this is the sweetest thing you could have done. Coming to see me and bringing me candy and flowers. It is almost worth spraining my ankle for.

SAM: Could I take a look at it?

ALICE: Why not? Everybody else has! Though I never heard of a butcher who was a doctor.

SAM: Well, I've known plenty of doctors who were butchers. Boy, that does look pretty bad. I wouldn't put meat like that on my counter.

ALICE: Sam, you always know just the right thing to say.

> *Now we'll move to other great outdoor snacks.*

Freckled Face Fried Chicken _____

6 cups oil
2 eggs, beaten
1 teaspoon leaf oregano
1 teaspoon leaf rosemary
1 teaspoon minced onion

2 cloves garlic, crushed
2 fryer chickens, cleaned and
   sectioned
2 cups all-purpose flour
Salt and pepper to taste

In a medium bowl combine 2 cups of oil, the eggs, oregano, rosemary, onion, and garlic. Pour the mixture over the chicken in shallow pan. Marinate the chicken in the refrigerator for 2 hours. Turn the chicken occasionally.

In a medium bowl mix the flour, salt, and pepper. Dip the chicken in the flour and coat well. In 2 large skillets heat 2 cups of oil each. Arrange the chicken in the skillets and brown on both sides. Cover the pans and reduce the heat. Cook over low heat for about 20 minutes, until the chicken is tender. Remove the pan from the heat and drain on paper towels. Eat immediately or refrigerate to take on a picnic the next day.

Makes 8 servings.

The Bears' Brie and Herb Picnic Omelets _____

9 eggs
3 tablespoons minced parsley
3 tablespoons chives
Salt and pepper to taste

4 ounces Brie, rind removed
   and cut into 3 pieces
6 tablespoons butter

In a medium bowl combine 3 eggs, 1 tablespoon of parsley, 1 tablespoon of chives, salt, and pepper. Beat well. Chop 1 piece of Brie. In a 6-inch skillet melt 2 tablespoons of butter. Coat the bottom of the skillet completely with butter. Add the egg mixture. Tilt the pan while cooking to keep the eggs from sticking. Cook until set but still creamy. Sprinkle chopped Brie over the surface. Reduce the heat and cook until the Brie is melted and the omelet is firm. Lift the edges with a fork and then roll up like a jelly roll. Make 2 more omelets with the remaining ingredients. Chill. When ready to eat slice into 1-inch slices.

Makes 3 omelets.

Spring Break Picnic Salad with Feta Cheese

2 cups canned French-cut green beans, drained
6 new red potatoes, cooked
1 green bell pepper, seeded and sliced
1 large red onion, sliced
2 9¼-ounce cans water-packed tuna, drained
10 cherry tomatoes
¾ cup feta cheese, chunked
½ cup olive oil
3 tablespoons white wine vinegar
½ teaspoon salt
2 teaspoons country Dijon mustard
1 clove garlic, minced
Pepper to taste
1 tablespoon minced fresh basil
4 hard-boiled eggs, peeled and quartered
2 ounces anchovies, drained
⅓ cup chopped parsley

In a large serving bowl toss together the beans, potatoes, green pepper, onion, tuna, cherry tomatoes, and feta. In a separate bowl mix the oil, vinegar, salt, mustard, garlic, pepper, and basil together well. Pour the dressing over the salad and toss. Top with eggs, anchovies, and parsley.

Makes 8 to 10 servings.

Eve Plumb

Eve Plumb seemed destined to go into the entertainment business. She was born in a hospital across from the Disney studios and baptized in a movie theater—not quite a trunk in Pocatello, Idaho, but close enough. When she was six years old, a children's talent agent moved next door to her family and quickly convinced her mother to take her on a commercial audition. She got the job, first time out, which started an active career in commercials and television shows.

Then, at the seasoned age of ten, she auditioned for "The Brady Bunch." Eve maintains she got the role of Jan because she was blond and looked like Florence Henderson, but the big reason was her ability to handle both comedy and drama convincingly. She was a natural-born actress who made believable all the emotional ups and downs of being a middle child in a large family. The continued popularity of "The Brady Bunch" has led Eve to reprise her role as Jan in "The Brady Brides," *A Very Brady Christmas,* and *The Bradys.*

Eve has been seen in many television movies, including *Dawn: Portrait of a Teenage Runaway*, a gritty departure from Jan Brady, *Secrets of Three Hungry Wives, The Night the Bridge Fell Down, Little Women*, and the sequel *Alexander: The Other Side of Dawn.* She was in the motion picture comedy *I'm Gonna Git U Sucka* and has written, performed, and created improvisations at The Groundling Theatre in Los Angeles, including *Your Very Own T.V. Show* and *The Girl's Club.* Most recently, she dropped into Metropolis for an episode of "Lois and Clark."

Thank goodness for the talent agent who moved in next door!

Tank's Tasty Turkey Salad _____

3 cups cooked turkey
1 cup diced celery
1 small onion, sliced
½ cup sliced radishes
½ cup chopped parsley
2 tomatoes, cut in wedges
½ cup cooked broccoli
½ cup cooked peas

1½ cups cubed Cheddar cheese
4 cups cooked macaroni
1½ cups mayonnaise
⅓ cup lemon juice
⅓ cup sugar
1 teaspoon salt
⅛ teaspoon pepper

In a large salad bowl toss together the turkey, vegetables, Cheddar, and macaroni. Blend together the mayonnaise, lemon juice, sugar, salt, and pepper. Pour the dressing over the salad. Refrigerate for at least 1 hour before serving.

Makes 8 servings.

ALICE: Vichyssoise is such a pretty name for cold potato soup, don't you think?

The Big Fisherman's Feast _____

24 slices oatmeal bread (use St. Paddy's, recipe on page 43)
Soft butter
8 slices canned smoked salmon, drained
¼ cup lemon juice

½ teaspoon coarse black pepper
1 8-ounce can white tuna, drained
3 tablespoons mayonnaise
1 large red onion, cut in 8 slices

Spread one side of each slice of bread with butter. Spread salmon on 8 buttered slices and sprinkle with lemon juice and pepper. Top with one slice of bread each, butter-side up. In a small bowl mix the tuna with the mayonnaise and spread the mixture on each sandwich. Top with the onions and the remaining slices of bread, butter-side down. Wrap tightly in foil and you're ready to go fishing.

Makes 8 sandwiches.

Eve was a solid actor. They all had their special strengths, but she handled the dramatic moments the best.

Sam the Butcher's Favorite Sandwich _____

16 slices rye bread
Soft butter
8 slices Swiss cheese

8 slices liverwurst
8 slices red onion
Country Dijon mustard

Butter 8 slices of bread. Top each with a slice of cheese, liverwurst, and onion. Spread mustard on the remaining slices and top each sandwich.

Alice's Note: I haven't met a butcher who didn't like liverwurst.

Middle Child Crabby Eggs_____

12 hard-boiled eggs, peeled
½ cup finely flaked crab meat
3 teaspoons Parmesan cheese
3 tablespoons butter

2½ tablespoons mayonnaise
2 tablespoons minced chives
2 tablespoons minced parsley
Salt and pepper to taste

Cut the eggs in half lengthwise and remove the yolks without damaging the whites. Mash together the yolks and remaining ingredients until well blended. Spoon the filling evenly into the egg white cavities.

Makes 24 servings.

Brady Trivia Quiz #4

In "Sergeant Emma," what are five big differences between Alice and her cousin?
What two things do they have in common?

Answers on Page 195.

Sergeant Emma's Chipped Ham And Dried Apricots_____

2 cups dried apricots
4 cups boiling water
6 tablespoons oil
¼ cup all-purpose flour
2 14-ounce cans evaporated
  milk

2 cups water
2 teaspoons dry mustard
1 cup chopped canned ham

In a large bowl pour the boiling water over apricots. Set aside until softened. Drain. Cut the apricots into small pieces.

In a skillet heat the oil and add the flour. Cook for 2 minutes, stirring constantly. Slowly add the milk and remaining water. Stirring constantly, add the mustard. Cook for 5 minutes. Add the apricots and ham, and cook until heated through. Serve hot.

Makes 6 servings.

Eve Plumb Remembers Her Favorite Dish

66The Brady kitchen was always a hub of activity and Ann, playing Alice, was called on to portray chef extraordinaire of suburban family cooking. When it came to boiled water, however, we left it to the studio craftsmen to work their movie magic. People have asked if the food we had on the show was real. When it came to boiled water, the answer is yes! No expense was spared. We looked forward to boiled water scenes on the Brady set. Our indulgent schoolteacher would free us from our books and papers so we could watch the diligent preparations of the prop and special effects men—an invaluable education. After hours of lighting and rehearsal, Ann would step into the scene holding her 'prop' spoon, taking her place by the pot of boiling water. Sometimes the pot was covered, adding to the tension. If the pot boiled over, it would ruin the take and the whole process would have to begin again. Visitors to the set were awed by the boiled water scenes. How we managed to create light comedy amid all the difficult technology was amazing.

"But I think the best thing about 'boiled water day' on the Brady set was that when the scene was finished, the extra boiled water was put on the snack table for the whole cast and crew to enjoy. As we used to say, 'Hey, who doesn't love boiled water?'99

Grand Canyon or Bust Hiker's Mix

3 cups rolled oats, toasted
1 cup sesame seeds, toasted
1 cup sunflower seeds, toasted
1 cup almonds, toasted and chopped
1 cup walnuts, toasted and chopped
1 cup raisins
1 cup dried apricots

Easy! Mix everything together and store in a covered container in the refrigerator. Just scoop what you want to carry into a plastic bag.

Variation: Add M&M®s for an extra energy jolt!

Harvey Klinger Zucchini Fingers___

16 small zucchini
¾ pound ground turkey
1 clove garlic, finely minced
6 tablespoons olive oil

¾ cup parsley, chopped
3 tablespoons Parmesan cheese
1 large egg, beaten
¾ cup bread crumbs

Cut the zucchini tips off at both ends. Remove the centers with an apple corer. In a medium bowl blend the turkey, garlic, 3 tablespoons of olive oil, parsley, Parmesan, egg, and bread crumbs. Stuff the zucchini evenly with the turkey mixture. Place the stuffed zucchini in an oiled shallow baking dish. Brush the zucchini with the remaining oil. Bake at 325° for 1 hour and 20 minutes. Allow the zucchini to cool.

Refrigerate overnight for the next day's munchies at the football game.

Makes 8 servings.

Tiger's Home from the Pound Cake _____

1 cup soft butter
1¾ cups sugar
4 eggs
¼ cup Amaretto liqueur
½ teaspoon vanilla extract

1 teaspoon almond extract
½ cup milk
2½ cups sifted all-purpose flour
1 tablespoon baking powder
¼ cup confectioners' sugar

In a large bowl cream together the butter and sugar. Add the eggs one at a time to the butter mixture. Beat until fluffy. In a separate bowl blend together the Amaretto, vanilla, almond, and milk. In a medium bowl sift together the flour, baking powder, and salt. Add the dry ingredients to the butter mixture alternately with the milk mixture. Pour the batter into a large greased and floured loaf pan. Bake at 350° for 55 to 60 minutes. Cool on a rack. Dust with confectioners' sugar and wrap in aluminum foil or plastic wrap for traveling. Slice when you get there.

Makes 8 to 10 servings.

Revolving Messages

66Once we had lunch on top of the Space Needle in Seattle. The restaurant had set up a screen around our table so we could have a little privacy, but Susan and Mike wrote notes and pasted them to the window so that people sitting around the edges got to see them pass by as the restaurant turned. I never did find out what the notes said.**99**

Jan's Nothing to Snicker at Snickers® Pie

1½ cups graham cracker crumbs (about 15 whole crackers)
1 tablespoon plus 2 teaspoons sugar
6 tablespoons unsalted butter, melted

5 2.07-ounceSnickers® bars
1 3-ounce package chocolate-flavored pudding and pie filling mix
1 cup heavy or whipping cream

Butter an 8-inch pie plate. In a medium bowl combine the graham cracker crumbs and 1 tablespoon of sugar. Stir in the butter until well combined. Press the crumb mixture into the bottom and sides of the pie plate. Bake at 350° for 5 to 8 minutes or until set. Cool completely on a wire rack.

Cut 4 of the Snickers® bars in half lengthwise and then into ¼-inch pieces crosswise. Sprinkle the pieces in the bottom of the pie crust.

Prepare the pudding mix according to the package directions for pie filling. Spoon the filling over the Snickers® pieces in the pie shell. Cover the surface of the pie with plastic wrap and refrigerate for 3 hours.

Just before serving, in a small bowl beat the heavy cream with the remaining 2 teaspoons of sugar with an electric mixer at high speed until stiff peaks form. Cut the remaining Snickers® bar into pieces. Cut the pie into slices and garnish each slice with a dollop of whipped cream and a candy bar piece.

Makes 8 to 10 servings.

Family Treats

It is hard to believe that when the show first started, Florence and I were both taller than the kids.

Double Parked Baked Bean Sandwiches

1 27-ounce can Boston baked beans, drained
3 tablespoons grated red onion
5 tablespoons country Dijon mustard

½ cup butter
16 slices pumpernickel bread

In a medium bowl mash together the beans, onion, and mustard. Spread the butter on one side of each slice of bread. Spread the bean mixture evenly on 8 slices and cover with the remaining slices. The kids love the sweet taste of this sandwich.

Makes 8 sandwiches.

ALICE: I better take these cookies into Mr. Brady before the kids get a radar fix on them, and it's good-bye Charlie.

Grown-up's Peanut Butter Sandwich

2 slices pumpernickel bread
2 tablespoons crunchy peanut butter

2 thick slices deli salami
1 thick slice red onion

Spread peanut butter on both slices of bread. Top one slice with salami and onion. Cover with the remaining slice.

Alice's Note: A Mr. B. favorite. No comment.

Makes 1 sandwich.

Alice's Room

66 I did have a room that showed up on the show now and then. Take a sharp right past the stove, then walk to the next sound stage. The first time I used it, I wanted my little room to have a personal touch—there's the method in me again. I brought a suitcase full of knickknacks and photos from home that I thought would be 'Alice looking.' They gave a nice realistic feel to the rather humble set. When the kids' rooms were first decorated, they all brought things from home: school awards, pennants, pictures, and whatnot. This allowed the make believe to be a little more real. 99

Yankee Doodle Macaroni And Cheese

5 tablespoons butter
¾ cup minced onion
3 tablespoons all-purpose flour
½ teaspoon pepper
⅓ cup heavy cream
⅔ cup white wine

1⅓ cups ricotta cheese
1⅓ cups grated Cheddar cheese
¼ cup grated Parmesan cheese
1 16-ounce package elbow macaroni, cooked and drained

In a large saucepan melt the butter and sauté the onions until softened. Stir in the flour and pepper. Cook for 2 minutes. Add the wine and cream, and bring the mixture to a boil, stirring constantly. Reduce the heat and simmer gently, stirring constantly until the sauce thickens, about 3 minutes. Stir in the ricotta, Cheddar, and Parmesan. Heat just until the Cheddar is melted. Toss with macaroni and serve.

Alice's Note: You never go wrong with this dish.

Makes 8 servings.

Tabu Toast

1 cup grated Cheddar cheese
⅓ cup butter
3 teaspoons Dijon mustard
8 slices bacon, cooked and
  crumbled

16 slices white bread, crusts
  removed

In a medium bowl combine the Cheddar, butter, and mustard. Stir in the bacon. Spread the mixture evenly on the bread slices, roll each up, and secure with toothpicks. Arrange the rolls in a broiler pan. Place under a preheated broiler and toast until brown on both sides.

Alice's Note: This is finger food for the boys' sleepovers.

Makes 16 servings.

JAN: I am going to make my famous peanut-butter-and-pickle sandwiches. You can't burn those. Too soggy.

Bobby's Sloppy Joes

¼ cup butter
1 large white onion, chopped
2 cloves garlic, minced
1¾ tablespoons Worcestershire
  sauce
2 teaspoons firmly packed
  brown sugar

1¾ teaspoons dry mustard
1¼ cups ketchup
2 cups lean ground beef,
  cooked
8 hamburger buns
Soft butter

In a skillet melt the butter and sauté the onion and garlic until soft, about 5 minutes. Add the Worcestershire, brown sugar, mustard, salt, and ketchup. Reduce the heat and simmer slowly for 10 minutes. Add the meat and simmer until hot. Spread the inside of the buns with butter. Spoon some of the beef evenly onto each bun.

Alice's Note: This is most requested when friends are brought home for lunch.

Makes 8 sandwiches.

Christopher Knight

Christopher has the distinction of saying what is probably the most famous line in all of Bradydom— "pork chops and applesauce"— delivered as an impersonation of Lloyd Schwartz, who was impersonating Humphrey Bogart.

Christopher was born into an acting family. His father, Edward, performed Shakespeare in New York and later became co-owner of The Onion Company in Los Angeles. Christopher had shot about two dozen commercials and had appeared on such hit series as "Gunsmoke," "Bonanza," and "Mannix" before he became a member of the Brady family. He had also made a feature film with Don Murray, *The Narrow Chute*, about a rodeo rider.

Christopher has always loved animals, and in his spare time off the Brady sound stage he maintained a small zoo that included a boxer, two cats, a tortoise, a rat, a rabbit, tropical fish, and several dozen prize-winning pigeons. He also found time to become a golf fanatic at the age of fifteen—a young man of boundless energy.

Christopher had a keen interest in a singing career, and he especially enjoyed the episodes and specials with the singing Bradys. He and Maureen McCormick even released a record album together (now that was some duo). After "The Brady Bunch," Christopher appeared in several TV movies, including *Diary of a Hitchhiker*, and he guest starred on "The Love Boat," "Happy Days," and "Another World." He was a regular on the series "Joe's World" and returned for all the Brady reunions.

Always intrigued with new challenges, Christopher has worked as a casting assistant and as the general manager of a software development company. His fascination with the computer has led to an exciting new career with Visual Software, a company on the cutting edge of interactive videos.

Perhaps in the future he can play Bogie in his own interactive version of *Casablanca*.

Big Catch Fish Burgers _____

2 cups halibut, cooked and
  flaked
2 tablespoons sweet pickle
  relish
2 tablespoons scallions (or
  green onions), minced
3 tablespoons minced parsley
1 teaspoon fresh lemon juice

Pepper to taste
6 tablespoons mayonnaise
Soft butter
8 English muffins
8 slices bacon, cooked and
  halved
8 slices Swiss cheese

In a medium bowl combine the fish, relish, scallions, parsley, lemon juice, and pepper. Add enough mayonnaise to moisten the mixture. Toast and butter the English muffins. Spread the bottom halves of the muffins with fish spread. Top with 1 slice of cheese and 2 bacon halves.

Alice's Note: The girls love this burger when they're being healthy, but it's good anytime.

Makes 8 sandwiches.

CAROL: Well, that's another ad from Shultz's Delicatessen.
ALICE: Ah, what a combination...Shakespeare and salami.

Greg's Hungry Reuben Sandwich _____

16 slices rye bread
Soft butter
Russian dressing
1½ pounds cooked corned beef,
  thinly sliced

1 pound sauerkraut, drained
8 slices Swiss cheese

Lightly toast and butter the bread. Spread with dressing. Top half of the bread with corned beef, sauerkraut, and cheese, and cover with the remaining halves of the bread. Bake at 400° until the cheese melts, about 6 minutes or 15 to 25 seconds in the microwave.

Makes 8 sandwiches.

Chris had a natural charm about him, like a modern Huck Finn. He had an energy that the camera just loved.

Mr. Matthews' Fast Hustling Chili

1 pound lean ground beef
2 tablespoons minced onion
2 15-ounce cans chili beans
1 28-ounce can stewed
  tomatoes, drained

1 6-ounce can tomato paste
2 tablespoons catsup
½ teaspoon garlic powder
1½ teaspoons chili powder

In a large saucepan brown the meat and onion together over medium heat, about 8 minutes. Drain the fat. Stir in the remaining ingredients and bring to a boil. Reduce the heat to simmer and cook for 15 minutes.

Alice's Note: This is what the kids like to make when they feel like cooking and no one's home. It's easy and filling. And only one pot to clean.

Makes 8 servings.

Mrs. B's Vegetable Chili _____

2 tablespoons olive oil
1 large white onion, chopped
1 green bell pepper, chopped
3 cups diced summer squash
1 large zucchini, diced
1 red bell pepper, diced
1 cup quartered fresh
  mushrooms
4 carrots, peeled and chopped
2 large tomatoes, chopped

2 cups cooked kidney beans
½ cup dry white wine
1 6-ounce can tomato paste
1 teaspoon minced garlic
1 teaspoon salt
¼ teaspoon pepper
1½ tablespoons chili powder
1 teaspoon cumin
Grated Cheddar cheese

In a large saucepan heat the oil and sauté the onion until soft. Add the bell peppers, squash, zucchini, mushrooms, and carrots. Cook over medium heat for about 10 minutes. Stir in the remaining ingredients except the cheese. Heat to a boil. Reduce the heat to low, cover, and simmer until the vegetables are soft, stirring occasionally. Serve with grated Cheddar cheese.

Makes 8 to 10 servings.

Puffed the Magic Potato _____

2 cups cooked mashed potatoes
4 eggs, beaten
¼ cup all-purpose flour
1 tablespoon minced onion

1 tablespoon garlic powder
¾ teaspoon salt
Oil

In a medium bowl mix all of the ingredients well except the oil. In a large skillet heat ½ inch of oil. Form the potato mixture into 1-inch balls and drop in the hot oil. Cook until crisp and golden brown, turning once. Drain on paper towels. Serve immediately.

Alice's Note: These are a great alternative to french fries.

Makes 6 servings.

Chris Knight Remembers Ann B.

66Ann used to scare me. Not in a mean way. It was because she was very professional—no nonsense—and I was a very hyperactive kid. We all were, except Barry, who never seemed like a kid. I'd get punch drunk and let off a lot of energy. Florence got a little punchy sometimes, but Ann never did. She was always prepared, always ready to get the job done on the first take. To someone like me, those qualities were intimidating. In the scene where we were all put into jail on our way to the Grand Canyon, Ann, realizing she was locked up with us, said she expected all of us to act like professionals until the scene was done. We did, but it wasn't easy. Ann also was the first person to introduce me to tennis. She used to hit the ball against the outside studio wall during breaks, and I started doing it, too. She also got me started on needlepoint, embroidery, and hooking rugs. All this was great. It allowed me to focus all my attention on one thing. Her life fascinated me. For a long time she left the industry, and now she is beginning to re-enter it again. She's a remarkable lady.99

Get Your Bacon and Cheese Hot Dogs! _____

8 hot dogs   8 slices bacon
8 wedges Cheddar cheese

Split the hot dogs lengthwise and insert the cheese. Wrap the hot dogs in a spiral with the bacon slices. Anchor with toothpicks. Place each on a separate foil strip, cheese-side down. Grill over hot coals until the bacon is done, about 7 minutes.
    Makes 8 servings.

What's Up, Welsh Rabbit _____

¼ cup butter
¼ cup all-purpose flour
2 cups dark beer
2 teaspoons Worcestershire
  sauce
¼ cup country Dijon mustard

Salt to taste
4 cups grated sharp Cheddar
  cheese
8 slices whole wheat bread,
  toasted and buttered

In a large skillet melt the butter over medium heat. Slowly blend in the flour until smooth. Stirring constantly, slowly add the beer. Cook until the sauce thickens. Add the Worcestershire sauce, mustard, and salt, and blend well. Add the cheese and cook until there are no lumps. Arrange the bread slices on a platter or on individual plates and spoon the sauce over.

Alice's Note: I think this is a family favorite because there really isn't a little bunny in the recipe.

Makes 8 servings.

Pick Me Up, Cheese Sticks _____

1 cup all-purpose flour
¼ teaspoon pepper
¼ cup butter
⅓ cup grated sharp Cheddar
  cheese

2 tablespoons grated Parmesan
  cheese
1 tablespoon cold water

In a large bowl mix the flour and pepper. Cut in the butter until crumbly. Mix in the cheeses and add the water. Stir with a fork until the dough begins to form a ball. Turn out onto a floured surface and roll out to ¼-inch thickness. Cut into 3½-inch sticks. Arrange the sticks on a baking sheet. Bake at 350° until golden brown, about 10 minutes. Serve right away or at room temperature for snacks. Remember, teenagers are always hungry.

Makes about 8 servings.

The Old Bradys

❝ I always liked the episode in which Bob and Florence played their own grandparents. It was great fun. Bob was a convincing old man, with the old voice and one marvelous moment when he appeared about to explode into apoplexy. Playing old convincingly is hard to do. I've tried it. Of course, it's easier for me now than it was twenty-five years ago. Actually, if you've seen Florence recently, it turns out to be perfectly possible that she won't change any more in the next twenty-five years than she has in the past twenty-five years! ❞

Holiday Confetti Ice Cream _____

½ cup sugar
2 vanilla beans
6 egg yolks

3 cups heavy cream
1 cup M&M®s

In a metal bowl combine the cream and 1 vanilla bean. Cover and chill over night.

In a blender process the sugar and 1 vanilla bean until the bean is pulverized. In a medium bowl whisk together the sugar and egg yolks. In a saucepan bring the cream with the vanilla bean almost to a boil over medium heat. Remove the pan from the heat. Remove the bean and pour the cream into the egg mixture. Whisk until well blended. Return the mixture to the saucepan and cook over low heat until it begins to thicken. Do not boil. Remove the pan from the heat and refrigerate until cool. Freeze in an ice cream freezer until just beginning to harden. Fold in the M&M®s and return to the freezer.

Alice's Note: This is a great Fourth of July dessert or one to make the kids feel special on New Year's Eve.

Makes about 6 servings.

Cindy's Buttery Just Butter Cookies

1 cup butter, softened
2 cups all-purpose flour

½ cup sugar
1 cup finely chopped almonds

In a medium bowl combine all of the ingredients and mix well. Turn onto a floured surface and roll out to ¼-inch thickness. Cut into the desired shapes with 1½-inch cookie cutters and arrange on an ungreased cookie sheet. Bake at 350° for 10 minutes.

Variation: Try spreading your favorite perserves on one cookie and covering it with another for a great sandwich cookie.

Makes 3 to 4 dozen cookies.

CAROL: Westdale High School, 19—I can't make out the date.
ALICE: I know. It was easier before I used the steel wool.
MIKE: Alice Nelson, first place, school *modern* dance contest?
CAROL: Alice, that's great. Why didn't you tell us yourself you were such a good dancer?
ALICE: Well, actually, I didn't know it myself. You'd be surprised the moves you make when the elastic breaks in your gym bloomers.

Brace Yourself Honey Taffy

1 cup sugar
¾ cup honey
⅔ cup water
1 teaspoon salt

1 tablespoon cornstarch
2 teaspoons vanilla extract
2 tablespoons butter

In a large saucepan combine the sugar, honey, water, salt, cornstarch, and vanilla. Cook over medium heat, stirring constantly, until the mixture reaches 256° on a candy thermometer or until a small amount dropped in cold water forms a hard ball. Remove the pan from the heat and pour into a buttered square pan.

When the taffy is cool enough to handle, butter hands and pull the taffy until satiny and light in color. Pull into long strips ½-inch wide. Cut into 1-inch pieces. Wrap individually in waxed paper or plastic wrap. Have fun. Sometimes this recipe is more fun to make than eat.
Makes 6 to 8 servings.

Grandma Connie's Shortbread ____

2 cups all-purpose flour
½ cup confectioners' sugar
⅓ cup rice flour
½ teaspoon salt
1 cup butter, softened

In a large bowl sift the dry ingredients together. Add the butter and mix completely. Turn out onto a floured surface and knead until very soft. Roll into a log and cover with plastic. Refrigerate for at least 1 hour. Knead gently on a floured surface for about 2 minutes. Roll the dough out to ¼-inch thickness. Cut with a 2-inch cutter into 24 round cookies. Bake at 350° for 20 minutes or until the cookies are lightly golden around the edges. Cool on a rack.
Makes 2 dozen cookies.

Marcia's Dreamy Chocolate Peanutty Crumble Squares _____

½ cup butter or margarine
1 cup all-purpose flour
¾ cup instant oats, uncooked
⅓ cup brown sugar
½ teaspoon baking soda
½ teaspoon vanilla extract
4 2.23-ounce Snickers® bars, cut into 8 slices each

Grease the bottom of an 8-inch square pan. In a large saucepan melt the butter or margarine. Remove the pan from the heat and stir in the flour, oats, brown sugar, baking soda, and vanilla. Blend until crumbly. Press ⅔ of the mixture into the prepared pan. Arrange the Snickers® bar slices in the pan, about ½-inch from the edge of the pan. Finely crumble the remaining mixture over the sliced Snickers® bars. Bake at 350° for 25 minutes or until edges are golden brown. Cool in the pan on a cooling rack. Cut into bars or squares to serve.
Makes 24 bars.

Greg's Kaleidoscope Oatmeal M&M®s Cookie Pizza

½ cup butter, softened
¾ cup light brown sugar
1 egg
1½ teaspoons vanilla extract
1 cup all-purpose flour
½ teaspoon baking powder
½ teaspoon baking soda

1 cup quick-cooking oats
¼ cup chopped nuts
¼ cup sweetened coconut
1 12-ounce package (1¾ cups)
M&M®s Semi-Sweet
Chocolate Baking Bits,
divided

Grease a 12-inch pizza pan. In a medium bowl beat the butter, brown sugar, egg, and vanilla until light and fluffy. In a separate bowl combine the flour, baking powder, baking soda, and oats. Gradually add the dry ingredients to the creamed mixture. Stir in 1 cup of M&M®s Semi-Sweet Chocolate Baking Bits. Spread mixture into the prepared pizza pan. Sprinkle with the chopped nuts, coconut, and remaining ¾ cup candies. Press lightly into the dough. Bake at 350° for 15 to 20 minutes or until golden brown. Cool in the pan. Cut into wedges to serve.

Make 12 to 16 wedges.

Cindy's Double-Take Snickers® Cookies

¾ cup margarine, softened
⅓ cup sugar
⅓ cup light brown sugar
1 egg
1 teaspoon vanilla extract
1½ cups all-purpose flour

3 tablespoons cocoa powder
¾ teaspoon baking soda
¼ teaspoon salt
4 2.07-ounces Snickers® bars,
coarsely chopped

In a large bowl cream together the margarine, sugar, and brown sugar. Add the egg and vanilla, and beat until light and fluffy. Combine the flour, cocoa powder, baking soda, and salt. Gradually blend into the creamed mixture. Stir in chopped Snickers® bars until evenly blended. Drop by heaping tablespoonfuls about 2 inches apart onto ungreased cookie sheets. Bake at 350° for 9 to 13 minutes. Cool 1 minute on the cookie sheets. Remove to wire cooling racks. Store in tightly covered container.

Makes about 3 dozen 2½-inch cookies.

Brady Celebrations

Have you ever seen such organized kids on Christmas morning? I think we shot this sometime in September.

PETER: Wow!
ALICE: You like it?
PETER: I love it. What is is?
ALICE: What is your favorite dessert?
PETER: Strawberry shortcake.
ALICE: What is your next favorite?
PETER: Banana split.
ALICE: And the one after that?
PETER: Hot fudge sundae.
ALICE: Well, that's what it is, a straw-split-fudge-short!

George Glass Cornish Game Hens

1 cup butter
1⅓ cups chopped fresh parsley
¾ cup chopped scallions (or green onions)
3 tablespoons chopped fresh rosemary
2 tablespoons chopped fresh thyme

1¾ tablespoons leaf sage
¼ cup olive oil
Salt and pepper to taste
8 Cornish game hens, rinsed and patted dry

In a medium bowl cream together the butter, parsley, scallions, rosemary, and 1 teaspoon dry sage. Lift the skin from the breasts of the hens without removing it. Spread butter mixture under the skin of each. Tie skin down with string. In a small bowl combine the oil and remaining sage. Rub the mixture evenly over the hens. Season with salt and pepper. Roast at 450° for 20 minutes. Reduce the heat to 350° and continue cooking, basting frequently with the pan juices, for about 45 more minutes or until the juices run clear when the hen is pierced. Serve immediately.

Makes 8 servings.

I Get Misty Irish Steak

8 sirloin steaks
Salt
Coarse pepper

½ cup butter
1 cup heavy cream
¼ cup Irish Mist Liqueur

Season the steak with salt and pepper. In a large skillet melt ¼ cup of butter over medium heat. Add 4 steaks and cook for 4 minutes or longer on each side. Place on a warm platter. Repeat with the remaining steaks. Add the cream to the juice in the pan, and stir until blended. Add the liqueur and stir until blended. Pour the sauce over the steaks. Garnish with watercress if desired.

Makes 8 servings.

Sports Sunday Sandwich

1 large round loaf Italian bread
4 ounces chopped black olives, drained
1 red onion, sliced and rings separated
½ head iceberg lettuce, separated
1 large red bell pepper, seeded and very thinly sliced

½ cup Italian dressing
½ pound salami, sliced
½ pound bologna, sliced
½ pound pepperoni, sliced
½ pound Provolone cheese, sliced
½ pound Cheddar cheese, sliced
2 large tomatoes, sliced

Halve the bread horizontally. In a large bowl combine the olives, onion, lettuce, and bell pepper and toss with dressing. Spread half of the salad mixture on the bottom half of the bread. Top with single layers of half of the meats, cheeses, and tomatoes. Top with the remaining salad and repeat layers of meats, cheeses, and tomatoes. Cover with the top of the bread and press down. Cut like a pie to serve.

Alice's Note: You might consider making two of these. They go pretty quickly on those special company Sundays.

Makes about 8 servings.

I hope that Eve is not talking about one of my meals.

Voice Change Veggie Sandwich___

1 soft loaf French bread
4 cloves garlic minced
Black pepper to taste
1 tablespoon finely minced
  fresh oregano
2 tablespoons minced fresh
  basil
1 red bell pepper, seeded and
  thinly sliced

1 green bell pepper, seeded
  and thinly sliced
1 red onion, thinly sliced
2 large tomatoes, sliced
6 ounces olives, sliced
10 ounces Provolone cheese,
  sliced
10 ounces sharp Cheddar
  cheese, sliced

Slice the bread horizontally and pull out enough bread to make a slight cavity in each side. Brush olive oil on the cavity sides. Sprinkle both sides of the bread evenly with garlic, pepper, oregano, and basil. On the bottom of the loaf layer both the peppers, onion, tomatoes, olives, and cheeses. Cover with the top of the bread. Wrap the sandwich in plastic and let it stand at room temperature for 40 minutes, or longer if refrigerated.

Alice's Note: This is great to serve with Sports Sunday Sandwich (page 167) for those people who do not want meat.

Makes 8 servings.

Peter's Party Pizza

1 package active dry yeast
1 cup warm water (110°)
2 tablespoons olive oil
1 teaspoon salt
3 cups all-purpose flour
1 cup tomato sauce
¼ pound pepperoni, sliced or chopped
¼ pound salami, sliced or chopped

¼ pound mild Italian sausage, cooked and drained
½ cup sliced black olives (if desired)
1 cup grated mozzarella
1 tablespoon minced basil
6 tablespoons fresh Parmesan cheese, grated

In a large bowl dissolve the yeast in warm water. Set aside for 5 minutes. Add the oil, salt, and flour, 1 cup at a time, until the dough is kneadable. Turn onto a floured surface and knead for about 5 minutes. Set the dough aside for 30 minutes.

Lightly oil a pizza pan. Roll the dough out into a 14-inch circle and place it in the pan. Form a ridge around the edge. Spread the tomato sauce over the crust. Top with the remaining ingredients except the Parmesan cheese. Sprinkle with Parmesan cheese. Drizzle a little oil over all. Bake at 400° for 20 to 25 minutes, until the crust is brown.

Makes 6 to 8 servings.

Me and Tango Too

66 The Roaring Twenties episode reminded me of what great fun doing the Charleston was. I loved that dance (which was before my time—honest!). In our before-we-started-working days, a friend of mine, Richard Deacon, and I used to pool our loose change, go to Ciro's, sit at the bar (no cover charge), and make a beer last until the band played something we could dance to. The Charleston was our specialty, but we were terrific at the Tango, too. Then we would proceed to do comedy dancing. Hard to describe, but a hoot to do. Richard was six-foot-four, and we were very, very funny together, if I do say so. We never had to buy more than one beer. People would send us free drinks for as long as we cared to hang around and dance. Ah, youth! 99

Double Date Dark Double Fudge Cupcakes

1½ cups all-purpose flour	1½ teaspoons vanilla extract
½ cup cocoa	4 ounces semisweet chocolate
1⅓ cups sugar	1 ounce unsweetened
1½ teaspoons baking soda	chocolate
1½ teaspoons baking powder	6 tablespoons butter, melted
¼ teaspoon instant coffee	2 egg yolks
1½ cups water	1⅓ cups confectioners' sugar
½ cup butter	2 tablespoons milk
3 eggs	

In a large mixing bowl sift together the flour, cocoa, sugar, baking soda, and baking powder. In a small bowl dissolve the coffee in 2 tablespoons of hot water. Add the coffee to the remaining water to make 1½ cups. Add the coffee water, ½ cup of butter, eggs, and vanilla to the flour mixture and beat gently until smooth. Pour into 24 muffin cups lined with paper cupcake liners, filling ⅔ full. Bake at 350° for 20 to 25 minutes. The tops will spring back when pressed lightly. Cool for 5 minutes, then turn out onto a rack to finish cooling.

In the top of a double boiler over simmering water or in the microwave melt the chocolates and 6 tablespoons of butter. Cool for 5 minutes. Beat in the egg yolks, confectioners' sugar, and milk until the frosting is smooth. Frost the cupcakes immediately.

ALICE: You two guys, eat your own lunches, will ya? Don't go trading off to other kids. It makes me feel unwanted.

BOBBY: Unwanted? Your sandwiches get more for trade-ins than anybody else's in the whole school!

ALICE: Really?

CINDY: Yeah. Once I traded one of your peanut-butter-and-jelly sandwiches for a turtle!

ALICE: Thanks. That's a real compliment.

Mr. Wonderful White Cake _____

2 cups all-purpose flour
1½ cups sugar
3½ teaspoons baking powder
1 teaspoon salt
1 cup milk
1 teaspoon vanilla extract

½ cup butter
4 egg whites
⅓ cup soft butter
3 cups confectioners' sugar
2 teaspoons vanilla extract
2 tablespoons cream

In a large bowl mix the flour, sugar, baking powder, salt, milk, 1 teaspoon of vanilla, and ½ cup of butter. Beat until smooth, about 3 minutes. Add the egg whites and beat for 2 more minutes. Pour the batter into 2 greased and floured cake pans. Bake at 350° for 30 to 35 minutes or until a toothpick inserted in the center comes out clean. Cool.

Blend ⅓ cup of butter and the confectioners' sugar. Add the vanilla and milk, and stir until smooth. Layer on the cooled cake.

Variations: For something a little different use almond instead of vanilla extract in the cake, Amaretto instead of vanilla in the frosting, and warm water instead of milk. Or just add M&M®s to white frosting for a colorful look.

Makes 10 servings.

Answers to Trivia Quiz #3

a. 55¢
b. $1.40
c. 69¢
d. 35¢
e. 92¢

Chin-ups Chewy Chocolate Cookie Cake

1½ cups butter
4 cups all-purpose flour
½ pound good quality sweet
  chocolate
⅓ cup warm water

½ teaspoon salt
1 pound good quality sweet
  chocolate
2 cups heavy cream, chilled
Confectioners' sugar

In a large bowl cut the butter into the flour with a pastry cutter until the mixture is crumbly. In the top of a double boiler over simmering water melt ½ pound of chocolate. Add the water and salt, and stir until smooth. Fold the chocolate mixture into the flour. When smooth, divide into 3 parts. Wrap in wax paper and chill for 20 minutes.

Roll out each piece between waxed paper to an 8x11-inch rectangle. Fold each piece up like a letter and wrap in fresh waxed paper. Chill an additional 2 hours. Roll out each section between waxed paper into a 10-inch circle. You now have 3 10-inch circles. Trim with a sharp knife to make even. Place each circle on waxed paper on an ungreased baking sheet. Bake at 325° for 30 minutes.

Cool for 5 minutes, then remove the waxed paper and cool on the baking sheet. Repeat with each layer. When the layers are completely cooled, start the filling.

In the top of a double boiler over simmering water, melt 1 pound of chocolate. Remove. Pour the cream into a chilled bowl and whip until very stiff. Fold the chocolate into the whipped cream. Spread the chocolate filling between layers of cake evenly and thickly. Sprinkle the cake with confectioners' sugar and semisweet chocolate curls.

Variation: To make it really pretty, sift the confectioners' sugar over a patterned paper doily. Remove the doily carefully to maintain the design. Chill the cake very well. Remove the cake from the refrigerator 1 hour before serving.

Makes 8 servings.

MIKE: Something wrong, Alice?
CAROL: Alice, I told you, peel the onions under the cold water.
ALICE: What! And miss a good cry?

Jan's Ginger Cookies

2¼ cups all-purpose flour
1 cup soft butter
1 cup confectioners' sugar
1 tablespoon lemon juice

2 teaspoons ginger
¾ teaspoon baking soda
¼ teaspoon salt
1 tablespoon milk

In a large bowl combine the flour, butter, sugar, and lemon juice. Blend in the remaining ingredients. Turn the dough onto a floured surface and roll out to ⅛-inch thickness. Cut with cookie cutters into favorite designs or use a sharp knife and create some. Arrange the cookies on an ungreased baking sheet. Bake at 400° for 6 to 8 minutes. The cookies should be golden brown. Cool slightly before removing from the cookie sheet.

Makes 3 to 4 dozen.

Oh My Nose Oatmeal Cookies

¾ cup butter
½ cup sugar
1 egg
2 tablespoons water
1 teaspoon vanilla extract

⅔ cup all-purpose flour
1 teaspoon cinnamon
½ teaspoon baking soda
3 cups quick cooking oats

In a large bowl cream together the butter and sugar. Add the egg and mix throughly. Stir in the water and vanilla. Add the flour, cinnamon, baking soda, and oats, and mix well. Roll into 1½-inch balls and place them on a cookie sheet. Flatten each to 2 inches in diameter. Arrange the cookies 1 inch apart. Bake at 350° for 15 minutes. The edges will be done, but the centers will still be soft. Cool on racks.

Variation: Add 1 cup raisins, chocolate chips, or M&M®s to this recipe.

Makes 2 dozen cookies.

Jelly Wafer Blues

1 cup soft butter
2 cups all-purpose flour
⅓ cup heavy cream

Sugar
Jelly or preserves
(your favorites)

In a large bowl cream together the butter and flour. Mix in the cream and blend completely. Turn the dough out onto a floured surface. Roll out the dough in sections to ⅛-inch thickness. Cut in 1½-inch circles. Coat with sugar and prick with a fork 4 times. Arrange the cookies on an ungreased baking sheet. Bake at 375° for 8 minutes. Cool. Spread half of the cookies with jelly and top with the remaining cookies.
    Makes 2½ dozen cookies.

Dark Shadow Sugar Cookies

1 cup butter
2 cups firmly packed dark
  brown sugar
2 eggs
1 tablespoon fresh lemon juice

½ cup milk
3½ cups all-purpose flour
1 teaspoon baking soda
1 teaspoon salt

In a large bowl cream together the butter and sugar. Mix in the eggs, lemon juice, and milk. Add the flour, soda, and salt, and mix thoroughly. Cover and chill for at least 1 hour. Drop the dough by rounded teaspoons on a greased cookie sheet. Bake at 400° for 8 to 10 minutes, until the cookies spring back when pressed with a finger.
    Makes 6 dozen.

Alice's Day Off Milky Way®
Cheesecake

1½ cups chocolate wafer
  crumbs
4 tablespoons margarine or
  butter, melted
1 envelope unflavored gelatin
1 cup skim milk
4 2.15-ounce Milky Way® bars,
  sliced

2 8-ounce packages light cream
  cheese, softened
2 tablespoons sugar
1 teaspoon vanilla extract
1 cup heavy or whipped cream
Fresh strawberries for garnish
  (optional)

In a medium bowl combine the wafer crumbs and butter. Press the mixture into the bottom and 2 inches up the sides of an 8-inch springform pan. Chill.

In a saucepan sprinkle the gelatin over the milk. Stir over low heat until the gelatin is dissolved. Add the Milky Way® bars and continue to stir over low heat until the mixture is smooth. Cool slightly.

Meanwhile, beat the cream cheese and sugar until smooth. Beat in the Milky Way® mixture and vanilla. Add the whipping cream and beat at high speed for 4 minutes. Pour the mixture into the prepared crust. Chill until firm, about 4 hours.

If desired, garnish with additional whipped cream, sliced MIlky Way® bars, and fresh strawberries.

Makes 12 servings.

Grandma Brady's Milky Way® Wonder Cake

2 tablespoons vegetable shortening
¾ cup finely chopped nuts
5 2.15-ounce Milky Way® bars, coarsely chopped
1 cup buttermilk (or plain yogurt or sour cream), divided

1 cup butter or margarine
1½ cups sugar
½ teaspoon vanilla extract
4 eggs
2½ cups all-purpose flour
1 teaspoon salt
¾ teaspoon baking soda

Grease a 10- to 12-cup bundt pan or a 10-inch tube pan with the shortening. Coat the pan with the chopped nuts. In a heavy saucepan over low heat melt the candy with ¼ cup of buttermilk, stirring frequently, until the candy is melted and the mixture is smooth. Set the pan aside.

Cream together the butter and sugar until light and fluffy. Blend in the vanilla. Add the eggs, one at a time, beating well after each addition. In a separate bowl combine the flour, salt, and baking soda. Add the dry ingredients to the creamed mixture alternately with the remaining ¾ cup of buttermilk. Mix just until the dry ingredients are moistened. Blend in the candy mixture. Spoon the batter into the prepared pan. Bake at 350° for 55 to 60 minutes or until a wooden pick inserted in the center comes out clean. Cool for 20 minutes, then invert onto a wire rack. Cool thoroughly.

Makes 10 servings.

Bobby's M&M®s Peanut Butter Jumbos

1 cup margarine or butter
1 cup peanut butter
1 cup sugar
1 cup firmly packed brown
  sugar

2 eggs
2 cups all-purpose flour
1 teaspoon baking soda
1½ cups M&M®s chocolate
  candies

In a large bowl beat together the margarine, peanut butter, sugar, and brown sugar until light and fluffy. Blend in the eggs. In a separate bowl combine the flour and baking soda. Add the dry ingredients to the margarine peanut butter mixture, blending well. Stir in the M&M®s. Drop the dough by ¼ cupfuls onto a greased cookie sheet about 3 inches apart. Bake at 350° for 14 to 15 minutes. Remove the cookies to a wire rack to cool thoroughly.

Makes 2 dozen 4-inch cookies.

Very Brady Holidays

That's me as Sergeant Emma, getting the Bradys into fighting shape.

Westdale High Family
Frolics Frittata

4 white potatoes, scrubbed and
  quartered
½ cup thinly sliced white onion
¼ cup olive oil
5 ounces cooked ham, cut in
  1-inch cubes

12 eggs
½ cup minced parsley
2 teaspoons fresh marjoram
1½ cups grated Gruyère
Salt and pepper to taste

In a large pot boil the potatoes in salted water until just soft, about 15 minutes. Drain and cool. Slice to ¼-inch thickness. In a 2-quart baking dish combine the onions and oil. Bake at 400° for 10 minutes. Remove the dish from the oven and reduce the heat to 350°. Layer the ham over the onions. Layer the potatoes over the ham. In a small bowl beat together the eggs, parsley, and marjoram. Pour the mixture over the potatoes. Sprinkle with cheese, salt, and pepper. Bake about 25 minutes. The frittata should be golden brown. A beautiful breakfast dish.

    Makes 10 to 12 servings.

CAROL: I haven't worn these pants for years. I'm surprised they still fit.

ALICE: You watch your figure, Mrs. Brady. I watch mine, too. And it has done some things that have shocked me.

Brady Brunch Poached Salmon

5 cups water
1¼ cups dry white wine
¼ cup fresh lemon juice
1 teaspoon salt
1 large onion, sliced
8 whole peppercorns
½ teaspoon nutmeg
½ teaspoon cinnamon
1 bay leaf
3 pounds fresh salmon, center
  cut with skin

5½ tablespoons peanut oil
3 tablespoons safflower oil
3½ tablespoons white wine
  vinegar
⅓ cup fresh lemon juice
1½ tablespoons chopped fresh
  dill
Salt and pepper to taste
Romaine leaves

In a large saucepan combine the water, white wine, ¼ cup of lemon juice, 1 teaspoon of salt, onion, peppercorns, nutmeg, cinnamon, and bay leaf. Simmer for 20 minutes. Remove the pan from the heat and cool to room temperature.

Wrap the fish in cheesecloth and tie the opening. Lower the fish into the liquid until completely covered. Add more water if necessary. Bring the liquid to a simmer, cover, and poach until the fish is just opaque. Remove the fish carefully and discard the liquid. Unwrap the fish and remove the skin and bones. Cut into 8 pieces. Refrigerate until chilled.

In a small bowl blend together the peanut oil, safflower oil, vinegar, ⅓ cup of lemon juice, and dill, and season with salt and pepper to taste. Arrange the lettuce leaves on a platter and top with the salmon. Spoon ½ of the vinaigrette over the salmon. Serve with the remaining vinaigrette on the side.

Makes 8 servings.

Lemon Pecan Bread, Yea, Yea, Yea!

½ cup butter, softened
¾ cup sugar
2 egg yolks
Grated rind of one lemon
1½ cups all-purpose flour
¼ teaspoon baking soda

1½ teaspoons baking powder
½ cup fresh lemon juice
1 cup shelled pecans, chopped
2 egg whites, stiffly beaten
¼ cup lemon juice
¼ cup confectioners' sugar

In a large bowl cream together the butter and sugar. Beat in the egg yolks and lemon rind. In a separate bowl sift together the flour, baking soda, and baking powder. Add the dry ingredients to the creamed mixture alternately with ½ cup of the lemon juice. Gently fold in the pecans. Fold in the egg whites. Pour the batter into a large greased loaf pan. Bake at 350° for 50 minutes or until a toothpick inserted in the center comes out clean.

Heat ¼ cup of lemon juice and blend in the confectioners' sugar. Drizzle the glaze over the hot loaf. Cool in the pan.

Makes 1 loaf.

Hanna Banana Bread

1 cup butter, softened	2 teaspoons baking soda
1½ cups sugar	1 teaspoon salt
4 eggs	6 large bananas, mashed
4 cups all-purpose flour	2 teaspoons vanilla extract

In a large bowl cream together the butter and sugar until fluffy. Add the eggs and beat well. In a separate bowl sift together the flour, baking soda, and salt. Add the dry ingredients to the creamed mixture. Mix well. Fold in the mashed bananas and vanilla. Pour the batter evenly into 2 greased 9x5-inch loaf pans. Bake at 350° for 50 minutes or until a toothpick inserted in the center comes out clean. Cool for 10 minutes in the pans, then remove to racks.

Makes 2 loaves.

ALICE: Mr. Brady, if a miracle happens, don't question it. Just lean back and accept it.

Super Duper Spiced Tea

9½ cups water	2 cups orange juice
6 whole cloves	½ cup fresh lemon juice
12 cinnamon sticks	Sugar to taste
1 teaspoon whole allspice	
⅓ cup English Breakfast tea leaves	

In a large saucepan combine the water, cloves, cinnamon, and allspice. Bring the mixture to a boil. Pour the boiling liquid over the tea in a large bowl. Set aside for 5 minutes. Stir in the orange and lemon juices. Return the tea to the saucepan and reheat, but do not boil. Strain into a large teapot or into cups. Serve with sugar.

Makes 12 servings.

Susan Olsen

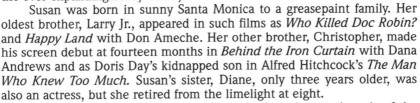

Is a photographic memory a blessing or a curse? Ask Susan Olsen, who seems to remember more about the making of "The Brady Bunch" than anyone, other than Lloyd Schwartz. Susan is constantly told she should write her own Brady memoir. Maybe someday, but right now she is far too busy with her own projects to spend time adding to the ever expanding Brady library.

Susan was born in sunny Santa Monica to a greasepaint family. Her oldest brother, Larry Jr., appeared in such films as *Who Killed Doc Robin?* and *Happy Land* with Don Ameche. Her other brother, Christopher, made his screen debut at fourteen months in *Behind the Iron Curtain* with Dana Andrews and as Doris Day's kidnapped son in Alfred Hitchcock's *The Man Who Knew Too Much.* Susan's sister, Diane, only three years older, was also an actress, but she retired from the limelight at eight.

Susan was a seasoned veteran of seven when she got the role of the youngest Brady. She had made commercials starting at the age of three, took a few years off, and, as she told Milton Berle, made her comeback at five (or was it six?) when she was picked from kindergarten to sing "I'm a Believer" on Pat Boone's daytime variety show. Then along came "Ironside," in which she appeared for one season, and roles in episodes of "Gunsmoke" and "Julia."

Susan appeared in a few of the Brady spin-offs after the series ended, but she was most noticeably missing from *A Very Brady Christmas* because she was on her honeymoon. As any wise, multi-talented person would do, she turned her creative energies to design work. Her glow-in-the-dark sneakers, which were manufactured by Converse, the footwear giant, were a big hit. The children's line was called "Kids Glow," and the adults' were labeled "Glow All Stars."

Susan continues her design work with textile prints and she has illustrated books. Unlike her sister, she has never lost the acting bug and still appears on talk shows and television specials.

Someday, of course, she will have to write that memoir.

Love and the Older Man's Apple Cider

2½ cups boiling water
2½ teaspoons black tea leaves
¼ cup sugar
1 cup orange juice

½ cup brandy
5 cups apple cider
Lemon slices

In a medium bowl pour the boiling water over the tea leaves and set the bowl aside for 5 minutes.

In a large bowl strain the tea over the sugar. Stir until the sugar dissolves. Stir in the orange juice and cool. Add the brandy and cider. Float lemon slices on top.

Makes 8 servings.

All Laugh, No Glory

66Watching the show as much as I have lately, I'm reminded how nice it is to play a supporting role. The leads have to work so hard and carry most of the load, then I stick my head in and get the laugh line! I got some very good lines, too. Of course, being a character-part type, I've spent most of my life playing support. So I've had a lot of practice.99

Never Too Young Non-alcoholic Eggnog

1 egg yolk
⅛ teaspoon nutmeg
½ cup milk

½ tablespoon sugar
1 egg white, whipped stiff

In a small bowl beat together the egg yolk, nutmeg, and milk. Add the sugar and beat until blended. With a spoon gently stir in the egg white.

Makes 1 serving.

The Family Feeling

66It's been fun to keep up the family feeling. As the kids got older and started having dates and prospective spouses, they always brought them on the set to meet 'the family.' And we felt like a family. That was the reason the show worked so well.99

Brady Brick of Cheese

2 cups shredded Cheddar cheese
1 3-ounce package cream cheese

¼ teaspoon crushed garlic
¼ cup walnuts, chopped
1½ tablespoons chili powder
½ teaspoon cumin

In a medium bowl blend the Cheddar and cream cheese well. Add the garlic and walnuts. Form the mixture into a brick and chill for at least 2 hours. In a shallow pan or on waxed paper mix the chili powder and cumin. Press the cheese brick into the seasoning mixture, turning to coat evenly. Chill until ready to serve.

Makes 10 to 12 servings.

Lloyd Schwartz

66Lloyd made wonderful contributions to the show. Among his many jobs, he was in charge of keeping track of the kids. Once, when someone told him to keep a real tight rein on them so they wouldn't run around and hurt themselves, he simply said, 'No,' and proceeded to let them act like kids and run around when they weren't working. My impression was that they all adored him. He was really very good with them. I know I loved him. Still do!99

Only Child Chicken Pâté _____

2 pounds chicken breasts,
  boned and skinned
¾ cup unsalted butter
⅔ cup thinly sliced white
  onions
¼ cup thinly sliced shallots
3 egg whites
1½ teaspoons salt
¼ teaspoon freshly ground
  pepper

⅛ teaspoon allspice
2¼ cups whipping cream,
  chilled
½ cup chicken broth
2¼ cups packed spinach leaves
2 cups packed basil leaves
¾ cup whipping cream, chilled

In a food processor purée the chicken in 2 batches to a smooth paste. Refrigerate for 1 hour. Melt the butter in a small skillet over low heat. Add the onions and shallots, and cook until soft, about 15 minutes. Let the mixture cool.

Combine half of the chicken with half of the onion mixture in the food processor and purée until smooth. Add half of the egg whites and process until smooth. Transfer the mixture to a bowl and refrigerate until chilled. Repeat with the remaining chicken.

Combine both chicken mixtures in a large bowl. Blend the salt, pepper, and allspice with the chicken mixture. Slowly add the cream to each batch. Set the bowl aside. In a large skillet bring the chicken broth to a boil. Add the spinach and basil and toss until just wilted, about 40 seconds. Drain and squeeze out the liquid. Purée the spinach mixture with ¾ cup of cream and ¼ of the chicken mixture until smooth.

Line a 9x5-inch loaf pan with plastic wrap, leaving a 5-inch overhang. Pour half of the chicken mixture into the pan. Cover with half of the spinach mixture. Repeat the layers. Tap the pan on a work surface to settle the pâté. Fold the overhanging plastic over the top of the pâté. Cover the pan tightly with foil. Place the loaf pan in a roasting pan. Fill the larger pan with water up ⅔ of the side of the loaf pan. Bake at 350° for 1 hour and 15 minutes. Cool and refrigerate overnight.

For serving, unmold onto a platter and let the pâté stand for 1 hour before cutting.

Makes 16 servings.

Two Petes in a Pod Chick Pea Salad

2 red onions, finely sliced
2 medium cloves garlic, minced
2 anchovy filets, mashed
2 teaspoons oil from anchovy can
4½ tablespoons lemon juice
¼ cup olive oil
3 tablespoons chopped parsley
4 teaspoons chopped capers
2 teaspoons chopped fresh thyme
4 cups canned chick peas, drained
Salt and pepper to taste
4 large celery stalks, sliced diagonally

In a large bowl mix the onions, garlic, anchovies, and anchovy oil. Add the lemon juice, olive oil, parsley, capers, and thyme, and stir to blend. Fold in the chick peas and season to taste with salt and pepper. Let the salad sit at room temperature for 2 hours. Stir occasionally. Chill. Just before serving add the celery.

Makes 6 to 8 servings.

SAM: There's a little something special in here for you, Alice. Four extra lamb chops in pink panties.

Love It or Leave It Liver Pâté

1 pound pork liver
1 large white onion, chopped
8 anchovies
3 eggs
½ teaspoon salt
¼ teaspoon pepper

In a blender or food processor purée the liver, onion, and anchovies. Add the eggs, salt, and pepper and mix well. Spread the mixture in a small glass loaf pan. Place the loaf pan in a roasting pan. Fill the larger pan with ½-inch of water. Bake at 250° for 1 hour. Cool in the dish.

Serve with chunks of French bread.

Makes 8 servings.

Crème de la Cream of Celery Soup

2 tablespoons butter
1 pound celery, finely chopped
1 cup minced onion
1 cup chicken stock

2 cups skim milk
2 tablespoons cornstarch
½ cup heavy cream

In a saucepan melt the butter and sauté ½ of the celery and all of the onion for 5 minutes. Pour in the stock and simmer for 10 to 15 minutes. Heat ¾ cup of milk. Strain the soup and return it to the pan. Add the hot milk and bring the mixture to a boil. Stir in the cornstarch and gradually add the remaining milk. Bring the mixture to a boil again for 1 minute. Add the rest of the celery and the cream. Simmer for 2 minutes, stirring constantly.

Makes about 4 servings.

Leaky Vase Potato and Leek Soup

2 tablespoons butter
3 leeks, white part only, finely sliced
4 potatoes, peeled and finely sliced

4 cups milk
Salt and pepper to taste

In a saucepan melt the butter and sauté the leeks until soft. Add the potatoes with enough water to cover. Simmer until well-cooked, about 30 minutes. Add the milk and season with salt and pepper to taste. Serve hot or cold.

Alice's Note: If you serve cold, sprinkle with diced cucumbers.
Makes 4 servings.

Say "Cheeeese" Soup

2 tablespoons butter
2 tablespoons all-purpose flour
6 cups chicken stock
1 cup grated Parmesan cheese

1 cup grated Gruyère cheese
1 cup cream
Salt and pepper to taste
1 tablespoon chopped chives

In a saucepan melt the butter over medium heat. Blend in the flour, stirrring constantly. Add the chicken stock and simmer for 15 minutes.

Add the Parmesan, Gruyère, and cream, and season with salt and pepper to taste. Sprinkle some of the chives on each serving.

Makes 8 servings.

CAROL: What in the world is all that shouting about?
ALICE: Oh, it's just a little disagreement, Mrs. Brady.
CAROL: About what?
ALICE: Well, it seems that Marcia accused Jan of telling You-Know-Who about You-Know-Whom, and pretty soon it would be all over You-Know-What.
CAROL: Alice, I want to thank you for clearing that up for me.
ALICE: Any time.

Bogie's Pork Chops (and applesauce!) with Lemon and Vermouth

½ cup unsalted butter
2 tablespoons oil
8 boneless pork chops
Salt to taste
2 teaspoons coarsely ground
  black pepper

⅔ cup dry vermouth
¼ cup fresh lemon juice
1 tablespoon finely grated
  lemon zest

In a large skillet melt 2 tablespoons of butter and the oil. Season the chops on both sides with salt and pepper. Place 4 chops in the skillet and cook on high until just brown on each side. Remove and keep warm on a platter. Repeat with another 2 tablespoons of butter and the remaining chops. Add the vermouth to the skillet and cook over medium heat until the liquid is reduced by half. Add the lemon juice and zest, and bring the sauce to a boil. Remove the pan from the heat and stir in the remaining butter until melted. Spoon the sauce over the pork chops and serve (with applesauce!).

Alice's Note: The perfect rice recipe to serve with this follows.

Makes 8 servings.

Newlyweds' Rice with Fresh Herbs

2 tablespoons butter	2 teaspoons salt
2 tablespoons oil	½ teaspoon pepper
1 cup finely chopped white	¼ cup finely chopped parsley
onion	¼ cup finely chopped thyme
3 cups long grain white rice	¼ cup finely chopped chervil
6 cups water	¼ cup finely chopped tarragon

In a large saucepan melt the butter. Add the oil and onion and cook on high until the onion is translucent, 2 to 3 minutes. Add the rice and cook, stirring constantly, for 1 minute. Add the water and stir in the salt and pepper. Bring the mixture to a boil. Reduce the heat, cover, and simmer until the rice is done, about 20 minutes. Stir in the herbs and serve.

Makes 8 servings.

Luscious Lamb with Basil Stuffing And Red Wine Sauce

3 tablespoons unsalted butter	Olive oil
2½ cups chopped white onions	1 cup water
2 medium cloves garlic, minced	1 large carrot, sliced
Salt and pepper to taste	3 stalks celery, sliced
¾ cup minced fresh basil	diagonally
½ teaspoon leaf tarragon	1½ cups dry red wine
1 6½-pound leg of lamb, boned	¼ cup unsalted butter, softened
and butterflied	

In a large skillet melt 3 tablespoons of butter over medium heat. Add the onion and garlic, and stir until soft. Add the basil and tarragon, and season with salt and pepper to taste. Cool.

Arrange the lamb cut-side-up on a work surface. Cut shallow incisions in the thick part of meat to form an even, flat surface. Spread the onion mixture over the lamb to 1 inch of the edge. Roll up the lamb. Tuck in the ends. Tie with string at 1-inch intervals. Place seam-side down on a rack in a roasting pan. Rub the top and sides with oil, and sprinkle with salt and pepper. Pour the water into the roasting pan. Add the carrot and celery. Roast at 350° for 1 hour and 20 minutes or until a meat thermometer registers 135° for medium-rare. Transfer the meat to a platter and keep warm.

Add the wine to the roasting pan and bring it to a boil. Strain the mixture into a small saucepan. Boil until reduced to about ¾ cup. Cool slightly and whisk in ¼ cup of butter. Remove the string from the lamb and place the lamb on a serving platter. Top with sauce and serve.

Alice's Note: Serve with Heavy Herbed Potatoes (below).

Makes 8 servings.

Do the Height Choreography

❝We were always having to do height choreography. Bob was six-foot-four, Florence was shorter than me, and the kids were shorter (for a while) than any of us. Who was standing, who was sitting, which step you were standing on—all this had to be taken into account. It looked a little strange at times. Even I know it's easier to stir standing up, but when I did a scene with Susan, there I'd be sitting and stirring.❞

Heavy Herbed Potatoes _____

8 baking potatoes, peeled and
    sliced thinly
⅔ cup olive oil
2 tablespoons minced fresh
    parsley
1 leek, white end only, thinly
    sliced

1 medium clove garlic, minced
2 tablespoons minced fresh
    chives
Salt and pepper to taste

Soak the potatoes in cold salted water for 5 minutes.

In a large bowl combine the oil, parsley, leek, garlic, and chives, and season with salt and pepper to taste. Drain the potatoes and add them to the bowl. Coat well. Spread the potatoes in a 3-quart baking dish. Bake at 350° for 1 hour or until the edges are golden brown.

Makes 8 servings.

I hope this isn't a comment about Alice's cooking.

Four Men Living All Together Rib Roast

1 8-pound rib roast

Place the roast fat-side up in a shallow roasting pan. (Ribs are their own rack). It is unnecessary to baste. Insert a meat thermometer in the center, not touching bone or resting on fat. Roast the meat at 325° until the thermometer reads between 140° (rare), 160° (medium), and 170° (well done). Allow the roast to sit for 15 to 20 minutes before carving. Serve with salt, pepper, and horseradish. Garnish with sprig of rosemary.

Alice's Note: Prime ribs are great because from placing the rib in the oven to carving, there is no work involved. It is a great holiday entrée that gets rave reviews. The guests even do their own seasoning at the table.

Makes 8 servings.

Sibling Rivalry Red Snapper_____

1 cup finely chopped white
  onions
¼ cup butter, melted
2 cups bread crumbs
1 cup fresh mushrooms,
  chopped
½ cup fresh parsley
2 tablespoons lemon juice
1 egg

1 clove garlic, minced
¼ teaspoon marjoram
Salt and pepper to taste
10 pounds red snapper,
  cleaned and patted dry
Oil
1 cup butter, melted
¼ cup lemon juice

In a large skillet sauté the onion in ¼ cup of butter until the onion is soft and translucent. Add the bread crumbs, mushrooms, parsley, 2 tablespoons of lemon juice, egg, garlic, and marjoram, and season with salt and pepper. Mix lightly. Remove the skillet from the heat. Rub the cavity of the fish with salt and pepper. Evenly stuff the fish. Close the opening and truss with string. Place extra stuffing in a covered baking dish. Brush the fish with oil. Place the fish in a shallow roasting pan. Bake at 350° for 1 hour and 30 minutes. The fish should flake easily with a fork.

In a small bowl combine 1 cup of melted butter and ¼ cup of lemon juice. Baste the fish every 15 minutes or so. About 20 minutes before the fish is done, place the dish of extra stuffing in the oven to bake.

Makes 10 to 12 servings.

ALICE: I think that's plenty of food, Mr. Brady.
MIKE: Oh, I don't know, Alice. Four fishermen get mighty hungry, you know.
CAROL: That's right, a couple of hours out on that water makes them awfully hungry.
ALICE: Makes me awfully seasick.
CAROL: Isn't it funny how some people get seasick and some people don't?
ALICE: I think I'm allergic to waves. Even when I take a bath, I have to be careful not to move around too much.

Pork Tenderloin with Apricots _____

½ cup all-purpose flour
Salt and pepper to taste
2½ pounds pork tenderloins,
   patted dry
Oil
½ cup apricot brandy
1 cup beef stock

1 cup butter
8 ripe apricots, halved and
   pitted
½ teaspoon cinnamon
½ teaspoon allspice
½ teaspoon nutmeg

Slice the pork into 24 thin slices. In a shallow bowl season the flour with salt and pepper. Coat the pork with the flour and shake off the excess. In a large skillet heat a thin layer of oil over medium heat. Cook the pork until the pink is gone on both sides. Turn off the heat. Remove the pork to a serving platter and keep it warm.

Pour the fat from the skillet. Add the brandy to the skillet, return the pan to the heat, and ignite. When the flames die down, add the stock. Boil until reduced to a third. Remove the pan from the heat and whisk in 2 tablespoons of butter. Return the pan to the heat and slowly whisk in the remaining butter. Add the apricots and heat through. Add the cinnamon, allspice, and nutmeg, and stir for about 30 seconds. Spoon the apricot sauce over the pork.

Makes 4 servings.

EVE: But Alice, Sam was meant for you, and you understand him.

ALICE: I understand this turkey, too, but that doesn't mean I have to go bowling with it.

Welcome Aboard Company Chicken _____

1 large clove garlic, finely
  minced
¼ cup chopped fresh oregano
½ cup fresh lemon juice
½ cup olive oil
1 cup dried apricots, diced
½ cup pitted black olives
½ cup capers
¼ cup finely chopped parsley

¼ cup finely chopped cilantro
5 large bay leaves
Salt and pepper to taste
4 2½-pound chickens, cleaned
  and quartered
1 cup firmly packed brown
  sugar
1 cup dry white wine

In a nonmetal container with a cover combine the garlic, oregano, lemon juice, olive oil, apricots, olives, capers, parsley, cilantro, and bay leaves, and season with salt and pepper. Place the chicken in the container and marinate the chicken overnight.

Arrange the chicken in a shallow baking pan or pans. Spoon the marinade evenly over it. Sprinkle with brown sugar evenly. Pour the wine evenly over all. Bake at 350° for 50 minutes or until the juices run clear when the thigh is pierced.

Serve on a platter with the olives, apricots, and capers spooned over the chicken. Serve the remaining juice on the side.

Makes up to 15 servings, for those big occasions.

Answers to Trivia Quiz #4

1. Emma likes a long morning jog and workout before breakfast.
2. Emma conducts bedroom inspections with a white glove.
3. Emma serves chipped beef on toast for "chow."
4. Emma is not afraid of mice (Alice will climb up on the kitchen table to avoid the little critters).
5. Emma has no sense of humor.

The two things they have in common are their looks, and they both enjoy a "good cry."

Our Pilgrim Fathers' Thanksgiving Turkey

1 turkey, giblets removed, washed and patted dry
Salt

Perfect Stuffing (recipe follows)
Butter, softened

Rub the turkey cavity lightly with salt. Stuff the turkey just before roasting. Fill the wishbone area and fasten the skin back down. Fold the wings across the back with tips together. Fill the body cavity with stuffing, but do not overfill. Tuck the legs under the band of skin at the rear. Place breast-side up in a shallow roasting pan and brush with butter. Insert a meat thermometer into the thickest part of the breast or inside the thigh without touching bone. Bake at 325° for 30 minutes per pound. The meat is done when the thermometer registers 185°, or 165° if the turkey is stuffed, or when the drumstick moves easily up and down. The meat will feel soft between fingers. Remove the turkey from the oven and let it sit for 20 minutes before carving. Remove the stuffing to a bowl and place the turkey on a platter. Retain the juices for gravy.

John Carver's Perfect Stuffing

1 cup butter
9 cups bread cubes
1 cup minced white onion
1¼ cups chopped celery
2 teaspoons salt

1¾ teaspoons crushed sage
1 teaspoon leaf thyme
½ teaspoon pepper
½ cup giblet broth

Melt the butter and pour it into a large mixing bowl. Add the bread and toss. Mix in the remaining ingredients except the broth. Add the broth slowly, using only enough to make the bread very slightly moist.

You are now ready to stuff your turkey.

Makes 8 servings.

The camera always loved Florence—from any angle.

John Smith's Giblets

Giblets from turkey
Salt and pepper to taste
1 bay leaf

½ onion, minced
½ teaspoon leaf thyme
½ teaspoon leaf sage

Rinse the giblets. In a medium saucepan cover the giblets with water and add the seasonings. Simmer over very low heat. Skim the foam from the broth as it cooks. Cook for 1 hour and 30 minutes or until the gizzard is tender. Reserve the broth for the stuffing and gravy. The giblets can be chopped and added to the gravy.

Priscilla Alden's Gravy

3 tablespoons butter
3 tablespoons all-purpose flour
1 ¼ cups milk
Turkey pan drippings

Chopped giblets
Giblet broth
Salt and pepper to taste

In a medium skillet melt the butter and slowly add the flour, stirring constantly. Slowly add the milk, making a white sauce. Slowly add the pan drippings, stirring constantly. Add the giblets. If the gravy becomes too thick, add broth a little at a time. If too thin, add flour. Season with salt and pepper to taste.

Makes 6 to 8 servings.

It's a Sunshine Day Scalloped Potatoes

2 tablespoons butter
1 large onion, thinly sliced
1 large clove garlic, minced
2 pounds potatoes, peeled and
thinly sliced

Salt and pepper to taste
1¾ cups cream
Bread crumbs

In a large skillet melt 1½ tablespoons of butter and sauté the onion over medium heat for about 3 minutes. Add the garlic and cook 1 minute more. Transfer the onions and garlic to a 3-quart baking dish. Add the potatoes and season with salt and pepper. Toss gently. Pour the cream over all, and sprinkle lightly and evenly with bread crumbs. Dot with the remaining butter. Bake at 400° for 10 minutes. Reduce the temperature to 350° and bake another 35 minutes. Serve immediately.

Makes 6 servings.

Lost Sketches Asparagus

2 pounds asparagus, bottoms of
stems trimmed
½ cup grated Parmesan cheese
Salt and pepper to taste

¼ cup butter, melted
¼ cup finely chopped fresh
basil

Blanch the asparagus lightly in boiling water, until just soft. Butter a medium baking dish. Sprinkle a third of the Parmesan over the bottom. Layer a third of the asparagus on top. Season with salt and pepper. Drizzle a third of the butter over the asparagus. Repeat the layers of cheese, asparagus, salt, pepper, and butter twice. Sprinkle 2 tablespoons of Parmesan over all, and top with the basil. Cover and bake at 325° for 20 minutes or until the cheese bubbles. Serve immediately.

Makes 8 servings.

Crunchy Cashew Green Beans ____

¼ cup butter, melted
1 teaspoon salt
¾ teaspoon pepper

2 pounds green beans, cleaned
  and lightly blanched
1¼ cups cashews

In a skillet melt the butter and add the salt and pepper. Drain the beans and transfer them to a serving bowl. Pour the butter over the beans. Add the cashews and toss. Serve immediately.

Alice's Note: This dish can accompany almost any meal where a green vegetable is wanted.

Makes 8 servings.

ALICE: I wonder if I sent in the wrong jingle?
MIKE: Wrong one?
ALICE: Yeah. I had another one:
    Everpressed is just right for you.
    If you are no matter who.
    Try our fabrics real soon.
    In flannel, silk, or gabardoon.
CAROL: Gabardoon?
ALICE: That's a pun.
MIKE: You mean poon.

Golden Mint Potatoes with Peas__

½ cup dry white wine
½ cup olive oil
20 small new red potatoes,
  cooked and quartered

2 cups shelled fresh peas
2 cups sour cream
½ cup chopped fresh mint
Salt and pepper to taste

In a small bowl mix the wine and oil. Place the potatoes in a large bowl. Pour the oil mixture over the potatoes and toss to coat well. Add the peas, sour cream, and mint. Toss gently. Season with salt and pepper. Chill before serving.

Makes 6 servings.

You're So Fresh Fruit Cake _____

1 cup corn oil
1 cup walnuts
1 cup grated coconut
1 cup raisins
2 cups rolled oats
1 cup peaches, peeled, pitted,
   and mashed

1 cup apricots, peeled, pitted,
   and mashed
1 cup apples, cored, skinned,
   and mashed
1 teaspoon vanilla extract
½ teaspoon almond extract

In a large bowl mix all of the ingredients together. The dough will be slightly crumbly. If too dry add a couple of tablespoons of orange juice. Spread in 2 9-inch greased cake pans. Bake at 350° for 40 minutes or until the bottom is golden brown.

Alice's Note: If you like, prepare a glaze by mixing ½ cup of orange juice and ½ cup sugar to make a syrup that can be drizzled over the cake. Without it this is one of the healthiest fruit cakes you've ever eaten.

Makes 8 to 10 servings.

Brady Kids' Cranberry Pie _____

12 ounces fresh cranberries,
   rinsed and drained
1 cup water
1¼ cups sugar
2 egg yolks
1½ tablespoons all-purpose
   flour

1 cup sour cream
1 9-inch pie crust, baked
1 cup whipping cream,
   whipped

In a large saucepan combine the cranberries, water, and 1 cup of sugar. Cook over medium heat for 10 minutes or until thick, stirring frequently.

Beat the egg, ¼ cup of sugar, and the flour. Add the mixture to the cranberries. Stir in the sour cream and cook for about 4 minutes. Pour the filling into the pie crust. Refrigerate overnight.

Top with whipped cream before serving.

Alice's Note: A wonderful way to serve those traditional cranberries.

Makes 8 servings.

GREG: Sure I had pie. I even had seconds. This will be my third helping.

ALICE: This will be your third on first, but it is only your second on seconds. Well, at least you know you know first and second, right? Well, this will be your third on first, or your second on seconds.

GREG: Alice, I think you are a little pie happy.

Power of the Press Pecan Pie————

4 eggs
1 cup firmly packed brown sugar
½ cup corn syrup
¼ cup molasses
1 teaspoon salt
¼ cup butter, melted

1 teaspoon vanilla extract
2 cups pecans, shelled and chopped
1 9-inch unbaked pie crust
⅓ cup pecans, shelled and halved

In a large bowl beat the eggs. Add the brown sugar, corn syrup, molasses, salt, butter, and vanilla. Mix well. Sprinkle the chopped pecans in the bottom of the pie crust and pour the egg mixture over them. Edge with pecan halves for decoration. Bake at 400° for 10 minutes. Reduce the heat to 325° and bake for 25 minutes or until set. Cool to room temperature before slicing.

Makes 8 servings.

GREG: She's a real mod girl. So I figure I better look really heavy.

ALICE: Humph. I look really heavy no matter what I wear.

Greg Wants a Car Carrot Cake _____

3 cups all-purpose flour
3 cups sugar
1 teaspoon salt
1 tablespoon baking soda
1 teaspoon cinnamon
1½ cups oil
4 large eggs

1 tablespoon vanilla extract
1 teaspoon almond extract
1½ cups walnuts, chopped
1⅓ cups grated carrots
¾ cup very finely chopped
   pineapple

In a large bowl sift together the dry ingredients. Add the oil, eggs, vanilla, and almond extracts. Mix well and add the walnuts, carrots, and pineapple, stirring them in gently. Pour the batter into 2 greased and floured 9-inch round cake pans. Bake at 350° until the edges pull away from the sides, about 30 minutes. Cool completely before frosting.

Frosting:

6 tablespoons butter
1 teaspoon vanilla extract
3 tablespoons fresh lemon juice

1 8-ounce package cream
   cheese
3 cups confectioners' sugar

In a medium bowl cream the butter, vanilla, lemon juice, and cheese. Add the sugar slowly and stir until there are no lumps. Spread the frosting on the cake.

PETER: A doc's got to know every disease in these books if he wants to make people well.
ALICE: I'll tell you an easier way to make 'em well. Tell 'em how much it will cost to be sick.

The Bad and the Long Running

66 We always got terrible reviews, right from the start, and we were often used as an example of how bad a situation comedy could be. After 20 years it's easy to laugh at this, but at the time we all held our breath every six or seven episodes waiting to see if we were going to be picked up to go on. I don't think anybody took us seriously until they realized that we had knocked off some 13 series that were our competition. I'll tell you one thing, if I'd known we were going to last this long, I'd have taken notes! This book would have been a lot easier to write. At the time, it just seemed like a pleasant children's show, and, like a lot of actors I've known, I was glad to have the job. But, here we are! I guess that the show just seemed too good to be true. A nice show about nice people who were mostly very nice to each other. Gosh, that doesn't sound so terrible, does it? 99

A Very Brady Pumpkin and Ice Cream Pie

¾ cup canned pumpkin
1 quart natural vanilla ice
  cream
¼ cup honey
⅛ teaspoon nutmeg

¼ teaspoon ginger
1 teaspoon cinnamon
⅛ teaspoon cloves
¼ teaspoon salt
1 9-inch pie crust, baked

In a large bowl mix all of the ingredients except the pie crust. Blend well. Pour the filling into the pie crust, and freeze until ready to serve.

Alice's Note: Very rich pie.

Makes 8 servings.

Brace Your Braces Peanut Brittle __

1½ teaspoons baking soda
1 teaspoon vanilla extract
1 teaspoon water
1½ cups sugar
1 cup water

½ cup honey
½ cup corn syrup
3 tablespoons butter
1 pound shelled unroasted
   peanuts

In a small bowl combine the baking soda, vanilla, and 1 teaspoon of water. Set the mixture aside.

In a large saucepan combine the sugar, 1 cup of water, honey, and corn syrup. Cook over medium heat until a candy thermometer registers 240° or until a small amount of the syrup dropped in cold water forms a soft ball. Stir in the butter and peanuts, and cook to 300° or until a small amount dropped in cold water separates into hard brittle threads. Remove the pan from the heat immediately and stir in the soda mixture. Divide the brittle evenly between two warm buttered 15½x12-inch baking sheets. Allow the brittle to cool and then break into pieces.

Makes about 2 pounds.

Peter's Perfect Pitch Peanut Butter and M&M®s Cookies _____

¾ cups (6 ounces) margarine,
   softened
¾ cup peanut butter
¾ cup sugar
½ cup light brown sugar
2 eggs
1 teaspoon vanilla extract

1⅔ cups all-purpose flour
¾ cup quick-cooking oats
1½ teaspoons baking soda
½ teaspoon salt
1 12-ounce package (2¾ cups)
   M&M®s Semi-Sweet
   Chocolate Baking Bits

In a large bowl cream the margarine, peanut butter, sugar, and brown sugar. Add the eggs and vanilla, and beat until light and fluffy. In a separate bowl combine the flour, oats, baking soda, and salt. Gradually add the dry ingredients to the creamed mixture. Stir in the M&M®s Semi-Sweet Chocolate Baking Bits until evenly blended. Drop by heaping tablespoonfuls about 3 inches apart onto ungreased cookie sheets. Bake at 350° for 8 to 12 minutes until lightly browned. Cool 1 minute on cookie sheets. Remove to wire cooling racks. Store in a tightly covered container.

Makes about 3 dozen 2½-inch cookies.

Feel Good Foods

Same family, same staircase, years later. Did I get smaller or did they get taller?

Here is an interesting combination of foods that are good for you and foods that make you feel good. There are some that even do both. What a wonder!

Great Grandpa Hank's Granola Waffles _____

1½ cups granola
1¾ cups milk
2 eggs
½ cup butter
1½ cups all-purpose flour
1 tablespoon baking powder
¼ teaspoon salt

½ teaspoon baking soda
Oil
¾ cup honey
¼ cup fresh lemon juice
¼ cup raisins
¼ cup chopped almonds

In a large bowl combine the granola and milk. Set the bowl aside for 10 minutes.

Beat in the eggs and butter. In a separate bowl sift together the flour, baking powder, salt, and baking soda. Add the dry ingredients to the granola. Beat until well blended. Heat a waffle iron and grease with oil if necessary. Cook the waffles until golden.

In a small saucepan combine and heat the honey and lemon juice. Pour the syrup into a serving dish and stir in the raisins and almonds. Serve on the side with the waffles.

Makes 6 to 8 servings.

Whole Wheat Pizza Dough, Re, Mi! _____

1 package active dry yeast
1⅛ cups warm water (110°)
1 teaspoon honey
4½ teaspoons oil

1 teaspoon salt
1¼ cups all-purpose flour
1¼ cups whole wheat flour

In a small bowl dissolve the yeast in ½ cup of water and set aside for 5 minutes.

In a large mixing bowl combine the yeast mixture, honey, remaining water, oil, and salt. Stirring constantly, alternately add the flour and whole wheat flour gradually. When the dough is kneadable, turn it onto a floured surface. Knead until smooth and elastic. Transfer the dough to an oiled bowl, turning over so the dough is coated with oil. Cover the bowl and let the dough rise until double in bulk. The dough may be used now or it can be refrigerated for 3 days or frozen for 2 months.

Makes dough for 1 20-inch pizza.

The Three Musketeers Cheese Pizza with Spinach and Garlic_____

Oil
4 large cloves garlic, minced
2 pounds spinach, lightly cooked, drained, and chopped
5 tablespoons olive oil
¾ teaspoon salt
Coarse black pepper

½ cup ricotta cheese, drained
5 ounces Asiago cheese, finely chopped
5 ounces mozzarella cheese, finely chopped
1 recipe Whole Wheat Pizza Dough, Re, Mi! (page 210)

In a 10-inch skillet heat ½ cup of oil over low heat. Add the garlic and cook until tender, about 5 minutes. Add the spinach and cook until heated through. Season with salt and pepper to taste. Set the spinach aside.

Punch the pizza dough down. Cover the dough with a cloth towel and let it rest for 10 minutes. Roll the dough out to a 20-inch circle. Brush the sides and bottom of the dough with the remaining oil. Transfer the dough to an oiled baking sheet that has been sprinkled with cornmeal. Spread the spinach mix evenly over the surface. Top with ricotta. Sprinkle Asiago and mozzarella evenly over all. Bake at 475° until the bottom of the crust is golden, about 20 minutes. Serve immediately.

Alice's Note: The great thing about this recipe is that it can be altered so simply by using different vegetables (zucchini, broccoli, etc.) or by adding meat (ground beef, sausage, etc.). The best alteration, of course, is the simple tomato sauce for pizza recipe that follows.

Mike Lookinland

One of the great unanswered Brady questions is, "Will Bobby ever walk again?" On "The Bradys" the youngest of the bunch fulfilled his childhood dream of becoming a race car driver, but Lady Luck was looking the other direction. Bobby crashed and ended up in a wheelchair—then the series was canceled! A perpetual cliffhanger in TV history.

How's this for a happy ending? Not only does he walk again, but he moves to Salt Lake City, marries a lovely woman, Kerry, has a son, Scott, becomes an accomplished first camera assistant for motion pictures, takes long hikes in the American wilderness, and learns to cook up recipes that compete with some of Alice's best? Well, don't cry for Bobby anymore, because this happy ending is true.

Mike began his acting career at age seven when he got into commercials because of his wholesome looks. He did spots for Cheerios and Band-Aids, and he was the Eldon Toy boy. This led to his first offer to appear in a television series in the role of Eddie Corbett on "The Courtship of Eddie's Father," which he turned down in favor of "The Brady Bunch."

Mike was very much in demand during this time, making guest appearances on "The Jonathan Winters Show," "Funny Face" with Jodie Foster, "The Wonderful World of Disney" drama "Bayou Boy," the TV movie *Dead Men Tell No Tales,* and he was the voice of Oblio in the acclaimed animated special "The Point" with Dustin Hoffman. He also found time for the Cub Scouts, playing the piano and organ in his family's folk singing group, and building and launching model rockets.

After the Brady series ended, Mike won a role in the feature film *The Towering Inferno* with Paul Newman and Steve McQueen. Later he returned for all the many Brady reunions. As he grew up, his interest switched from in-front-of-the-camera to behind-the-camera. Mike attended the University of Utah, originally majoring in chemical engineering, but he changed to film studies. He worked as a production assistant for Robert Redford's Sundance Institute, which led to a job with Rocky Mountain Motion Pictures.

Now just change Bobby to Mike, and you have that happy ending we all expect from "The Brady Bunch."

Tabu Tomato Sauce_____

4¼ teaspoons olive oil
2½ pounds plum tomatoes,
   seeded and coarsely chopped
¼ cup tomato paste

¾ teaspoon salt
¼ teaspoon sugar
2 tablespoons finely minced
   fresh basil

In a large saucepan heat the oil over medium heat. Add all of the ingredients except the basil and cook for about 50 minutes, stirring frequently. Mix in the basil just before using. This can be refrigerated 3 days ahead of use. Don't add basil until it is to be used.

Makes about 3 cups of sauce.

Radical Ratatouille Pizza_____

Olive oil
1 large onion, sliced and rings
   separated
3 cloves garlic, minced
3 small zucchini, sliced
1 yellow squash, cubed
1 red bell pepper, seeded and
   sliced in rings
1 green bell pepper, seeded
   and sliced in rings

Salt and pepper to taste
5 plum tomatoes, sliced
1 teaspoon minced fresh
   rosemary
Cornmeal
1 recipe Whole Wheat Pizza
   Dough, Re, Mi! (page 210)
½ cup Provolone cheese sliced
½ cup grated Parmesan cheese

In a large skillet heat the oil and sauté the onions for 3 minutes. Add the garlic and cook for 1 minute. Add the squashes and bell peppers and cook for 2 minutes, making sure the vegetables are totally coated with oil. Cover the skillet and cook the vegetables for 20 minutes. Season with salt and pepper to taste. Add the tomatoes and rosemary, and simmer for 10 minutes. Remove the pan from the heat. Cool to room temperature.

Sprinkle cornmeal in 2 10-inch deep dish pizza pans. Divide the pizza dough in half and roll out each half on a floured surface. Place the dough in the pizza pans and form ridges on the edges of both. Spoon half of the vegetable mixture evenly over each. Top with Provolone cheese and sprinkle with Parmesan. Bake at 425° for 25 minutes or until the cheese is bubbly and the crust is browned.

Alice's Note: This is an adult pizza the kids will love too.

Makes 4 servings.

Totally Cosmic Baked Apples _____

8 large baking apples, peeled and cored
⅓ cup firmly packed brown sugar
¾ teaspoon ginger
1 teaspoon cinnamon
1⅓ cups water
½ cup honey
1¼ tablespoons lemon juice
3 tablespoons butter

Arrange the apples standing up in a buttered baking dish. Mix together the brown sugar, ginger, and cinnamon in a mixing bowl. Spoon equally into the center of each apple. In a saucepan heat the water, honey, and lemon juice and stir until the honey melts. Pour the syrup over and around the apples. Dot each apple with a cube of butter. Bake at 375° for 40 minutes or until the apples are easily pierced with a knife, but not mushy. Every 10 minutes spoon the juices over the apples as they bake.

Serve with ice cream if desired. There's no better way to get your apple a day.

Makes 8 servings.

Trouble in Paradise

66When we were in Hawaii, Mike got the most awful sunburn. Of course, all of them had been warned to watch the tropical sun but, after all, they really were kids. Bless his heart, Mike was just miserable. There was one piece of business—climbing a rope ladder, I think—that he couldn't do at all, but he was a real pro in the clinches. He never said a word of complaint, just huddled under a lot of towels just before the take.99

Mom's Chicken Noodle Soup _____

1 3-pound broiler chicken
Salt and pepper to taste
1½ cups noodles (your choice
  or whatever Mom has in the
  kitchen)

3 tablespoons chopped onion
1 bay leaf

Wash the chicken and place it in a large pot. Cover the chicken with water and season with salt and pepper to taste. Bring to a boil, reduce the heat, and simmer for 1 hour and 30 minutes or until the chicken is tender. Remove the chicken from the bone and cut it into bite-size pieces. Return the meat to the broth and add the remaining ingredients. Bring to boiling again, reduce the heat, and simmer until the noodles are done.

Alice's Note: Other vegetables may be added at the same time as noodles for different tastes (spinach, mustard greens, carrots, celery, and so on). But when you are not feeling your best the basic is the best cure. It has now been acknowledged by experts that Mom's soup really works.

Makes about 6 servings.

Tightened Braces Tomato Soup ____

¼ cup butter
8 scallions, thinly sliced
8 large tomatoes, peeled and
  diced
1 clove garlic, finely minced

4 cups chicken broth
3 tablespoons lemon juice
1 tablespoon sugar
Salt and pepper to taste

In a saucepan melt the butter and add the scallions, tomatoes, and garlic. Cover and simmer for 5 minutes. Add the remaining ingredients and bring the soup to a boil. Reduce the heat and simmer another 10 minutes.

Alice's Note: This is all that kids like Jan want on days when their braces have been tightened. There is something about the warmth of the soup and the acidity of the tomato that is soothing. Of course it could also be that you don't have to chew.

Makes 6 to 8 servings.

Chocolate Mousse
À la Bullwinkle

3 teaspoons unflavored gelatin   1½ cups sugar
3 tablespoons cold water   3 cups whipping cream
6 tablespoons boiling water   1 teaspoon vanilla extract
1⅓ cups cocoa

In a small bowl combine the gelatin and cold water. Set aside a few minutes to soften. Add the boiling water and stir until the gelatin is dissolved. In a separate bowl mix the cocoa and sugar. Add the cream and vanilla, and beat until stiff peaks form. Add the gelatin and beat until blended. Spoon into 8 dessert dishes and refrigerate until set, about 40 minutes. Top with whipped cream if desired.
   Makes 8 servings.

On the really blue days, what do you need but chocolate?

Hot Erupting Volcano
Fudge Sundae

5 tablespoons butter   2 cups cocoa
½ teaspoon salt   ¾ cup heavy cream
1 teaspoon vanilla extract   1 quart all-natural vanilla ice
⅓ cup sugar   cream (how about the recipe
⅓ cup firmly packed brown   on page 218)
   sugar   Peanuts, cherries, bananas, or
⅓ cup corn syrup   M&M®s for garnish

In a saucepan melt the butter and add the salt, vanilla, sugar, brown sugar, and corn syrup. Stirring constantly over low heat, slowly add the cocoa alternately with the cream. When thoroughly blended serve over ice cream. Garnish with peanuts, cherries, bananas, or if you are really in a chocoholic frenzy, M&M®s.
   Makes 4 servings.

Mike was the only true blond of the boys, and so for the longest time he had to have it dyed—until Sherwood allowed him to revert to his natural color.

Brownies of Doom

1 cup all-purpose flour
1 teaspoon baking powder
¼ teaspoon baking soda
½ teaspoon salt
⅔ cup extra-chunky peanut
   butter
¼ cup butter, softened

½ cup firmly packed brown
   sugar
½ cup sugar
2 eggs
1 teaspoon vanilla extract
1 cup semisweet chocolate
   chips

In a medium bowl sift together the flour, baking powder, baking soda, and salt. In a large mixing bowl cream the peanut butter, butter, brown sugar, and sugar until fluffy. Add the eggs and vanilla and beat until smooth. Add the dry ingredients and beat until blended. Fold in the chocolate chips. Pour the batter into a buttered 9-inch square pan. Bake at 350° for 30 minutes or until golden. Cool in the pan. Cut in squares.

Makes 12 squares.

Lights Out Malted Milk with Vanilla and Chocolate Ice Cream ___

⅔ cup milk
2½ tablespoons malt

1 scoop chocolate or vanilla ice cream

In a blender combine the milk, malt, and ice cream. Blend until frothy.

Alice's Note: You can use other flavors of ice cream or fruit or just have the malted milk plain. It's a great summer drink. And a treat for someone having a bad day.

Makes 1 serving.

Mike Lookinland's Recipe for Cement Oatmeal: Hire Irv!

66After the original run of the show, they trimmed away scenes to make room for more commercials. The beginnings of scenes got shorter, then a few seconds of a sight gag were cut. I remember one moment that has disappeared forever. The prop man, Irving, used to make food that was deliberately inedible. After all, there were six hungry kids on the prowl, and the last thing Irving wanted was to be turned into a short order cook. He would spray the food so it would shine and look fresh on camera, but this would also make it very unappetizing. In one scene Susan Olsen and I were eating oatmeal. Susan was letting the hard lumps of oatmeal roll off her spoon into the bowl. The oatmeal hit the bowl like little clumps of cement, and this was in the final version! I couldn't believe it. But I haven't seen that moment in many years, so it must have been replaced by a commercial. Too bad. It was very funny!99

Wheeler Dealer Chocolate and Walnut Bread _____

½ cup warm water (110°)
1 package active dry yeast
3½ cups all-purpose flour
1½ tablespoons sugar
1½ teaspoons salt

4 eggs
¾ cup butter, softened
1 8-ounce package semisweet
chocolate chips
1 cup chopped walnuts

In a large bowl dissolve the yeast in the warm water. Set the bowl aside for 5 minutes.

Add the flour, sugar, salt, and eggs, and beat until blended. Add the butter and blend until the batter is smooth. Cover and let rise until doubled in bulk. Punch down and add the chocolate chips and walnuts. Spoon into 2 greased 9x5-inch loaf pans. Bake at 350° for 45 minutes. Cool for 10 minutes, then remove to racks. This is a breakfast bread, but it's a great snack anytime.

Makes 2 loaves.

Mmmmm! M&M®s Toffee _____

1 cup chopped pecans
½ cup butter
¾ cup firmly packed brown
sugar

½ cup M&M®s

Spread the pecans in a buttered 9-inch square cake pan. In a saucepan melt the butter and add the sugar. Heat to a boil stirring constantly. Cook until all of the sugar has melted. Spread the sugar mixture over the pecans and allow the mixture to cool just until the sugar starts to harden. Sprinkle M&M®s over the top and gently press into the toffee. Chill until firm.

Variations: With the new colors of M&M®s you can make a Christmas toffee with green and red ones or an Easter toffee with the pastels. Let your imagination run wild.

Makes 12 servings.

Law and Disorder Chocolate Chip Cookies

1 cup butter
¾ cup sugar
¾ cup firmly packed brown
  sugar
2 eggs
2 teaspoons vanilla extract

2¼ cups all-purpose flour
1 teaspoon baking soda
½ teaspoon salt
2 cups semisweet chocolate
  chips

In a large bowl cream together the butter, sugar, brown sugar, eggs, and vanilla. In a separate bowl mix the flour, baking soda, and salt. Blend the dry ingredients into the butter mixture. Stir in the chocolate chips. Drop by tablespoon onto an ungreased cookie sheet. Bake at 375° for 9 to 10 minutes, until lightly golden brown.

Variation: For those special holiday occasions and a little color substitute M&M®s for chocolate chips.

Makes 5 dozen cookies.

Double Trouble Chip Cookies

1 cup butter, softened
1 cup peanut butter
2 eggs, beaten
1½ cups sugar
½ cup firmly packed brown
  sugar

2 cups all-purpose flour
1 teaspoon baking soda
1 6-ounce package semisweet
  chocolate chips
1 6-ounce package peanut
  butter chips

In a large bowl cream the butter with the peanut butter. Beat in the eggs, sugar, and brown sugar until smooth. Add the flour and baking soda and mix until blended. Stir in the chocolate and peanut butter chips. Drop by rounded teaspoonfuls onto a buttered cookie sheet. Bake at 325° for 12 to 15 minutes or until golden. Cool on racks.

Makes 6 dozen cookies.

Personal Favorites

Ah, a housekeeper's work is never done.

Here are some special treats from the cast of 'The Brady Bunch,' Sherwood, and my friend Barbara. I wish I had had these recipes back in those days when I was trying to find new ways to boil water.

Ann B.'s One and Only Beef Jerky

Beef brisket
⅓ cup soy sauce
⅔ cup lemon juice
Worchestershire sauce
  (not much)
Ground red pepper (optional)
Garlic salt (optional)
Coarse ground pepper
  (optional)

Tabasco sauce (optional)
Smoke flavoring (optional)
Rosemary (optional)
Smashed dried onions
  (optional)
Cumin (optional, a little goes a
  long way)
Anything else that occurs to
  you

Cut off all the fat from the beef. Slice into manageably sized pieces. Arrange the beef strips in a shallow dish.

In a small bowl combine one part soy sauce and two parts lemon juice. Add any or all of the remaining ingredients that appeal to you. Pour the marinade over the beef.

Drain. Spread the beef out on aluminum foil and put it in an oven that has a gas pilot. Don't light the oven. After 3 or 4 days it will be black and ugly and taste wonderful.

Alice's Note: I used to call this "My Secret Recipe for Beef Jerky That I Give to Everybody" because I kept hoping that someone would make it, then send me some. It takes 3 or 4 days to make, and I was always on the road a lot and didn't have time. I have lots of time now, so don't send me any. Try it. If you like it, give it to someone you like. If you don't like it, give it to someone you don't like.

Makes 4 to 6 servings.

Barry and Tiger, too.

Florence's Divine Stuffed Rigatoni

2 tablespoons olive oil
1 cup chopped onion
1 large clove garlic, crushed
2 tablespoons sugar
1⅓ cups tomato paste
1¾ cups tomatoes, crushed
2 cups water
1 teaspoon dried oregano leaves
1 teaspoon dried basil leaves
¾ teaspoon salt
⅛ teaspoon crushed red pepper

1 pound large rigatoni
2 15-ounce cartons ricotta cheese
1 cup grated mozzarella cheese
⅓ cup chopped spinach, cooked and drained
½ pound ground beef, cooked and drained
2 tablespoons grated onion
¼ teaspoon black pepper
¼ teaspoon salt
¼ cup grated Parmesan cheese

In a saucepan heat the oil and sauté 1 cup of onion and the garlic. Stir in the sugar, tomato paste, tomatoes, water, oregano, basil, salt, and red pepper. Bring the sauce to a boil, reduce the heat, and simmer for 1 hour.

Cook the rigatoni according to the package directions. Drain.

In a large bowl mix the ricotta, mozzarella, spinach, beef, 2 tablespooons of onion, pepper, and salt. Stuff the rigatoni with the mixture. Place a layer of shells in a baking dish. Cover with a layer of sauce and Parmesan cheese. Continue layering until all of the ingredients are used. Bake at 350° for 45 minutes.

Makes 8 servings.

Florence

Florence's Chicken Oregano_____

4 boneless chicken breasts	**⅓ cup Parmesan cheese**
½ cup butter (or olive oil)	**2 cups sliced mushrooms**
1 teaspoon leaf oregano	**1 16-ounce box spaghetti**
Garlic powder	**1 tablespoon oil**
Pepper to taste	

Arrange the chicken in a baking pan. Dot with 3 tablespoons of butter and sprinkle with some of the oregano and the garlic powder. Bake at 375° for 45 minutes to 1 hour. Add the mushrooms for the last 10 minutes of baking.

Cook the spaghetti according to the package directions, adding 1 tablespoon of oil to the water. Drain.

Sprinkle ¼ cup of Parmesan, a little more of the oregano, and pepper on the bottom of a platter. Place the spaghetti on top of the spices on the platter. Sprinkle Parmesan cheese, remaining oregano, and pepper over the spaghetti. Melt 5 tablespoons of butter and pour it over the noodles. Place the chicken and mushrooms over the noodles and serve.

Makes 4 servings.

Robert Reed's Pumpkin Chiffon Pie

The following is from Karen Rietz, Robert Reed's mother: "I have one recipe that my son particularly enjoyed, but I think he felt guilty every time he ate it because it is so rich."

3 egg yolks, beaten
¾ cup packed dark brown sugar
1½ cups cooked pumpkin
½ cup milk
½ teaspoon salt
½ teaspoon ginger
½ teaspoon cinnamon
¼ teaspoon cloves
1 envelope unflavored gelatin
¼ cup cold water
1 cup whipping cream
¼ cup sugar
1 9-inch pie shell, baked
Whipped cream for garnish

In the top of a double boiler combine the egg yolks, brown sugar, pumpkin, milk, salt, ginger, cinnamon, and cloves. Cook over boiling water, stirring constantly, for about 10 minutes. The pumpkin mixture will thicken. In a small bowl soften the gelatin in cold water. Add it to the pumpkin mixture. Chill the pumpkin mixture until partly set. Beat the whipping cream with the sugar until peaks form. Fold the whipped cream into the partly set pumpkin mixture. Pour the filling into a well-cooled pie shell and chill until set. Garnish with whipped cream.

Makes 6 to 8 servings.

Maureen and Eve

Robert Reed's
Chicken Rosemary Cajun _____

The following is dedicated to the memory of Robert Reed from his daughter, Karen, and her mother, Marilyn. This was Robert's favorite recipe.

1 large fryer or roasting chicken (3½ to 4-pounds)
½ teaspoon chicken seasoning mix (see below)
1 red apple, cored, peeled, and cut into thin strips
½ stalk celery, chopped into large pieces
1 small onion, sliced

½ strip bacon
1 teaspoon butter
1½ teaspoons chicken seasoning mix
1 teaspoon rosemary
½ cup water
½ cup vinegar
½ cup red wine

Wash the chicken and pat it dry with a towel. Season the inside of the chicken cavity with ½ teaspoon of the chicken seasoning. Place the apple, celery, onion, and bacon inside the cavity. Truss the chicken legs by pulling them through pieces of the skin at the cavity opening, so that both legs are secure. Simply cut a small slit through the skin on each side of the chicken and tuck the crossed leg through the slit. Rub the softened butter into the chicken with your hands, then season with 1½ teaspoons of chicken seasoning mix and the rosemary. Place the chicken in a baking dish. Bake at 425° for 20 minutes. When the chicken is done, remove it from the oven and place it on a warm platter. Pour any excess fat from the pan. Deglaze the pan with water, vinegar, and wine, making sure to dissolve all pan drippings. Slice the warm chicken and spoon the sauce over it. Serve warm. Only 235 calories per serving.

Chicken seasoning mix: In a small bowl mix 2 tablespoons of salt, 1 teaspoon of black pepper, 1 teaspoon of white pepper, ½ teaspoon of red pepper, 2 teaspoons of garlic powder, 2 teaspoons of onion powder, ¼ teaspoon of ground bay leaves, ¼ teaspoon of filè powder, ¾ teaspoon of sweet basil, and ½ teaspoon of paprika

Makes 8 servings.

Robert

One for All

66To have an excuse to talk with all the kids again (adults, excuse me!) has been a pleasure. Time melts away like the chocolate on one of Alice's cakes (excuse me, again). I think we are all happy to help with things that are really for us. It seems, at times, that it's mostly other people who come out ahead. All of us on the show have been exploited to one degree or another over the years, so it's just more fun to do things for each other. I miss them all. I really do.99

That's me as Schultzy on "The Bob Cummings Show."

Mo's Fabulous Meatballs _____

1½ pounds ground turkey
   breast
⅔ cup cracker crumbs
⅓ cup minced onion
1 egg
1½ teaspoons salt
¼ teaspoon ginger
¼ cup milk
1 tablespoon butter

2 tablespoons cornstarch
½ cup firmly packed brown
   sugar
1 13½-ounce can pineapple
   tidbits, syrup reserved
⅓ cup vinegar
1 tablespoon soy sauce
⅓ green bell pepper, chopped

In a large bowl combine the turkey, cracker crumbs, onion, egg, salt, ginger, and milk. Mix well. Shape into balls by rounded tablespoons. In a large skillet melt the butter and brown the meatballs. Remove and keep warm. Pour out the fat. In a small bowl mix the cornstarch and sugar. Add the pineapple syrup, vinegar, and soy sauce, and stir until smooth. Pour the mixture into the skillet and stir constantly over medium heat until the mixture thickens and begins to boil. Stirring constantly, boil for 1 minute. Add the meatballs, pineapple, and green pepper, and heat through. Serve immediately.

    Makes 6 servings.

Robert Reed

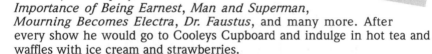

Robert Reed's characterizations suggest the work of a handful of actors, rather than one talented performer. He pursued his dramatic undergraduate education at Northwestern University, where he studied with the remarkable Alvina Krause. During this time he played Romeo, Richard III, and Othello; other plays included *The Importance of Being Earnest, Man and Superman, Mourning Becomes Electra, Dr. Faustus*, and many more. After every show he would go to Cooleys Cupboard and indulge in hot tea and waffles with ice cream and strawberries.

Summers were spent at Alvina Krause's Summer Playhouse in the Poconos Mountains, a training ground where Robert got to try his hand at stage design. From there he set sail for London, where he won a spot at the famed Royal Academy of Dramatic Arts and performed with fellow students Brian Bedford, Albert Finney, and Peter O'Toole. When he returned to the United States, Robert joined the award-winning off-Broadway troupe The Shakespearewrights and starred in *Romeo and Juliet* and *A Midsummer Night's Dream.* He went on to become a resident member of Chicago's Studebaker Theatre where he appeared with E. G. Marshall (with whom he later co-starred in the Emmy-winning "The Defenders") and appeared opposite Geraldine Page in Eugenie Leontovitch's production of *A Month in the Country.* Robert also appeared in *Androcles and the Lion* directed by Sir Cedric Hardwig, the original company of Richard Rodgers' *Avanti!,* the Broadway comedy *Barefoot in the Park,* and two successful national tours of *The Owl and the Pussycat* and *California Suite.* He was last seen on Broadway in *Deathtrap and Doubles.*

Arriving in Hollywood, Robert quickly began to land numerous roles in television. The turning point in his career proved to be a guest stint as a young attorney on "Father Knows Best." The role led directly to his being cast in "The Defenders." Next Robert had the distinction of appearing in two hit series: "The Brady Bunch," where he brilliantly played straightman to a housekeeper, and "Mannix." In the phenomenally successful "Rich Man, Poor Man," he appeared as the decadent millionaire Teddy Baylan; and he portrayed Dr. Adam Rose in the series "Nurse."

Robert was honored with Emmy nominations for his performances in "Rich Man, Poor Man," "Medical Center—The Third Sex," and "Roots." Just prior to his death in May 1992, he began teaching at U.C.L.A., where he could pass on all his knowledge and love of Shakespeare.

It's too bad he didn't have more time.

The Mod Squad a la Brady.

Maureen's Chicken à l'Orange

2 2½-pound broiler chickens
2 tablespoons minced onions
¼ teaspoon leaf tarragon
2 tablespoons butter
½ cup orange juice
Salt to taste
⅛ teaspoon dry mustard

¼ cup currant jelly
2 tablespoons grated orange
  peel
2 tablespoons port
1 orange, peeled and sectioned
1 tablespoon all-purpose flour

Wash the chickens and pat them dry. Place the chickens breast-side up in a shallow roasting pan. In a skillet melt the butter and sauté the onions and tarragon leaves until soft. Add the orange juice, salt, mustard, jelly, and peel, and cook over medium heat until the jelly melts. Stir constantly. Reduce the heat to low and add the port and orange sections. Cook for 1 minute. Remove the pan from the heat. Baste the chicken with half of the sauce. Roast at 325° for 2 hours and 30 minutes or until the juices run clear when the thigh is pricked. Baste frequently with the juice in the pan.

In a small saucepan stir the flour into the remaining sauce and heat. Cook until the mixture thickens and boils. Stir for 1 minute. Place the chicken on a serving platter and pour the sauce over it.

Makes 8 servings.

Barry's Yogurt Chicken

2 boneless breasts of chicken, halved, skinned, and fat removed

Salt and pepper to taste
½ cup plain yogurt
Grated Parmesan cheese

Wash the chickens and pat them dry. Salt and pepper both sides of the chicken. Rub the yogurt into both sides. Place the chicken in a baking dish with a cover. Sprinkle with Parmesan cheese and cover. Bake at 325° for 40 to 45 minutes. For the last few minutes remove the cover and brown the chicken. Watch closely.

Makes 4 servings.

Maureen

Sherwood and his singing Bradys. Yes, Virginia, there was a Hippie Era.

Barry's Showstopper Zucchini and Swiss Cheese Pie

Butter
¼ cup bread crumbs
1½ tablespoons olive oil
1 medium white onion, diced
2 cloves garlic, minced
3 small tomatoes, seeded and diced
3 medium zucchini, thinly sliced

Pepper to taste
⅓ cup milk
3 large eggs, beaten
⅓ pound grated Swiss cheese
¼ cup grated Parmesan cheese
1 tablespoon butter

Grease a 9-inch pie plate with butter and sprinkle evenly with the bread crumbs until the bottom and sides are coated. Sauté the onion and garlic in the oil for 10 minutes over medium heat. Stir in the tomatoes and cook for 5 minutes. Increase the heat and add the zucchini and pepper. Cook until the zucchini just begins to soften, about 5 minutes. Remove the pan from the heat and let it stand for 5 minutes. In a separate bowl mix the milk and eggs. Add the milk mixture to the zucchini mixture. Pour half of the filling into the pie plate. Top with Swiss cheese. Pour in the other half of the zucchini mixture. Sprinkle Parmesan cheese over the top and dot with butter. Bake at 375° for 30 minutes or until a tester comes out clean. Let the pie cool for 10 minutes before slicing.

Makes 6 to 8 servings.

California Winter Boiled Water___

1 to 2 cups ice   **Stove**
Medium saucepan

Place the ice in the saucepan, and place the saucepan on the stove. Turn on the burner, making sure it's the one under the pan. Set on low as not to burn the ice. Gradually raise the heat 'til boiling.

Warning: Always boil water uncovered. If you place a top on the pot, it will boil over the minute you turn your back and make a horrible noisy mess. Boiling water is not for the faint of heart.

One more on the stairs, this one with autographs.

Eve's Boiled Water

❝This is a recipe handed down in my family. My grandmother first boiled water on the Oklahoma prairie, and although times may have 'moderned up some,' as she might say, it's a tradition that lives on. I found this recipe in an old trunk in her handwriting.❞

Gramma's Winter Boiled Water ____

1 to 2 cups snow (not yellow)   **Wood**
Pot   **Matches**

Place the snow in the pot, make a "teepee" of wood, and light with matches. (Cow chips make good kindlin'.) Hang the pot over the fire, once started, and keep an eye on it to make sure it burns regular and hot 'til the water boils. Makin' boiled water at night keeps varmints away.

Eve's Note: Wow. We can only imagine the hardships they endured. Gramma's recipe has nourished our family for years, and I have my own version. I use ice from the ice maker in the freezer— much easier than making ice from scratch like my mother had to do.

No comment!

Chris' Rigatoni with Broccoli And Chicken

3 large chicken breasts, boned
  and skinned
Seasoned flour
1¼ pounds rigatoni
Olive oil
½ pound broccoli, cut in florets

½ cup butter
3 cloves garlic, minced
½ cup cream sherry
Pepper
½ cup grated Parmesan cheese
Salt

Pound the chicken breasts between sheets of waxed paper until about ¼-inch thick. Dust with seasoned flour. Cut each breast into ¼-inch horizontal slices. Set aside.

Bring 5 quarts of water to a boil. Add the rigatoni and cook until tender. Drain and rinse in cold water. Lightly drizzle with olive oil and toss to prevent sticking.

In a separate pan bring 2 quarts of water to a boil. Drop the broccoli into hot water and cook for 30 seconds. Be careful not to overcook. Remove and drain. Set the broccoli aside. In a large skillet melt the butter over medium heat. Do not allow the butter to brown. Add the garlic and cook for 1 minute. Add the chicken and cook for 1 minute on each side. Add the broccoli. Increase the heat (the skillet should be smoking slightly at this point) and add the cream sherry. The sherry will ignite. Carefully shake the skillet back and forth until the flames subside, about 1 minute. Add the cooked rigatoni, pepper, and half of the cheese. Toss to mix the pasta in the skillet. Season to taste with salt. Serve on large pasta plates. Sprinkle with the remaining cheese.

Makes 8 to 10 servings.

ALICE: First long dress I've had since high school. Same color, just not quite the same size.

Once more onto the staircase, this time for "The Brady Brides."

Susan's South of the Border Beef Filet _____

1 tablespoon butter
1 large onion, chopped
1 green bell pepper, chopped
1 red bell pepper, chopped
2 tablespoons tomato paste
½ cup hot beef bouillon
¾ teaspoon salt
⅛ teaspoon white pepper

½ teaspoon Tabasco sauce
4 4-ounce beef filets
½ teaspoon fresh ground
   pepper
2 tablespoons vegetable oil
2 tablespoons tequila
⅛ teaspoon cayenne pepper

In a skillet sauté the onions until golden. Add the green bell pepper and red bell pepper, and cook an additional 2 minutes. In a small bowl blend the tomato paste with the beef bouillon and pour the mixture over the onions and peppers. Season with the salt, white pepper, and Tabasco sauce. Cover and simmer for 10 minutes. Pat the meat dry and rub it with the black pepper. In a separate skillet heat the oil and cook the filets for 3 minutes on each side. On a warm platter arrange the onions and peppers. Place the filets on top. Make a sauce by adding tequila to the pan drippings. Season with the cayenne pepper. Pour the sauce over the filets. Serve immediately.

Makes 4 servings.

Susan's Super Easy Pot Roast _____

1 3- to 4-pound rounded rump
   roast
Pepper to taste
1 package onion soup mix
2 10½-ounce cans cream of
   mushroom soup
2 10½-ounce cans tomato soup
1 bundle celery
1 dozen carrots, peeled
4 onions, cut in half
4 potatoes, cut in half
½ cup red wine (optional)

Place the roast in a pan and sprinkle with pepper. Place the vegetables around the roast. In a medium bowl combine the soups and wine, and pour the mixture over the meat and vegetables. Cover with a tight lid or aluminum foil. Bake at 350° for 1 hour, then open and baste. Cover and continue cooking for 20 minutes per pound or to individual taste.

Makes 6 to 8 servings.

Oops! How did this get in here? Schultzy (me) with the totally delightful Bob Cummings.

Doing a little P.R. for "A Very Brady Christmas."

Mike's Scintillating Chili

1 pound ground beef
1 cup chopped onion
½ cup chopped green bell
  pepper
2 cloves garlic, minced
2 16-ounce cans whole
  tomatoes, cut up
2 16-ounce cans dark red
  kidney beans, drained

1 8-ounce can tomato sauce
1 12-ounce can diced tomatoes
  with chili peppers
3 teaspoons chili powder
½ teaspoon dried basil, crushed
¼ teaspoon salt
1¼ teaspoons pepper
½ teaspoon cumin
Tabasco sauce to taste

In a large saucepan cook the ground beef, onion, green pepper, and garlic until the meat is brown. Drain the fat. Stir in the undrained tomatoes, kidney beans, tomato sauce, and spices. Bring to a boil. Reduce the heat, cover, and simmer for at least 1 hour.

Makes 4 to 6 servings.

Well, here I am as Schultzy again. That was before I traded in my tennis racket for a spatula.

Mike's Spaghetti Sauce _____

2 pounds extra lean ground
  beef
2 tablespoons olive oil
2 pounds mild bulk Italian
  sausage
6 large stalks celery, diced
3 green bell peppers, diced
1 pound fresh mushrooms,
  sliced

1 28-ounce can stewed
  tomatoes
1 large onion, diced
2 15-ounce cans tomato sauce
1 12-ounce can tomato paste
6 bay leaves
Oregano to taste
Salt and pepper to taste
2 cloves of garlic, minced

In a skillet brown the ground beef. In a saucepan heat the olive oil and braise the sausage. Add the ground beef to the sausage and add the remaining ingredients. Simmer for at least 1 hour.

Makes 8 servings.

Mike's Clam Chowder _____

¾ cup melted butter
1 cup all-purpose flour
1 cup diced potatoes
1 cup diced celery
1 cup diced onions
1 cup diced green bell peppers
1 cup diced leeks
¾ cup chopped clams
¾ tablespoon pepper

1½ tablespoons salt
6 bay leaves
1 teaspoon Tabasco sauce
¾ cup sherry
2 cups water
¾ cup clam juice
¾ tablespoon whole thyme
2 quarts half and half

Combine the melted butter and flour in an ovenproof container. Bake at 325° for 30 minutes.

In a saucepan combine all of the ingredients except the half and half. Simmer until the potatoes are cooked. Blend the butter and flour mixture into the chowder and cook until thick, stirring constantly. Remove the pan from the heat and stir in the half and half. Heat to serving temperature.

Makes 6 to 8 servings.

Mike's Dreamy Chocolate Cheesecake _____

½ cup butter or margarine,
   melted over low heat
2 cups Famous Chocolate
   Wafers, finely crushed
¼ cup sugar
4 ounces German sweet
   chocolate, melted
4 8-ounce packages cream
   cheese
1¼ cups sugar

2 teaspoons instant coffee
2 tablespoons water or white
   rum
Pinch salt
4 large eggs
2 cups sour cream
¼ cup sugar
1 teaspoon white rum
   (optional)

In a food processor combine the melted butter, crumbs, and ¼ cup of sugar. Press the crumb mixture into the bottom and sides of a 10-inch springform pan.

In the top of a double boiler over simmering water melt the chocolate. In a mixer or food processor combine the cream cheese and 1¼ cups of sugar and beat for 2 minutes or until soft. In a cup or small bowl dissolve the coffee in the water. Add the dissolved coffee, melted chocolate, and salt to the cheese mixture and blend together. Beat in the eggs one at a time with an electric mixer on low. Pour the filling into the crust. Bake at 350° for 45 minutes. Remove the cheesecake from the oven and let it stand for 10 minutes.

In a medium bowl mix together the sour cream, ¼ cup of sugar, and rum. Spread the topping over the baked filling and return the cake to the oven for 10 minutes. Remove and refrigerate immediately. Serve cold.

Alice's Note: You can freeze this. Just defrost about 1 day before serving. Halve this recipe for a 7-inch pan.

Sherwood and Florence

Allan Melvin

Allan Melvin was born in Kansas City, the son of a film salesman. He grew up in New York City and developed an early interest in show business from his father and from an aunt and uncle who performed in vaudeville.

He attended the School of Ethical Culture. While working as a movie usher, he practiced imitating voices and doing impressions. In 1946 he won an Arthur Godfrey talent show, which got him a start in radio, where he worked on such shows as "Lorenzo Jones" and "Pepper Young's Family."

From there he performed in a nightclub doing standup comedy and impressions written especially for him by his longtime friend, novelist Richard Condon. When Condon's book *Stalag 17* was made into a Broadway play in 1951, Allan originated the role of Reed and played it for two years.

He made his television debut on "The Phil Silvers Show" in 1954 as the resourceful Sergeant Henshaw. Allan moved to California in 1961 and has been busy in one series after another since then. Besides gruff-but-big-hearted Sam the Butcher, Alice's love interest and bowling partner in "The Brady Bunch," he has had guest roles on "The Andy Griffith Show," "Gomer Pyle," "The Dick Van Dyke Show," and "My Favorite Martian."

Allan played the role of next-door-neighbor Barney Hefner on "All in the Family" and, subsequently, "Archie Bunker's Place." He has also done many familiar cartoon voices, notably Bluto in "Popeye" and "McGilla, Gorilla," as well as numerous radio commercials.

In his spare time Allan plays golf and enjoys his weekend retreat in Laguna. He and his wife, Amalia, live in Los Angeles.

A remarkable career for someone who used to overcharge for his lamb chops!

Sam's Currant Scots Scones _____

It's a braw bricht snack wi' a cuppa!

2 cups all-purpose flour
3 teaspoons baking powder
½ teaspoon salt

¼ cup butter
1½ cups milk
¼ cup dried currants

In a large bowl sift together the flour, baking powder, and salt. Rub the butter into the dry ingredients. Add the milk, stirring into a soft paste. Add the currants. Turn the mixture onto a floured board and roll until about ½-inch thick. Cut into triangles and place on a greased baking pan. Bake at 450° for 15 minutes. Split, butter, and serve with jam or jelly.

Makes about 6 servings.

The whole crew of "A Very Brady Christmas."

Sherwood's Chicken Curry _____

2 onions, finely chopped
2 cloves garlic, crushed
1 1-inch piece fresh ginger,
   grated
¼ cup curry powder
2 large ripe tomatoes, skinned,
   seeded, and diced
2 teaspoons paprika
2 whole cloves

1 2-inch stick cinnamon
2 cups coconut milk
2 teaspoons salt
2 fresh chili peppers, seeded
1 3½- to 4-pound stewing
   chicken, cut up
¼ cup cream or sour cream
2 tablespoons chopped fresh
   mint

In a saucepan heat a small amount of oil and sauté the onions, garlic, and ginger. Add the curry powder and cook for 3 to 4 minutes. Add the tomatoes, paprika, cloves, cinnamon, coconut milk, salt, and chili peppers. Cover and simmer for about 15 minutes, then add the chicken and simmer for 45 minutes to 1 hour, until the chicken is tender. Remove the chili peppers. Add the cream and mint. Heat through and serve with accompaniments.

Makes 4 to 6 servings.

Sherwood's Shrimp Marinara _____

2 pounds cooked shrimp
¼ cup olive oil
2 cloves garlic, sliced
1 1-pound 13-ounce can
   tomatoes, sieved or puréed
1½ teaspoons salt

1 teaspoon oregano
1 teaspoon chopped parsley
¼ teaspoon pepper
¼ cup red wine (optional)
3 cups white rice

Shell, wash, and drain the shrimp. In a large skillet heat the oil and sauté gently over medium high heat for 5 minutes. Remove the shrimp from the skillet and keep warm. Add the garlic and sauté until golden. Stir in the tomatoes, salt, oregano, parsley, pepper, and wine. Cook rapidly, uncovered, for 15 minutes or until thickened, stirring occasionally. If the sauce becomes too thick, add ¼ to ½ cup water. Add the shrimp, and reheat gently. Meanwhile cook the rice. Serve immediately with the shrimp sauce.

Makes 8 servings.

The Bishop's Wife

❝One of my oldest and dearest friends is Barbara Frey, the wife of Episcopal Bishop William C. Frey. They lived in Central America for ten years, and she makes some remarkably good Mexican dishes. To quote a Brady line, 'hot, super hot, and whooo! Pass the fire extinguisher!' Barbara loves to tell stories about me, like the time I was helping set the table for a woman's forum of about fifty ladies and wham! I dropped a gallon jar of mayonnaise on the freshly cleaned carpet just as the guests were arriving. The rug, as she would say, had a short, meaningful life. She also tells this story, 'One of Ann's favorite things to do to unsuspecting guests was to serve coffee in white china mugs that had little green frogs in the bottom. She would watch (as would all of us who knew) with great solemn restraint as they stirred in cream and sugar and tried to decide whether it would be rude to say, "There's something in my cup!" ' Here are a few of my favorite recipes that Barbara fixes so beautifully.❞

Barbara's Green Chili Casserole

1 16-ounce can green chilies, rinsed in cold water
1 large onion, sliced and separated

1 cup grated Cheddar cheese
1 cup mozzarella cheese
4 eggs, beaten

In a 2-quart casserole dish layer the chilies, onion, and mixed cheeses. Pour the beaten eggs over the casserole. Bake at 350° for 1 hour.

Makes 8 servings.

Barbara's Summer Nachos _____

Lettuce
Tortilla chips
Diced cooked turkey
Black beans, drained
Chopped green onions

Chopped tomatoes
Grated cheese
Salsa (homemade or
   commercial)
Sour cream

In a large shallow bowl or on a serving platter layer all of the ingredients except the salsa and sour cream in the order given. Serve the salsa and sour cream on the side.

Quick Killer Salsa _____

4 tomatoes, chopped
4 jalapeños, finely chopped
1 tablespoon chopped garlic
1 large onion, chopped
1 large bunch cilantro, chopped

¼ cup vinegar
¼ cup olive oil
Salt to taste
1 teaspoon ground cumin
   (optional)

In a serving dish mix all the ingredients together. Serve as dip or on Barbara's Summer Nachos (above).

PETER: What's a five-letter word for exhausted?
ALICE: Alice!

Ann B. Davis

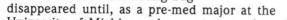

Schultzy to some, Alice to many, Ann B. Davis to everyone, this endearing actress has had a full career in television and theater. Ann B.'s first professional gig was at the age of six when she and her twin sister, Harriet, put on a puppet show and took in two dollars at the box office. After that the acting bug disappeared until, as a pre-med major at the University of Michigan, she went to see her older brother, Evans, in *Oklahoma!* That did it. She switched majors and graduated with a degree in drama and speech, then served her apprenticeship at the Erie Playhouse in Pennsylvania. Ann B. headed west and made the rounds performing at the Barn Theater in Porterville, the Wharf Theater in Monterey, and the San Francisco Theater Guild. Finally she followed the yellow brick road to Hollywood, where she performed at the Cabaret Concert, a coffeehouse a long way from the Strip. A friend's boyfriend, who happened to be a casting director, saw her and suggested that she might be right for the "gal Friday" part on a new sitcom starring Bob Cummings. The rest is television history.

At the audition were Cummings, financial backer George Burns ("Say good night, Gracie!") and producer Paul Henning, who later created "The Beverly Hillbillies." After Ann B. read for the part, George Burns simply said, "I think we'll be calling you." Three hours later she got the call telling her that the role of Charmaine "Shultzy" Schultz was hers. She played Schultzy for five seasons, was nominated for the Emmy four years in a row, and received the award twice. After "The Bob Cummings Show" she hit the road again.

Ann B. discovered that because of her television role audiences accepted her in starring roles in summer stock and dinner theater. She played opposite Lyle Talbot in Thornton Wilder's *The Matchmaker* for several seasons. She's since appeared in all fifty states appearing in *Auntie Mame, Blithe Spirit, Funny Girl,* and *The Nearlyweds,* a play written expressly for her by Lloyd Schwartz. Ann B. was picked by George Abbott to replace Carol Burnett in *Once Upon a Mattress,* and toured in the national company of *No, No Nanette* with Don Ameche and Evelyn Keyes. She has long been a dedicated supporter of the USO, and has entertained the troops in Vietnam, Korea, and Thailand.

Ann B. returned to Hollywood to play the physical-education teacher, Miss Wilson, in "The John Forsythe Show." Then Sherwood Schwartz said the immortal line, "I don't want somebody like Ann B. Davis, I want Ann B. Davis!" Thus was born Alice, the calm, comic relief in the topsy-turvy Brady household. Never has one housekeeper done so much for so many, forever smiling and always everybody's best buddy in time of need. Whatever Mike Brady paid Alice, it certainly was the deal of the century.

As for the silver screen, Ann B. was in *Lover Come Back* with Rock Hudson and Doris Day, *A Man Called Peter*, *Pepe*, and *All Hands on Deck*, and she recently made a cameo appearance as Alice in *Naked Gun 33⅓: The Final Insult*. In 1960 she received a star on the Hollywood Walk of Fame—not bad for a girl from Schenectady, New York.

In 1976 Ann B. sold her house in Los Angeles, gave up her orange Porsche 914, and moved to Denver to join an Episcopalian community run by Bishop William C. Frey and his wife Barbara. For several years she put acting aside for other priorities in her life, only returning for a "Brady Bunch" movie-of-the-week or special. Her community relocated to Ambridge, Pennsylvania, recently. Perhaps because of the move, the lure of the road beckoned, and she happily joined the national tour of *Crazy For You*.

You can take the actress out of the theater, but you can't get the theater out of the actress. Welcome back, Ann B.

Sherwood Schwartz, creator of "The Brady Bunch," says that one of his "most cherished mementos are two very special puppets which Ann B. Davis had made for me. One puppet, obviously me, is holding a script and pulling the strings on another puppet, obviously Ann B. Davis (a.k.a. Alice in her blue uniform). The concept is very flattering to me, but believe me, Ann B. Davis is nobody's puppet."

Books and Stuff

In a time long, long ago none of us thought that "The Brady Bunch" would end up being the subject of books, magazines, and newsletters. If anybody had suggested such an idea, they would have been laughed off the set. The rather unkind notices we received at the time certainly did not hint that the Bradys would one day become the subject of scholarly research. But bless my pot roast, it has.

Here is a list of the books currently in print that will tell you more than you ever wanted to know about the Bradys and the folks that made it all possible—or, sometimes, impossible:

One of our own spilled the beans in *Growing Up Brady: I Was A Teenage Greg* by Barry Williams with Chris Kreski, and a foreword by Robert Reed. This behind-the-scenes look at the Bradys spent more than three months on *The New York Times* bestseller list. *Growing Up Brady* is published by Harper Paperbacks, a division of HarperCollins Publishers.

The Brady Bunch Book by Andrew J. Edelstein and Frank Lovece, as thick as a romance novel, is full of tidbits that I never knew. It has a short foreword by Florence Henderson and is published by Warner Books, Inc.

Elizabeth Moran has put together a groovy—did people really say that?—book titled *Brady Mania: Everything You Always Wanted To Know About America's Favorite TV Family—And A Few Things You Probably Didn't*. Published by Bob Adams, Inc., It is a lot of fun to thumb through.

Currently, there are two Brady Bunch publications. You can get more information about these by writing to Erin and Don Smith, P.O. Box 1754, Bethesda, Maryland 20827-1754, or Rob Delker, who just started a new publication, *The Whole Truth*, by Scoop Brady, at P.O. Box 68321, Milwaukie, Oregon 97268-0321.

Acknowledgments

Considering the fact that everybody who has ever known me will burst into laughter when they see my name connected with a cookbook, my first and primary thanks must go to Ron Newcomer. Personally, I can't cook. Well, I don't cook—maybe a steak or a chop, but nothing that merits me giving any advice whatsoever—with the exception, of course, of my secret recipe for Beef Jerky, which somebody gave me eons ago. Ron and his wife Diane Smolen did all the gathering, choosing, checking, testing, and whatever else one does for a cookbook. To him I give all the credit and many, many thanks. What I supplied are the anecdotes, which are as accurate as the passage of time will allow, some pictures, and twenty years of television exposure as the world's most perfect housekeeper.

For that reputation I thank Sherwood Schwartz (who once moved me to tears as he told me about his early ambitions to be a doctor, when he ran into anti-Semitic prejudices and switched to being a gag writer). I thank Sherwood for creating a series with moral values that outlasted the fashions and styles of the day and has presented to several generations now a scenario of "life as it ought to be." Thank you for pointing to the hope that is in us.

I thank Mickey Freeman, my publicist since my "Bob Cummings Show" days, who had the idea for this book and put the right people together to get it done.

And, of course, my thanks to The Bunch, who all came through with recipes and stories, filling in the blanks and making me look good. Thank you, Florence. You were wonderful and you never change. And thank you "kids." You all have grown up to be very fine young men and women. I'm extremely proud to know you.

I also thank Lloyd Schwartz for his support, Patricia Kennedy, Bill Birnes, Gene and Lou Schaeffer, Marian Smolen, Nick Toth, Elizabeth Moran, and a special thanks to Darlene Schwartz for all of her help over and beyond the call of duty.

Index

Alice's Day Off Milky Way® Cheesecake, 174
Alice's Ever Popular Meat Loaf, 73
Alice's Famous Whole Wheat Buttermilk
    Waffles, 22
Alice's No Tears Onion Soup, 59
almond torte, Bobster's perfect, 135
Ann B.'s One and Only Beef Jerky, 218
appetizers, *see also* snacks
    Barbara's Summer Nachos, 242
    Brady Brick of Cheese, 183
    Crab Dip Supremes, 186
    Love It or Leave It Liver Pâté, 187
    Mo's Fabulous Meatballs, 224
    Only Child Chicken Pâté, 184
    Pick Me Up, Cheese Sticks, 160
    Quick Killer Salsa, 242
    Stuffed Gooey Gouda Cheese, 186
apples
    Cindy's Golden Apple Pancake, 20
    Everybody Can't Be George Washington's
        Apple Crumble, 136
    Johnny Apple Juice Tea, 125
    Love and the Older Man's Apple Cider,
        182
    Newton's Applesauce, 51
    Real McCoy Cider Chicken, 91
    Snow White Apple Crisp, 111
    Totally Cosmic Baked Apples, 210
apricots
    Pork Tenderloin with Apricots, 194
    Sergeant Emma's Chipped Ham and Dried
        Apricots, 147
    Welcome Aboard Company Chicken, 195
asparagus, lost sketches, 198
Attack of the Eggplant Parmigiana, 102
Aunt Jenny's Minestrone with Sausage, 53

bacon and cheese hot dogs, 159
Baked Bananas à la Brady, 110
baked beans
    Benedict Arnold's Best Baked Beans, 133
    Double Parked Baked Bean Sandwiches,
        152
baked chicken, divine decadence, 89

bananas
    Baked Bananas à la Brady, 110
    Hanna Banana Bread, 180
    Jungle Jim Banana Milk, 19
Banquet Night Hostess London Broil, 65
Barbara's Green Chili Casserole, 241
Barbara's Summer Nachos, 242
barbecue, *see also* hamburgers
    Bell Bottoms Barbecued Short Ribs,
        129
    En Guarde! Barbecued Swordfish, 133
    Get Your Bacon and Cheese Hot Dogs!,
        159
    Outstanding Citizen Rosemary Chicken,
        132
    Quarterback Sneak Hot Dogs, 132
    Sunday Barbecue Grilled Shrimp with
        Green Salsa, 98
bar cookies, *see* cookies
barley and mushroom casserole on Broadway,
    99
Barry's Showstopper Zucchini and Swiss
    Cheese Pie, 228
Barry's Yogurt Chicken, 227
basil stuffing and red wine sauce, lamb with,
    190
B.B.'s French Omelet, 27
beans
    Benedict Arnold's Best Baked Beans, 133
    Brady-riffic Black Bean Soup, 51
    Cousin Emma's Military Tomatoes and
        Green Beans, 105
    Crunchy Cashew Green Beans, 199
    Double Parked Baked Bean Sandwiches,
        152
Bears' Brie and Herb Picnic Omelets, The,
    142
Beebe Gallini's Brussels Sprouts and Red Bell
    Peppers, 106
beef
    Alice's Ever Popular Meat Loaf, 73
    Ann B.'s One and Only Beef Jerky, 218
    Banquet Night Hostess London Broil, 65
    Bell Bottoms Barbecued Short Ribs, 129

Black Forest Spiced German Pot Roast, 69

Bobby's Sloppy Joes, 154

Brady Cowboy Breakfast Steak, 36

Carol Brady's Spiced Beef and Vegetables, 70

Clinton Avenue Homemade Corned Beef, 46

Drysdale's Home Run Stuffed Green Peppers, 75

Elopement Enchilada Casserole, 80

Everybody's Smiling Beef and Eggplant Casserole, 84

Far Out Hungarian Goulash, 73

Fast and Easy Rider Pepper Steak, 64

Figaro, Figaro, Figaro Burgers, 131

Fighting Irish Beef Casserole, 77

Fillmore Flank Steak with Garlic-Ginger Sauce, 65

Four Men Living All Together Rib Roast, 192

Headed West Best Sandwich, 114

House of Cards Hamburgers, 130

I Get Misty Irish Steak, 167

Jesse James T-bone Steak, 129

Judge Alice's Pot Roast, 68

Meat Cutters' Ball Beef Tenderloin, 61

Mike's Scintillating Chili, 234

Mr. Matthews' Fast Hustling Chili, 157

Old Dutch Oven Beef Stew, 75

Out of this World Round Steak and Gravy, 67

Outer Space Chimichangas, 78

Professor Whitehead's Beef Teriyaki, 67

Raquel the Goat's Greek Sandwiches, 48

Safety Monitor Stroganoff, 70

Sam's Cold Tenderloin with Horseradish Sauce, 63

Skip Farnum's Spanish Meat Loaf, 74

Silver Platters Steak, 64

Stage Fright Swedish Meatballs, 72

Susan's South of the Border Beef Filet, 232

Susan's Super Easy Pot Roast, 233

Two-handed Stuffed French Bread, 115

Bell Bottoms Barbecued Short Ribs, 129

Benedict Arnold's Best Baked Beans, 133

beverages

Exact Words Ice Tea, 124

Jolly Green Garden Tomato Juice, 18

Johnny Apple Juice Tea, 125

Juliet Is the Sun Julep, 38

Jungle Jim Banana Milk, 19

Kitty Karryall Cocoa, 17

Launch Pad Orange Juice, 16

Love and the Older Man's Apple Cider, 182

Lovely Lady Lemonade, 38

Never Too Young Non-alcoholic Eggnog, 182

Super Duper Spiced Tea, 180

Tutti Fruity Juice Food, 18

Big Catch Fish Burgers, 156

Big Fisherman's Feast, The, 145

Big River Salmon Spread, 45

black bean soup, Brady-riffic, 51

Black Forest Spiced German Pot Roast, 69

blueberry coffeecake, 33

Bobby's M&M®s Peanut Butter Jumbos, 176

Bobby's Pool Hustler Pancakes, 20

Bobby's Sloppy Joes, 154

Bobster's Perfect Almond Torte, 135

Bogie's Pork Chops (and applesauce!) with Lemon and Vermouth, 189

boiled water, California winter, 229

boiled water, Gramma's winter, 230

Brace Your Braces Peanut Brittle, 204

Brace Yourself Honey Taffy, 162

Brady Brick of Cheese, 183

Brady Brunch Poached Salmon, 178

Brady Cowboy Breakfast Steak, 36

Brady Family Favorite Quiche, 30

Brady-riffic Black Bean Soup, 51

Brady Six Spinach and Egg Casserole, 114

bread, quick

Country Custard Corny Corn Bread, 35

Hanna Banana Bread, 180

Marcia, Marcia, Marcia Muffins, 34

John Carver's Perfect Stuffing, 196

Lemon Pecan Bread, Yea, Yea, Yea!, 179

Mellow Out Orange Muffins, 34

St. Paddy's Whole Wheat Oatmeal Bread, 39

Tiger's Hush Puppies, 141

Wheeler Dealer Chocolate and Walnut Bread, 215

bread, yeast

Cyrano de Brady Breadsticks, 109

Great White Whale Bread, 39

South of the Border Bread, 29

Whole Wheat Sunny Buns, 108

Brie and herb picnic omelets, 142

brittle, brace your braces peanut, 204

Broadway Joe's Corned Beef Special, 47

broccoli

Chris' Rigatoni with Broccoli and Chicken, 231

Dear Libby's Chicken Loves Broccoli Salad, 117

Brownies of Doom, 213

Brussels sprouts and red bell peppers, 106

Bubbles' Cheesy Bubbling Potatoes, 101

Bugs' Sweet and Sour Carrots, 105

buns, whole wheat sunny, 108

burgers, see also hamburgers

Big Catch Fish Burgers, 156

butter cookies, Cindy's buttery just, 162

buttermilk
   Alice's Famous Whole Wheat Buttermilk
     Waffles, 22
   Bobby's Pool Hustler Pancakes, 20

cabbage
   Broadway Joe's Corned Beef Special, 47
   Soleful Cabbage, 97
   Surfin' Greg's Coconut Cabbage Salad,
     126
Caesar salad, secret admirer, 56
cakes
   Chin-ups Chewy Chocolate Cookie
     Cake, 172
   Double Date Dark Double Fudge
     Cupcakes, 170
   Grandma Brady's Milky Way® Wonder
     Cake, 175
   Greg Wants a Car Carrot Cake, 202
   Mr. Wonderful White Cake, 171
   Oahu Pineapple Spice Cake, 111
   Sunshine Sisters' Sour Cream Pound
     Cake, 137
   Tiger's Home from the Pound Cake, 149
   You're So Fresh Fruit Cake, 200
California Dreamin' Shellfish Stew, 52
California Raised Doughnuts, 24
California Winter Boiled Water, 229
candy
   Brace Your Braces Peanut Brittle, 204
   Brace Yourself Honey Taffy, 162
   Mmmmm! M&M®s Toffee, 215
Carol Brady's Spiced Beef and Vegetables, 70
carrots
   Bugs' Sweet and Sour Carrots, 105
   Greg Wants a Car Carrot Cake, 202
cashew green beans, crunchy, 199
casseroles
   Barbara's Green Chili Casserole, 241
   Brady Six Spinach and Egg Casserole, 114
   Carol Brady's Spiced Beef and Vegetables,
     70
   Elopement Enchilada Casserole, 80
   Everybody's Smiling Beef and Eggplant
     Casserole, 84
   Fighting Irish Beef Casserole, 77
   Italian Spaghetti Western, 80
   Jan's Crusty Cauliflower Casserole, 101
   Johnny Bravo's Turkey au Gratin, 120
   Mushroom and Barley Casserole on
     Broadway, 99
   Scoop Brady's Crab Saint Barts, 99
   Tiki Cave Turkey Casserole, 120
   Trading Stamps Turkey Florentine, 119
cauliflower casserole, Jan's crusty, 101
celery
   Crème de la Cream of Celery Soup, 188
   Mike's Top Secret Shrimp and Celery
     Salad, 50

cheesecake
   Alice's Day Off Milky Way® Cheesecake,
     174
   Color Television Coffee Cake, 112
   Mike's Dreamy Chocolate Cheesecake,
     236
cheese
   Attack of the Eggplant Parmigiana, 102
   Barbara's Green Chili Casserole, 241
   Barry's Showstopper Zucchini and Swiss
     Cheese Pie, 228
   Bears' Brie and Herb Picnic Omelets, The,
     142
   Brady Brick of Cheese, 183
   Brady Family Favorite Quiche, 30
   Count of Monte Cristo Sandwiches, The,
     117
   Crab Dip Supremes, 186
   Evil Stepmother Sour Cream Enchiladas,
     95
   Fried Ham and Cheese Hot Rod
     Sandwich, 48
   Get Your Bacon and Cheese Hot Dogs!,
     159
   Goofy Hole-in-One Eggs, 26
   Melancholy Danish Prince, 44
   Mrs. Desi Arnaz, Jr., Lasagna, 83
   Not-So-Ugly Duckling Country Eggs, 28
   Peach of an Omelet, A, 28
   Pick Me Up, Cheese Sticks, 160
   Say "Cheeeese" Soup, 188
   South of the Border Bread, 29
   Spring Break Picnic Salad with Feta
     Cheese, 143
   Stuffed Gooey Gouda Cheese, 186
   Tabu Toast, 154
   Tattletale Tuna Sundwich, 42
   Three Musketeers Cheese Pizza with
     Spinach and Garlic, The, 207
   Très Cheesiest Quiche, 30
   Twice Married Potatoes with Cheese and
     Chilies, 103
   Voice Changer Veggie Sandwich, 168
   What's Up, Welsh Rabbit, 160
   Yankee Doodle Macaroni and Cheese,
     153
chicken
   Barry's Yogurt Chicken, 227
   Count of Monte Cristo Sandwiches, The,
     117
   Chris' Rigatoni with Broccoli and
     Chicken, 231
   Davy Jones' Fan Club Sandwich, 44
   Dear Libby's Chicken Loves Broccoli
     Salad, 117
   Divine Decadence Baked Chicken, 89
   Evil Stepmother Enchiladas, 95
   Florence's Chicken Oregano, 220
   Freckled Face Fried Chicken, 142

Funky Chicken au Gratin, The, 89
Grandma Connie's Curried Chicken
    Spread, 40
Greg's Chicken Surprise Salad, 118
Incident at Vermicelli with Chicken and
    Roasted Peppers, 92
Maureen's Chicken à l'Orange, 226
Mom's Chicken Noodle Soup, 211
Only Child Chicken Pâté, 184
Orange Blossom Roasted Chicken Special,
    The, 90
Outstanding Citizen Rosemary Chicken,
    132
Psychedelic Bachelor Pad Paella, 94
Real McCoy Cider Chicken, The, 91
Robert Reed's Chicken Rosemary Cajun,
    222
Sherwood's Chicken Curry, 240
Shove It in the Oven Fried Chicken, 87
Welcome Aboard Company Chicken, 195
Zacchariah T. Brown's Golden Chicken
    Sandwich, 42
chick pea salad, two Petes in a pod, 187
chili
    Mike's Scintillating Chili, 234
    Mr. Matthew's Fast Hustling Chili, 157
    Mrs. B's Vegetable Chili, 158
chimichangas, beef, with green chili salsa, 78
chocolate
    Brownies of Doom, 213
    Chin-ups Chewy Chocolate Cookie
        Cake, 172
    Chocolate Mousse à la Bullwinkle, 212
    Double Date Dark Double Fudge
        Cupcakes, 170
    Double Trouble Chip Cookies, 216
    Hot Erupting Volcano Fudge Sundae, 212
    Law and Disorder Chocolate Chip
        Cookies, 216
    Lights Out Malted Milk with Vanilla and
        Chocolate Ice Cream, 214
    Marcia's Dreamy Chocolate Peanutty
        Crumble Squares, 163
    Mike's Dreamy Chocolate Cheesecake,
        236
    Wheeler Dealer Chocolate and Walnut
        Bread, 215
chowder, Mike's clam, 236
Chris' Rigatoni with Broccoli and Chicken,
    231
cider chicken, the real McCoy, 91
cider, apple, with brandy, 182
Cindy's Buttery Just Butter Cookies, 162
Cindy's Double-Take Snickers® Cookies, 164
Cindy's Golden Apple Pancake, 20
clams
    California Dreamin' Shellfish Stew, 52
    Easy Steaming Clams, 141
    Mike's Clam Chowder, 236

Clinton Avenue Homemade Corned Beef, 46
cocoa, Kitty Karryall, 17
coconut cabbage salad, surfin' Greg's, 126
coffee cake
    color television, 112
    I'm so blueberry, 33
Color Television Coffee Cake, 112
cookies
    Bobby's M&M®s Peanut Butter Jumbos,
        176
    Brownies of Doom, 213
    Cindy's Buttery Just Butter Cookies, 162
    Cindy's Double-Take Snickers Cookies,
        164
    Dark Shadow Sugar Cookies, 174
    Double Trouble Chip Cookies, 216
    Grandma Connie's Shortbread, 163
    Greg's Kaleidoscope Oatmeal M&M®s
        Cookie Pizza, 164
    Jan's Ginger Cookies, 173
    Jelly Wafer Blues, 174
    Law and Disorder Chocolate Chip
        Cookies, 216
    Marcia's Dreamy Chocolate Peanutty
        Crumble Squares, 163
    Oh My Nose Oatmeal Cookies, 173
    Peter's Perfect Pitch Peanut Butter and
        M&M®s Cookies, 204
    Sam's Currant Scots Scones, 239
corn bread
    Country Custard Corny Corn Bread, 35
corn dogs, Santa Monica, 50
corned beef
    Broadway Joe's Corned Beef Special, 47
    Clinton Avenue Homemade Corned Beef,
        46
    Honeymoon Heavenly Hash, 36
Cornish game hens, George Glass, 166
Count of Monte Cristo Sandwiches, The,
    117
Country Custard Corny Corn Bread, 35
Cousin Emma's Military Tomatoes and Green
    Beans, 105
crab
    Crab Dip Supremes, 186
    Middle Child Crabby Eggs, 147
    Scoop Brady's Crab Saint Barts, 99
cranberry pie, 200
Crème de la Cream of Celery Soup, 188
crisp, apple, 111
croissant French toast, Marcia's, 121
crumbles
    Everybody Can't Be George Washington's
        Apple Crumble, 136
    Fruit of the Gods Crumble, 138
Crunchy Cashew Green Beans, 199
cupcakes, double date dark double fudge,
    170
currant scones, 239

curry
 Grandma Connie's Curried Chicken
  Spread, 40
 Sherwood's Chicken Curry, 240
Cyrano de Brady Breadsticks, 109

Dark Shadow Sugar Cookies, 174
Davy Jones' Fan Club Sandwich, 44
Dear Libby's Chicken Loves Broccoli Salad, 117
desserts, *see also* cakes, cookies, crumbles,
  pies
 Bobster's Perfect Almond Torte, 135
 Chocolate Mousse à la Bullwinkle, 212
 Dreamy Dentist Delicious Strawberry
  Shortcake, 138
 Hot Erupting Volcano Fudge Sunday, 212
 Marcia Gets Peachy Peach Ice Creamed,
  135
 Snow White Apple Crisp, 111
 Totally Cosmic Baked Apples, 210
dill dressing shrimp and celery salad with, 50
dips, *see* appetizers
Divine Decadence Baked Chicken, 89
Do-It-Yourself Flour Tortillas, 77
Double Date Dark Double Fudge Cupcakes,
  170
Double Parked Baked Bean Sandwiches, 152
Double Trouble Chip Cookies, 216
dough, whole wheat pizza, 206
Doughnut Glaze for Raised Doughnuts, 25
doughnuts
 California Raised Doughnuts, 24
 Doughnut Glaze for Raised Doughnuts, 25
Dr. Cameron's Vinaigrette Dressing, 58
Dreamy Dentist Delicious Strawberry
  Shortcake, 138
Dr. Vogel's Vegetable Soup, 60
Drysdale's Home Run Stuffed Green Peppers,
  75

Easy Steaming Clams, 141
eggnog, never too young non-alcoholic, 182
eggplant
 Attack of the Eggplant Parmigiana, 102
 Everybody's Smiling Beef and Eggplant
  Casserole, 84
eggs
 B.B.'s French Omelet, 27
 Bears' Brie and Herb Picnic Omelets, The,
  142
 Brady Family Favorite Quiche, 30
 Brady Six Spinach and Egg Casserole, 114
 Goofy Hole-in-One Eggs, 26
 Here's the Story Soufflé du Potato, 103
 Middle Child Crabby Eggs, 147
 Not-So-Ugly Duckling Country Eggs, 28
 Peach of an Omelet, A, 28
 Sunshine Day Baked Eggs, 26
 Très Cheesiest Quiche, 30

Westdale High Family Frolics Frittata, 178
Elopement Enchilada Casserole, 80
enchiladas
 Elopement Enchilada Casserole, 80
 Evil Stepmother Sour Cream Enchiladas,
  95
 En Guarde! Barbecued Swordfish, 133
entrées, *see* beef, casseroles, chicken, ham,
  lamb, pasta, pork, tuna, turkey
Everybody Can't Be George Washington's
  Apple Crumble, 136
Everybody's Smiling Beef and Eggplant
  Casserole, 84
Evil Stepmother Sour Cream Enchiladas, 95
Exact Words Ice Tea, 124

Far Out Hungarian Goulash, 73
Fast and Easy Rider Pepper Steak, 64
Father of the Year French Dressing, 58
Figaro, Figaro, Figaro, Burgers, 131
Fighting Irish Beef Casserole, 77
Fillmore Flank Steak with Garlic-Ginger
  Sauce, 65
fish, *see also* crab, flounder, red snapper,
  salmon, shrimp, swordfish, trout, tuna
 Big Catch Fish Burgers, 156
 Frontier Scouts' Fabulous Fish Fry, 140
 Psychedelic Bachelor Pad Paella, 94
 Soleful Cabbage, 97
flank steak with garlic-ginger sauce, 65
Florence's Chicken Oregano, 220
Florence's Divine Stuffed Rigatoni, 219
flounder, fringed vest, 98
flour tortillas, 77
Fluffy's Fab French Toast, 23
Four Men Living All Together Rib Roast, 192
Freckled Face Fried Chicken, 142
French toast
 Fluffy's Fab French Toast, 23
 Honey Bunch French Toast, 23
 Marcia's Croissant French Toast, 121
fried chicken
 Freckled Face Fried Chicken, 142
 Shove It in the Oven Fried Chicken, 87
Fried Ham and Cheese Hot Rod Sandwich, 48
Fringed Vest Flounder, 98
frittata, potato and ham, 178
Frontier Scouts' Fabulous Fish Fry, 140
fruit cake, 200
Fruit of the Gods Crumble, 138
fudge
 Double Date Dark Double Fudge
  Cupcakes, 170
 Hot Erupting Volcano Fudge Sundae, 212
Funky Chicken au Gratin, The, 89

garlic
 Fillmore Flank Steak with Garlic-Ginger
  Sauce, 65

Garlic (No Vampire) Potatoes, 104
Three Musketeers Cheese Pizza with
  Spinach and Garlic, The, 207
game hens, Cornish, 166
George Glass Cornish Game Hens, 166
Get Your Bacon and Cheese Hot Dogs!, 159
giblets, John Smith's, 197
ginger
  Fillmore Flank Steak with Garlic-Ginger
    Sauce, 65
  Jan's Ginger Cookies, 173
  Totally Cosmic Baked Apples, 210
glaze for raised doughnuts, 25
Golden Mint Potatoes with Peas, 199
Goofy Hole-in-One Eggs, 26
goulash, Hungarian, 73
Gramma's Winter Boiled Water, 230
Grand Canyon or Bust Hiker's Mix, 148
Grandma Brady's Milky Way® Wonder Cake,
  175
Grandma Connie's Curried Chicken Spread,
  40
Grandma Connie's Shortbread, 163
granola waffles, 206
gravy, Priscilla Alden's, 197
Great Grandpa Hank's Granola Waffles, 206
Great Scot's Breakfast Baps (Breakfast Rolls),
  33
Great White Whale Bread, 39
green beans
  Cousin Emma's Military Tomatoes and
    Green Beans, 105
  Crunchy Cashew Green Beans, 199
green chili casserole, 241
Green Chili Salsa, 79
green peppers, stuffed, 75
Greg Gets Grounded Grilled Lamb, 87
Greg Wants a Car Carrot Cake, 202
Greg's Chicken Surprise Salad, 118
Greg's Hungry Reuben Sandwich, 156
Greg's Kaleidoscope Oatmeal M&M's Cookie
  Pizza, 164
grilled shrimp with green salsa, 98
Groovy Old-fashioned Pancakes, 19
Grown-up's Peanut Butter Sandwich, 152

ham
  Brady Family Favorite Quiche, 30
  Count of Monte Cristo Sandwiches, The,
    117
  Fried Ham and Cheese Hot Rod
    Sandwich, 48
  Goofy Hole-in-One Eggs, 26
  Head Cheerleader Ham Loaf, 40
  Sergeant Emma's Chipped Ham and Dried
    Apricots, 147
  Sunshine Day Baked Eggs, 26
  Westdale High Family Frolics Frittata,
    178

hamburgers
  Figaro, Figaro, Figaro Burgers, 131
  House of Cards Hamburgers, 130
Hanna Banana Bread, 180
Harvey Klinger Zucchini Fingers, 149
Head Cheerleader Ham Loaf, 40
Headed West Best Sandwich, 114
Heavy Herbed Potatoes, 191
Here's the Story Soufflé du Potato, 103
hiker's mix, 148
Holiday Confetti Ice Cream, 161
honey
  Brace Yourself Honey Taffy, 162
  Honey Bunch French Toast, 23
  Sam Loves Alice Lamb Chops, 76
Honeymoon Heavenly Hash, 36
hot dogs
  Get Your Bacon and Cheese Hot Dogs!,
    159
  Quarterback Sneak Hot Dogs, 132
Hot Erupting Volcano Fudge Sunday, 212
House of Cards Hamburgers, 130
Hungarian Goulash, 73
hush puppies, 141

ice cream
  Holiday Confetti Ice Cream, 161
  Lights Out Malted Milk with Vanilla and
    Chocolate Ice Cream, 214
  Marcia Gets Peachy Peach Ice Creamed,
    135
  Very Brady Pumpkin and Ice Cream Pie,
    A, 203
I Get Misty Irish Steak, 167
I'm Just Wild About Saffron Rice, 91
I'm So Blueberry Coffee Cake, 33
Incident at Vermicelli with Chicken and
  Roasted Peppers, 92
Italian Spaghetti Western, 80
It's a Sunshine Day Scalloped Potatoes,
  198
jalapeño dressing, vegetable salad with, 57
Jan's Crusty Cauliflower Casserole, 101
Jan's Ginger Cookies, 173
Jan's Nothing to Snicker at Snickers® Pie,
  150
Jelly Wafer Blues, 174
jerky, Ann B.'s one and only, 218
Jesse James' T-bone Steak, 129
John Carver's Perfect Stuffing, 196
Johnny Apple Juice Tea, 125
Johnny Bravo's Turkey au Gratin, 120
John Smith's Giblets, 197
Jolly Green Garden Tomato Juice, 18
Judge Alice's Pot Roast, 68
julep, Juliet is the sun, 38
Juliet Is the Sun Julep, 38
Jungle Jim Banana Milk, 19

Kitty Karryall Cocoa, 17

lamb
Greg Gets Grounded Grilled Lamb, 87
Luscious Lamb with Basil Stuffing and Red
Wine Sauce, 190
Millicent's Meatball Sandwich, 49
Sam Loves Alice Lamb Chops, 76
lasagna, Mrs. Desi Arnaz, Jr., 83
Launch Pad Orange Juice, 16
Law and Disorder Chocolate Chip Cookies,
216
Leaky Vase Potato and Leek Soup, 188
Leapin' Salmon Fish Cakes, 95
leek soup, potato and, 188
lemon
Lemon Pecan Bread, Yea, Yea, Yea!, 179
Lovely Lady Lemonade, 38
Thyme to Change Vinaigrette, 57
lentil soup, 59
Lights Out Malted Milk with Vanilla and
Chocolate Ice Cream, 214
liver pâté, 187
Lost Sketches Asparagus, 198
Lost Locket Lentil Soup, 59
Love and the Older Man's Apple Cider, 182
Love It or Leave It Liver Pâté, 187
Lovely Lady Lemonade, 38
Luscious Lamb with Basil Stuffing and Red
Wine Sauce, 190

macaroni, *see also* pasta
Meet the Bradys Macaroni Salad, 127
Yankee Doodle Macaroni and Cheese,
153
marinara, Sherwood's shrimp, 240
malted milk with vanilla and chocolate ice
cream, 214
M&M's
Bobby's M&M's Peanut Butter Jumbos,
176
Greg's Kaleidoscope Oatmeal M&M's
Cookie Pizza, 164
Holiday Confetti Ice Cream, 161
Mmmmm! M&M's Toffee, 215
Peter's Perfect Pitch Peanut Butter and
M&M's Cookies, 204
Marcia Gets Peachy Peach Ice Creamed,
135
Marcia, Marcia, Marcia Muffins, 34
Marcia's Croissant French Toast, 121
Marcia's Dreamy Chocolate Peanutty
Crumble Squares, 163
Maureen's Chicken à l'Orange, 226
meatballs
Millicent's Meatball Sandwich, 49
Mo's Fabulous Meatballs, 224
Stage Fright Swedish Meatballs, 72
Meat Cutters' Ball Beef Tenderloin, 61

meat loaves
Alice's Ever Popular Meat Loaf, 73
Head Cheerleader Ham Loaf, 40
Skip Farnum's Spanish Meat Loaf, 74
Meet the Bradys Macaroni Salad, 127
Melancholy Danish Prince, 44
Mellow Out Orange Muffins, 34
Middle Child Crabby Eggs, 147
Mike's Clam Chowder, 236
Mike's Dreamy Chocolate Cheesecake, 236
Mike's Favorite Potato Salad, 126
Mike's Scintillating Chili, 234
Mike's Spaghetti Sauce, 235
Mike's Top Secret Shrimp and Celery Salad,
50
milk
Jungle Jim Banana Milk, 19
Lights Out Malted Milk with Vanilla and
Chocolate Ice Cream, 214
Milky Way® bars
Alice's Day Off Milky Way® Cheesecake,
174
Grandma Brady's Milky Way® Wonder
Cake, 175
Millicent's Meatball Sandwich, 49
minestrone with sausage, 53
mint
Juliet Is the Sun Julep, 38
Golden Mint Potatoes with Peas, 199
Mmmmm! M&M's Toffee, 215
Mom's Chicken Noodle Soup, 211
Monster Mashed Potato Cakes, 122
Monte Cristo sandwiches, 117
Mo's Fabulous Meatballs, 224
Most Popular Girl Pine Nut Pasta Sauce, 82
mountain trout, 96
mousse, chocolate, 212
Mr. Matthews' Fast Hustling Chili, 157
Mrs. B's Vegetable Chili, 158
Mrs. Desi Arnaz Jr.'s Lasagna, 83
Mr. Wonderful White Cake, 171
muffins
Marcia, Marcia, Marcia Muffins, 34
Mellow Out Orange Muffins, 34
mulled tea, spiced, 180
mushrooms
Peter's Volcanic Mushroom Sauce, 81
Warren Mulaney Mushroom Sauce, 82
Mushroom and Barley Casserole on
Broadway, 99

nachos, Barbara's summer, 242
Never Too Young Non-alcoholic Eggnog,
182
Newlyweds' Rice with Fresh Herbs, 190
Newton's Applesauce, 51
noodles
Far Out Hungarian Goulash, 73
Mom's Chicken Noodle Soup, 211

Safety Monitor Stroganoff, 70
Not-So-Ugly Duckling Country Eggs, 28

Oahu Pineapple Spice Cake, 111
oats
  Greg's Kaleidoscope Oatmeal M&M®s
    Cookie Pizza, 164
  Marcia's Dreamy Chocolate Peanutty
    Crumble Squares, 163
  Oh My Nose Oatmeal Cookies, 173
  St. Paddy's Whole Wheat Oatmeal Bread,
    39
Oh My Nose Oatmeal Cookies, 173
Old Dutch Oven Beef Stew, 75
omelets
  B.B.'s French Omelet, 27
  Bears' Brie and Herb Picnic Omelets, The,
    142
  Peach of an Omelet, A, 28
onion soup, 59
Only Child Chicken Pâté, 184
orange
  Launch Pad Orange Juice, 16
  Maureen's Chicken à l'Orange, 226
  Mellow Out Orange Muffins, 34
  Orange Blossom Roasted Chicken Special,
    The, 90
Our Pilgrim Fathers' Thanksgiving Turkey,
  196
Out of This World Round Steak and Gravy,
  67
Outer Space Chimichangas, 78
Outstanding Citizen Rosemary Chicken, 132
Over the Rainbow Pepper Salad, 125

paella, 94
pancakes
  Groovy Old-fashioned Pancakes, 19
  Bobby's Pool Hustler Pancakes, 20
  Cindy's Golden Apple Pancake, 20
pasta, see also macaroni, noodles
  Chris' Rigatoni with Broccoli and
    Chicken, 231
  Florence's Divine Stuffed Rigatoni, 219
  Incident at Vermicelli with Chicken and
    Roasted Peppers, 92
  Italian Spaghetti Western, 80
  Most Popular Girl Pine Nut Pasta Sauce,
    82
  Peter's Volcanic Mushroom Sauce, 81
  Tank's Tasty Turkey Salad, 145
  Veni, Vidi, Vici Veggy Vermicelli, 107
  Warren Mulaney Mushroom Sauce, 82
pâté
  Love It or Leave It Liver Pâté, 187
  Only Child Chicken Pâté, 184
peaches
  Marcia Gets Peachy Peach Ice Creamed,
    135

Peach of an Omelet, A, 28
peanut brittle, 204
peanut butter
  Bobby's M&M®s Peanut Butter Jumbos,
    176
  Double Trouble Chip Cookies, 216
  Grown-up's Peanut Butter Sandwich, 152
  Peter's Perfect Pitch Peanut Butter and
    M&M®s Cookies, 204
  peanutty crumble squares, chocolate, 163
peas
  Golden Mint Potatoes with Peas, 199
  Peter's Perfect Peas, 106
  Swingset Sour Green Pea Salad, 127
  Two Petes In A Pod Chick Pea Salad, 187
pecan pie, 201
peppers
  Beebe Gallini's Brussels Sprouts and Red
    Bell Peppers, 106
  Incident at Vermicelli with Chicken and
    Roasted Peppers, 92
  Over the Rainbow Pepper Salad, 125
pepper steak, 64
Personality Kid Roast Pork, 85
pesto, 83
Peter the Great Pesto, 83
Peter's Party Pizza, 169
Peter's Perfect Peas, 106
Peter's Perfect Pitch Peanut Butter and
  M&M®s Cookies, 204
Peter's Volcanic Mushroom Sauce, 81
Pick Me Up, Cheese Sticks, 160
pies
  Barry's Showstopper Zucchini and Swiss
    Cheese Pie, 228
  Brady Kids' Cranberry Pie, 200
  Jan's Nothing to Snicker at Snickers® Pie,
    150
  Power of the Press Pecan Pie, 201
  Robert Reed's Pumpkin Chiffon Pie, 221
  Very Brady Pumpkin and Ice Cream Pie,
    A, 203
pineapple
  Mo's Fabulous Meatballs, 224
  Oahu Pineapple Spice Cake, 111
pine nut pasta sauce, 82
pizza
  Greg's Kaleidoscope Oatmeal M&M®s
    Cookie Pizza, 164
  Peter's Party Pizza, 169
  Radical Ratatouille Pizza, 209
  Three Musketeers Cheese Pizza with
    Spinach and Garlic, The, 207
  Whole Wheat Pizza Dough, Re, Mi!, 206
pork, see also ham, sausage
  Alice's Ever Popular Meat Loaf, 73
  Aunt Jenny's Minestrone with Sausage, 53
  Bogie's Pork Chops (and applesauce!) with
    Lemon and Vermouth, 189

Personality Kid Roast Pork, 85
Pork Tenderloin with Apricots, 194
Stage Fright Swedish Meatballs, 72
Pork Tenderloin with Apricots, 194
potatoes
    Bubbles' Cheesy Bubbling Potatoes, 101
    Garlic (No Vampire) Potatoes, 104
    Golden Mint Potatoes with Peas, 199
    Heavy Herbed Potatoes, 191
    Here's the Story Soufflé du Potato, 103
    Honeymoon Heavenly Hash, 36
    It's a Sunshine Day Scalloped Potatoes,
        198
    Leaky Vase Potato and Leek Soup, 188
    Mike's Favorite Potato Salad, 126
    Monster Mashed Potato Cakes, 122
    Not-So-Ugly Duckling Country Eggs, 28
    Puffed the Magic Potato, 158
    Twice Married Potatoes with Cheese and
        Chilies, 103
    UFO Potatoes, 31
    Westdale High Family Frolics Frittata, 178
    Woodland Park Potatoes, 31
pot roast
    Black Forest Spiced German Pot Roast, 69
    Judge Alice's Pot Roast, 68
    Susan's Super Easy Pot Roast, 233
    Two-handed Stuffed French Bread, 115
pound cake
    Sunshine Sisters' Sour Cream Pound
        Cake, 137
    Tiger's Home from the Pound Cake, 149
Power of the Press Pecan Pie, 201
Priscilla Alden's Gravy, 197
Professor Whitehead's Beef Teriyaki, 67
Psychedelic Bachelor Pad Paella, 94
Puffed the Magic Potato, 158
pumpkin
    Robert Reed's Pumpkin Chiffon Pie, 221
    Very Brady Pumpkin and Ice Cream Pie,
        A, 203

Quarterback Sneak Hot Dogs, 132
quiche
    Brady Family Favorite Quiche, 30
    Trés Cheesiest Quiche, 30
quick breads, *see* breads
Quick Killer Salsa, 242

Radical Ratatouille Pizza, 209
Raquel the Goat's Greek Sandwiches, 48
ratatouille pizza, 209
red snapper, 193
red wine sauce, lamb with basil stuffing and,
    190
Real McCoy Cider Chicken, The, 91
reuben sandwich, 156
ribs
    Bell Bottoms Barbecued Short Ribs, 129

Four Men Living All Together Rib Roast,
    192
rice
    Drysdale's Home Run Stuffed Green
        Peppers, 75
    Everybody's Smiling Baked Beef and
        Eggplant Casserole, 84
    Fast and Easy Rider Pepper Steak, 64
    I'm Just Wild about Saffron Rice, 91
    Newlyweds' Rice with Fresh Herbs, 190
    Psychedelic Bachelor Pad Paella, 94
rigatoni
    Chris' Rigatoni with Broccoli and
        Chicken, 231
    Florence's Divine Stuffed Rigatoni, 219
roast beef sandwiches, 48
roast, rib 196, *see also* pot roast
Robert Reed's Chicken Rosemary Cajun,
    222
Robert Reed's Pumpkin Chiffon Pie, 221
rolls
    Great Scot's Breakfast Baps (Breakfast
        Rolls), 33
round steak and gravy, 67
rye
    Big River Salmon Spread, 45
    Broadway Joe's Corned Beef Special, 47
    Greg's Hungry Reuben Sandwich, 156
    Sam the Butcher's Favorite Sandwich,
        146

Safety Monitor Stroganoff, 70
saffron rice, 91
salad dressings
    Dr. Cameron's Vinaigrette Dressing, 58
    Father of the Year French Dressing, 58
    Thyme to Change Vinaigrette, 57
salads
    Dear Libby's Chicken Loves Broccoli
        Salad, 117
    Greg's Chicken Surprise Salad, 118
    Meet the Bradys Macaroni Salad, 127
    Mike's Favorite Potato Salad, 126
    Mike's Top Secret Shrimp and Celery
        Salad, 50
    Over the Rainbow Pepper Salad, 125
    Secret Admirer Caesar Salad, 56
    Spring Break Picnic Salad with Feta
        Cheese, 143
    Summer Picnic Watermelon Basket, 134
    Surfin' Greg's Coconut Cabbage Salad,
        126
    Swingset Sour Green Pea Salad, 127
    Tank's Tasty Turkey Salad, 145
    Two Petes In A Pod Chick Pea Salad, 187
    Vote for Brady Vegetable Salad, 57
salmon
    Big Fisherman's Feast, The, 145
    Big River Salmon Spread, 45

Brady Brunch Poached Salmon, 178
Leapin' Salmon Fish Cakes, 95
Sweet Salmon Pie, 96
salsa
    Green Chili Salsa, 79
    Quick Killer Salsa, 242
    Sunday Barbecue Grilled Shrimp with
        Green Salsa, 98
Sam Loves Alice Lamb Chops, 76
Sam's Cold Tenderloin with Horseradish
    Sauce, 63
Sam's Currant Scots Scones, 239
Sam the Butcher's Favorite Sandwich, 146
sandwiches
    Big Catch Fish Burgers, 156
    Big Fisherman's Feast, The, 145
    Bobby's Sloppy Joes, 154
    Broadway Joe's Corned Beef Special, 47
    Count of Monte Cristo Sandwiches, The,
        117
    Davy Jones' Fan Club Sandwich, 44
    Double Parked Baked Bean Sandwiches,
        152
    Fried Ham and Cheese Hot Rod
        Sandwiches, 48
    Grandma Connie's Curried Chicken
        Spread, 40
    Greg's Hungry Reuben Sandwich, 156
    Grown-up's Peanut Butter Sandwich, 152
    Headed West Best Sandwich, 114
    Melancholy Danish Prince, 44
    Millicent's Meatball Sandwich, 49
    Raquel the Goat's Greek Sandwiches, 48
    Sam the Butcher's Favorite Sandwich,
        146
    Slumber Party Sub, 46
    Sports Sunday Sandwich, 167
    Tattletale Tuna Sandwich, 42
    Two-handed Stuffed French Bread, 115
    Voice Change Veggie Sandwich, 168
    Zacchariah T. Brown's Golden Chicken
        Sandwich, 42
Santa Monica Corn Dogs, 50
sauces
    Mike's Spaghetti Sauce, 235
    Most Popular Girl Pine Nut Pasta Sauce,
        82
    Peter the Great Pesto, 83
    Peter's Volcanic Mushroom Sauce, 81
    Tabu Tomato Sauce, 209
    Warren Mulaney Mushroom Sauce, 82
sausage, minestrone with, 53
Say "Cheeeese" Soup, 188
scalloped potatoes, 198
scones, currant Scots, 239
Scoop Brady's Crab Saint Barts, 99
Secret Admirer Caesar Salad, 56
Sergeant Emma's Chipped Ham and Dried
    Apricots, 147

shellfish stew, 52
Sherwood's Chicken Curry, 240
Sherwood's Shrimp Marinara, 240
shortbread, 163
shortcake, strawberry, 138
Shove It in the Oven Fried Chicken, 87
shrimp
    Mike's Top Secret Shrimp and Celery
        Salad, 50
    Sherwood's Shrimp Marinara, 240
    Sunday Barbecue Grilled Shrimp with
        Green Salsa, 98
Sibling Rivalry Red Snapper, 193
Silver Platters Steak, 64
sloppy joes, 154
Slumber Party Sub, 46
Skip Farnum's Spanish Meat Loaf, 74
snacks, *see also* appetizers
    Grand Canyon or Bust Hiker's Mix, 148
    Harvey Klinger Zucchini Fingers, 149
    Tabu Toast, 154
Snickers®
    Cindy's Double-Take Snickers® Cookies,
        164
    Jan's Nothing to Snicker at Snickers® Pie,
        150
    Marcia's Dreamy Chocolate Peanutty
        Crumble Squares, 163
Snow White Apple Crisp, 111
Soleful Cabbage, 97
soups
    Alice's No Tears Onion Soup, 59
    Brady-riffic Black Bean Soup, 51
    Crème de la Cream of Celery Soup, 188
    Dr. Vogel's Vegetable Soup, 60
    Leaky Vase Potato and Leek Soup, 188
    Lost Locket Lentil Soup, 59
    Mike's Scintillating Chili, 234
    Mom's Chicken Noodle Soup, 211
    Mr. Matthews' Fast Hustling Chili, 157
    Say "Cheeeese" Soup, 188
    Tightened Braces Tomato Soup, 211
soufflé du potato, 103
sour cream
    Evil Stepmother Sour Cream Enchiladas,
        95
    Elopement Enchilada Casserole, 80
    Sunshine Sisters' Sour Cream Pound
        Cake, 137
South of the Border Bread, 29
spaghetti, Italian, 80
spaghetti sauce, 235
spinach
    Brady Six Spinach and Egg Casserole, 114
    Three Musketeers Cheese Pizza with
        Spinach and Garlic, The, 207
Sports Sunday Sandwich, 167
spreads
    Big River Salmon Spread, 45

Grandma Connie's Curried Chicken Spread, 40
Spring Break Picnic Salad with Feta Cheese, 143
S.S. Brady Tuna Fish Spread, 41
Sunflower Girls' Sunflower Seed Spread, 45
S.S. Brady Tuna Fish Spread, 41
Stage Fright Swedish Meatballs, 72
steak
  Banquet Night Hostess London Broil, 65
  Brady Cowboy Breakfast Steak, 36
  Fast and Easy Rider Pepper Steak, 64
  Fillmore Flank Steak with Garlic-Ginger Sauce, 65
  I Get Misty Irish Steak, 167
  Jesse James' T-bone Steak, 129
  Out of this World Round Steak and Gravy, 67
  Silver Platters Steak, 64
stew
  California Dreamin' Shellfish Stew, 52
  Old Dutch Oven Beef Stew, 75
St. Paddy's Whole Wheat Oatmeal Bread, 39
stroganoff, beef, 70
strawberry shortcake, 138
Stuffed Gooey Gouda Cheese, 186
stuffing, John Carver's perfect, 196
sub, slumber party, 46
sugar cookies, 174
Summer Picnic Watermelon Basket, 134
sundae, hot fudge, 212
Sunday Barbecue Grilled Shrimp with Green Salsa, 98
Sunflower Girls' Sunflower Seed Spread, 45
Sunshine Day Baked Eggs, 26
Sunshine Sisters' Sour Cream Pound Cake, 137
Super Duper Spiced Tea, 180
Surfin' Greg's Coconut Cabbage Salad, 126
Susan's South of the Border Beef Filet, 232
Susan's Super Easy Pot Roast, 233
sweet and sour carrots, 105
Sweet Salmon Pie, 96
Swingset Sour Green Pea Salad, 127
swordfish, barbecued, 133

Tabu Toast, 154
Tabu Tomato Sauce, 209
taffy, honey, 162
Tank's Tasty Turkey Salad, 145
Tattletale Tuna Sandwich, 42
tea
  Exact Words Ice Tea, 124
  Johnny Apple Juice Tea, 125
  Juliet Is the Sun Julep, 38
  Super Duper Spiced Tea, 180
tenderloins

Meat Cutters' Ball Beef Tenderloin, 61
Pork Tenderloin with Apricots, 194
Sam's Cold Tenderloin with Horseradish Sauce, 63
teriyaki, beef, 67
Three Musketeers Cheese Pizza with Spinach and Garlic, The, 207
Thyme to Change Vinaigrette, 57
Tiger's Hush Puppies, 141
Tightened Braces Tomato Soup, 211
toast, tabu, 154
toffee, M&M®s, 215
tomatoes
  Cousin Emma's Military Tomatoes and Green Beans, 105
  Greg Gets Grounded Grilled Lamb, 87
  Jolly Green Garden Tomato Juice, 18
  Tabu Tomato Sauce, 209
  Tightened Braces Tomato Soup, 211
torte, almond, 135
tortillas, flour, 77
Totally Cosmic Baked Apples, 210
Totally Mod Waffles, 21
Trading Stamps Turkey Florentine, 119
Trés Cheesiest Quiche, 30
trout, mountain, 96
tuna
  Big Fisherman's Feast, The, 145
  S.S. Brady Tuna Fish Spread, 41
  Sunflower Girls' Sunflower Seed Spread, 45
  Tattletale Tuna Sandwich, 42
turkey
  Brady Family Favorite Quiche, 30
  Harvey Klinger Zucchini Fingers, 149
  Johnny Bravo's Turkey au Gratin, 120
  John Smith's Giblets, 197
  Mo's Fabulous Meatballs, 224
  Our Pilgrim Fathers' Thanksgiving Turkey, 196
  Priscilla Alden's Gravy, 197
  Tank's Tasty Turkey Salad, 145
  Tiki Cave Turkey Casserole, 120
  Trading Stamps Turkey Florentine, 119
  Tutti Fruity Juice Food, 18
Twice Married Potatoes with Cheese and Chilies, 103
Two-handed Stuffed French Bread, 115
Two Petes In a Pod Chick Pea Salad, 187

UFO Potatoes, 31

vanilla and chocolate ice cream, malted milk with, 214
vegetable salad, 57
vegetable soup, 60
veggie sandwich, 168
veggy vermicelli, 107
Veni, Vidi, Vici Veggy Vermicelli, 107

vermicelli, veggy, 107
vinaigrette
    Dr. Cameron's Vinaigrette Dressing, 58
    Thyme to Change Vinaigrette, 57
Very Brady Pumpkin and Ice Cream Pie, A, 203
Voice Change Veggie Sandwich, 168
Vote for Brady Vegetable Salad, 57

waffles
    Alice's Famous Whole Wheat Buttermilk Waffles, 22
    Great Grandpa Hank's Granola Waffles, 206
    Totally Mod Waffles, 21
Warren Mulaney Mushroom Sauce, 82
watermelon basket, 134
Welcome Aboard Company Chicken, 195
Westdale High Family Frolics Frittata, 178
What America Means to Me Mountain Trout, 96
What's Up, Welsh Rabbit, 160
Wheeler Dealer Chocolate and Walnut Bread, 215
white cake, 171
whole wheat

Alice's Famous Whole Wheat Buttermilk Waffles, 22
Count of Monte Cristo Sandwiches, The, 117
Marcia, Marcia, Marcia Muffins, 34
St. Paddy's Whole Wheat Oatmeal Bread, 39
What's Up, Welsh Rabbit, 162
Whole Wheat Pizza Dough, Re, Mi!, 206
Whole Wheat Sunny Buns, 108
winter boiled water, California, 229
winter boiled water, Gramma's, 230
Woodland Park Potatoes, 31

Yankee Doodle Macaroni and Cheese, 153
yeast breads, *see* breads
yogurt chicken, 227
You're So Fresh Fruit Cake, 200

Zacchariah T. Brown's Golden Chicken Sandwich, 42
zucchini
    Barry's Showstopper Zucchini and Swiss Cheese Pie, 228
    Harvey Klinger Zucchini Fingers, 149

Ron Newcomer is president of New West Productions, and co-founder of the Scottsdale Culinary Festival. He is a member of the Dramatists Guild, and has had twelve plays produced. Currently he is working on a musical based on Orson Welles' Panic Broadcast, "The War of the Worlds," a mystery novel, *The Alfred Affair*, and *Indian Poker*, which will be published by Birch Lane Press.

Diane Smolen co-founded Musical Theatre of Arizona, and was a founding member of Shakespeare & Co., where she also directed and designed many productions. She comes from a large Air Force family that has lived all over the world. Currently she is putting together the recipes for a new cookbook that should delight children of all ages. Diane's two children, Miles and Meghann, are her toughest critics.